RSF: The Russell Sage Foundation Journal of the Social Sciences

Severe Deprivation in America

VOLUME 1 • NUMBER 1 • NOVEMBER 2015

RSF: The Russell Sage Foundation Journal of the Social Sciences   ISSN 2377-8261

The Russell Sage Foundation

The Russell Sage Foundation, one of the oldest of America's general purpose foundations, was established in 1907 by Mrs. Margaret Olivia Sage for "the improvement of social and living conditions in the United States." The foundation seeks to fulfill this mandate by fostering the development and dissemination of knowledge about the country's political, social, and economic problems. While the foundation endeavors to assure the accuracy and objectivity of each book it publishes, the conclusions and interpretations in Russell Sage Foundation publications are those of the authors and not of the foundation, its trustees, or its staff. Publication by Russell Sage, therefore, does not imply foundation endorsement.

Board of Trustees

Sara S. McLanahan, *Chair*

Larry M. Bartels
Kenneth D. Brody
Karen S. Cook
W. Bowman Cutter III
Sheldon H. Danziger
Kathryn Edin
Lawrence F. Katz

Nicholas Lemann
Peter R. Orszag
Claude M. Steele
Shelley E. Taylor
Richard H. Thaler
Hirokazu Yoshikawa

Mission Statement

RSF: The Russell Sage Foundation Journal of the Social Sciences is a peer-reviewed, open-access journal of original empirical research articles by both established and emerging scholars. It is designed to promote cross-disciplinary collaborations on timely issues of interest to academics, policymakers, and the public at large. Each issue is thematic in nature and focuses on a specific research question or area of interest. The introduction to each issue will include an accessible, broad, and synthetic overview of the research question under consideration and the current thinking from the various social sciences.

RSF Journal Editorial Board

Annette Bernhardt,
  University of California,
  Berkeley
Marianne Bertrand,
  University of Chicago
Karen S. Cook, Stanford
  University
Sheldon H. Danziger,
  Russell Sage Foundation
Nancy Folbre, University of
  Massachusetts
Janet C. Gornick, The
  CUNY Graduate Center
John A. Ferejohn, Stanford
  University

Larry V. Hedges,
  Northwestern University
Jennifer Hochschild,
  Harvard University
Rucker C. Johnson,
  University of California,
  Berkeley
Douglas S. Massey,
  Princeton University
James Sidanius, Harvard
  University
Mary C. Waters, Harvard
  University
Bruce Western, Harvard
  University

Copyright © 2015 by Russell Sage Foundation. All rights reserved. Printed in the United States of America. No part of this publication may be reproduced, stored in a retrieval system, or transmitted in any form or by any means, electronic, mechanical, photocopying, recording, or otherwise, without the prior written permission of the publisher. Reproduction by the United States Government in whole or in part is permitted for any purpose.

Opinions expressed in this journal are not necessarily those of the editors, editorial board, trustees, or the Russell Sage Foundation.

We invite scholars to submit proposals for potential issues through the *RSF* application portal: https://rsfjournal.onlineapplicationportal.com/. Submissions should be addressed to Suzanne Nichols, Director of Publications.

Russell Sage Foundation
112 East 64th Street
New York, NY 10065

ISSN (print):   2377-8253
ISSN (electronic): 2377-8261
ISBN: 978-0-87154-501-5

RSF: The Russell Sage Foundation Journal of the Social Sciences

VOLUME 1 NUMBER 1
NOVEMBER 2015

Severe Deprivation in America

ISSUE EDITOR
Matthew Desmond, Harvard University

CONTENTS

Severe Deprivation in America: An Introduction **1**
Matthew Desmond

Part I. Severe Deprivation Among the Young and Old

Trends in Deep Poverty from 1968 to 2011: The Influence of Family Structure, Employment Patterns, and the Safety Net **14**
Liana Fox, Christopher Wimer, Irwin Garfinkel, Neeraj Kaushal, JaeHyun Nam, and Jane Waldfogel

Compounded Deprivation in the Transition to Adulthood: The Intersection of Racial and Economic Inequality Among Chicagoans, 1995–2013 **35**
Kristin L. Perkins and Robert J. Sampson

Income, Poverty, and Material Hardship Among Older Americans **55**
Helen Levy

How Well Does the "Safety Net" Work for Family Safety Nets? Economic Survival Strategies Among Grandmother Caregivers in Severe Deprivation **78**
LaShawnDa Pittman

Part II. Extreme Poverty and Social Suffering

How Institutions Deprive: Ethnography, Social Work, and Interventionist Ethics Among the Hypermarginalized **100**
Megan Comfort, Andrea M. Lopez, Christina Powers, Alex H. Kral, and Jennifer Lorvick

Understanding the Dynamics of $2-a-Day Poverty in the United States **120**
H. Luke Shaefer, Kathryn Edin, and Elizabeth Talbert

When There Is No Welfare: The Income Packaging Strategies of Mothers Without Earnings or Cash Assistance Following an Economic Downturn **139**
Kristin S. Seefeldt and Heather Sandstrom

Severe Deprivation in America: An Introduction

MATTHEW DESMOND

A LIFE

Crystal Mayberry was born prematurely on a spring day in 1990 shortly after her pregnant mother was stabbed eleven times in the back during a robbery.[1] The attack induced labor. Both mother and daughter survived. It was not the first time Crystal's mother had been stabbed. For as far back as she can remember, Crystal's father had beat her mother. He smoked crack cocaine, and so did her mother; so did her mother's mother.

Crystal's mother found a way to leave, and her father soon after began a lengthy prison sentence. Crystal and her mother moved in with another man and his parents. That man's father began molesting Crystal. She told her mother, and her mother called her a liar. Not long after Crystal began kindergarten, Child Protective Services stepped in. At five, Crystal was placed in foster care.

Crystal was bounced around between dozens of group homes and sets of foster parents. She lived with her aunt for five years. Then her aunt returned her. After that, the longest Crystal lived anywhere was eight months. When adolescence arrived, Crystal had to fight more with the other girls in the group homes. She picked up assault charges and a scar across her right cheekbone. People and their houses, pets, furniture, dishes—these came and went. Food was more stable, and Crystal began taking refuge in it. She put on weight. Because of her weight, she developed sleep apnea.

When Crystal was sixteen, she stopped going to high school. When she turned eighteen, she aged out of foster care. By that time she had passed through more than twenty-five foster placements. She had been approved for Supplemental Security Income (SSI), mainly on account of bipolar disorder, and would receive $754 a month, or a little over $9,000 a year.

Crystal was barred from low-income housing for two years because of the assault charge she caught for fighting in the group home. Even if she had not been barred, she would still have found herself at the bottom of a waiting list that was six years long, which wasn't too bad considering that the wait in large cities like Washington, D.C., can extend to twenty years. Crystal secured her first apartment in the private market—a run-down two-bedroom unit in the inner city whose rent took 73 percent of her income. A few months later, Crystal experienced her first official eviction, which went on her record, making it likely that her appli-

Matthew Desmond is associate professor of sociology and social studies at Harvard University.

I thank Sheldon Danziger, Kathy Edin, Suzanne Nichols, Devah Pager, Robert Sampson, Mario Small, Bruce Western, the Russell Sage Foundation Trustees, and all who participated in the "Severe Deprivation in America" conference, hosted and sponsored by the Russell Sage Foundation on October 30–31, 2014. Direct correspondence to: Matthew Desmond at mdesmond@fas.harvard.edu, Department of Sociology, Harvard University, William James Hall, 33 Kirkland St., Cambridge, MA 02138.

1. I met Crystal while conducting ethnographic fieldwork in Milwaukee with low-income tenants and their landlords (Desmond 2012, 2016). Crystal Mayberry is a pseudonym.

cation for housing assistance would be denied. After her eviction, Crystal met a woman named Vanetta at a homeless shelter and, with her, secured another apartment. Then Crystal put Vanetta's friend through a window, and the landlord told Crystal to leave.

Crystal spent nights in shelters, with friends, and with members of her church. She learned how to live on the streets, walking them at night and sleeping on the bus or in hospital waiting rooms during the day. She learned to survive by relying on strangers. She met a woman at a bus stop and ended up living with her for a month. People were attracted to Crystal. She was gregarious and funny, with an endearing habit of slapping her hands together and laughing at herself. She sang in public, gospel mostly.

Crystal had always believed that her Supplemental Security Income was secure. You couldn't get fired from SSI, and your hours couldn't get cut. "SSI always come," she said. Until one day it didn't. Crystal had been approved for SSI as a minor, but her adult re-evaluation found her ineligible. Now Crystal's only source of income was food stamps. She tried donating plasma, but her veins were too small. Disconnected, Crystal burned through the remaining ties she had from church and her foster families. When her SSI was not reinstated after several months, she descended into street homelessness and prostitution. Crystal had never been a morning person but soon learned that was the best time to turn tricks, catching men on their way to work.

A CHALLENGE

Many of us who are poverty scholars have met people like Crystal. We learn a great deal from them, and our own lives are influenced by them. And many of us feel, on returning to the library from the field, that the tools provided by mainstream social science are outdated and leave us ill-equipped to deal with the complexities of the lives of people like Crystal.

Should we say Crystal is "poor"? She certainly is that—but living in mere poverty would be a tremendous blessing for Crystal. Poverty is defined officially as an income cutoff, a threshold. But there are many depths below the poverty line. Poverty is qualitatively different from "deep poverty" (half below the poverty line), which in turn is a world apart from "extreme poverty" (living on $2 a day) (Aron, Jacobson, and Turner 2013; Shaefer and Edin 2013). There is poverty, and then there is *poverty*. Recent debates about poverty measurement have focused largely on its material attributes: for example, how to account for taxes, transfers, and benefits, or whether to adopt a relative or absolute definition (Brady 2003; Meyer and Sullivan 2012). These debates are necessary and productive, but a relatively small income is but one of many obstacles preventing Crystal from living a full, productive, and healthy life. Like many people from disadvantaged families, she experienced setbacks at a very young age (even before birth) and never fully recovered from them. Poverty is more than a material condition (Sen 1999).

Should we place Crystal in a larger "structural framework"? If so, which one? Many of our structural theories, and their corresponding policy prescriptions, trace social problems back to a singular source, some big word that sits at the mouth of the river. Deindustrialization. Neoliberalism. Racism. Welfare reform. What would that singular source be in Crystal's life? The joblessness of her father? Her mother's addiction? The sexual abuse or violence? The broken foster system or schools that allowed her to fall through the cracks? Poverty is *multidimensional*, yet the one-dimensional focus of many of our structural accounts facilitates intellectual fragmentation and prevents researchers from building a comprehensive and systematic theory of poverty that articulates how movements and countermovements in different spheres of life (political, economic, residential, familial) collude to deepen or lessen American inequality.

Should we make sense of Crystal's young life by referencing "culture?" Can we do that and fully appreciate how traumas imprinted themselves on her body and mind? At seventeen, Crystal was examined by a clinical psychologist, who diagnosed her with, among other things, bipolar disorder, post-traumatic stress disorder, reactive attachment disorder, and borderline intellectual functioning. According to his report, Crystal "has limited ability to tolerate much in the way of frustration or anxiety and a proneness to act out her tensions without much in the way of forethought or deliberation.... She is still seen as being fragilely integrated." Did Crystal put that woman through a window because of the "culture of violence" pervading the inner city, or because she was a young person who had herself been brutalized and psychologically damaged—or both? The time is ripe to explore the relationship between culture, psychology, and inequality (Lamont and Small 2008; Patterson 2015). What is clear is that we cannot talk about agency without recognizing the deep imprint of past traumas, just as we cannot talk about "violent offenders" without recognizing that many of them were "violently offended" themselves as children, as Bruce Western's article demonstrates.

How should we begin to study the conditions that Crystal's young life embodies so tragically and completely? Should we design a randomized control trial or a quasi-experimental method to isolate the single most meaningful cause of Crystal's hardship? That seems quite impossible, as the lives of the poor are characterized by correlated and compounding disadvantages. Should we conduct a survey or analyze big data in the form of administrative records? Our most vulnerable citizens often are left out of survey samples and infrequently show up in administrative databases. Should we conduct fieldwork? Ethnography comes with its own set of analytical and ethical challenges, especially when studying the poor. These questions have led several contributors to this issue to develop methodological innovations to capture the complexities of poverty, including the ethnographic approach of Megan Comfort and her coauthors, who fully integrate clinical social work.

Besides these methodological challenges, the very language of "poverty" can be fuzzy and imprecise. This problem is accentuated by the fact that our analytical concepts have never been innocent of politics and moralizing (Gans 1995; O'Connor 2009). Our current terminology groups all families below a certain income threshold into a single category: the poor. But doing so can flatten crucial differences in how material scarcity and psychological turmoil are experienced. How can our concepts be refined or redefined? How can we capture with more precision variations or degrees of hardship and social suffering among low-income families? And what do we mean by "poverty" anyway?

SEVERE DEPRIVATION

These challenges motivated this journal issue on severe deprivation in America. By "severe deprivation," we mean economic hardship that is (1) acute, (2) compounded, and (3) persistent. Let us unpack these three components.

Acute hardship: Life far below the poverty line, characterized by a scarcity of critical resources and material hardship. No rich democracy matches the United States in the depth and expanse of its poverty. As of 2015, almost 50 million Americans lived below the federal poverty line. If America's poor founded a country, that country would have a bigger population than Spain. In 2010, 20.5 million people in the United States lived in deep poverty—that is, on incomes below half the federal poverty threshold—up by almost 8 million since 2000.[2] That same year one in every fifty Americans reported living in a household with an income consisting only of food stamps (DeParle 2010; Edelman 2012). Crystal lived on $25 a day before expenses and far less after she paid her rent.

Compounded hardship: "Poverty plus," or correlated and compounded adversity. This idea speaks to the clustering of different kinds of disadvantage across multiple dimensions (psychological, social, material) and institutions (work, family, prison). Although the literature on development economics has grappled with the problem of measuring multidimensional hardship (Alkire and Foster 2011; Sen 1976), students of poverty in America have only begun thinking through the conceptual and methodological challenges of this approach. The essence of poverty is not simply an economic condition but the *linked ecology* of social maladies and broken institutions. To this end, the articles in this issue develop new ways of combining—rather than isolating—dif-

---

2. In 2010 the number of Americans in deep poverty fell to 15 million after accounting for all public benefits. Most of those people were lifted into mere poverty (Edelman 2012, 82).

ferent forms of disadvantage, including Claire Herbert, Jeff Morenoff, and David Harding's analysis of the nexus between the prison and housing markets and Kristin Perkins and Robert Sampson's method of measuring "compounded disadvantage" that unites individual and ecological hardship (see also Sampson 2014). If, in the end, it comes down to *all of it*, then thinking that one institution or condition has supreme explanatory priority—that "the most important thing" is the family, the neighborhood, housing, employment, or education—may be the wrong direction for poverty research. This point applies to statistical methods that promote isolationist thinking as well as to qualitative approaches that tend to focus on a single dimension of a disadvantaged group instead of "studying the whole" (Desmond 2014; Halle 1984).

Persistent hardship: Enduring disadvantage often stubbornly impervious to change. This component of our definition focuses attention on three interrelated matters. The first involves the lasting effects of *early-life trauma,* including abuse, hunger, and violence experienced as a child or even as a fetus (Shonkoff et al. 2012). Many people below the poverty line speak of the traumas that set them on certain paths. Just ask Mrs. Lana of Eastwood, whose madness after her son's murder is captured by Laurence Ralph. The second matter is deprivation *experienced over long stretches,* even lifetimes. Here, questions regarding the coping strategies and effects of long-term social suffering come into play (Brooks-Gunn and Duncan 1997; Jencks 1992). The third element of persistent deprivation deals with *generational* poverty passed down from parents to children (Sharkey 2013). When we focus on generational deprivation, we not only recognize the resiliency of past wrongs on present-day problems but we may also find explanations for why some children born into poverty manage to climb out of it.

A critic might accuse the social scientists in this issue of "scraping the very bottom" and object to building a research agenda, let alone a public policy, this way. To this criticism we have three responses. First, thinking about severe deprivation is not just a matter of studying the poorest of the poor. Our collective project is to develop a set of analytical commitments that go beyond narrow and tidy approaches to economic vulnerability. It is more about a perspective, a certain intellectual posture, than about a specific population.

That being said, it may be just as orienting to speak of the "severely deprived" as a population as it was when scholars spoke of "the underclass" (Myrdal 1963; Jencks 1992; Wilson 1987), before that term became saddled with so much cultural baggage that researchers and journalists eventually let it die. We know startlingly little about life at the bottom of society (Gans 2014), even if many social problems we care about—from crime and violence to homelessness and teenage pregnancy—largely involve not simply "the poor" but people whose lives are characterized by economic hardship that is acute, compounded, and persistent. In fact, researchers who focus exclusively on, say, educational inequality, housing instability, legal entanglements, or neighborhood disadvantage often are studying the *very same families* whose lives are marred by severe deprivation. Our second response speaks to the need to develop an approach that encourages researchers and policymakers to understand those families holistically instead of specializing in one vector of their lives.

Third, we note that not only does severe deprivation rest at the heart of many social problems, but that it may not be as rare as scholars often think. When Americans compare the poverty of their fellow citizens with the desperation that grips the slum dwellers of Lagos or Caracas, or with the swollen-bellied families in the villages of rural India or inland China, they sometimes conclude that American poverty would be considered downright abundance in other parts of the word, that ours is an unfortunate but ultimately lesser hardship. On some key measures, this is undeniably true. But this line of thinking can cause us to overlook just how desperate the situation is for those Americans living at the very bottom. Sometimes such comparisons lead to the presumption that nobody in the United States lives "that bad." "Four billion people in the world earn less than $2 per day," write a group of scholars in the pages of a leading academic journal (Walsh, Kress, and Beyerchen 2005, 473). "No one in the U.S., Japan, or Germany lives in such poverty." No one? This is tragically far from true, at least as far as the United States is concerned. Luke Shaefer, Kathryn Edin, and Elizabeth Talbert find that the number of American children who experienced chronic extreme poverty, living on no more than $2 a day for seven months or more, has increased by over 240 percent since 1996.

A NEW POVERTY AGENDA

Poverty researchers from across the social sciences have the opportunity to reach collectively toward a new paradigm—not just a new way of thinking but a whole different approach to the study of vulnerability, violence, and marginality, one that carries methodological, policy-relevant, and normative implications. Most research is rooted in theories now a few decades old. These theories have stood the test of time because they are incisive, sweeping, and validated. But they also were developed before the United States began incarcerating more of its citizens than any other nation; before urban rents soared and poor families began dedicating the majority of their income to housing; before welfare reform caused caseloads to plummet; and before the crack epidemic tore apart poor minority communities. In recent years, the very *nature* of poverty in America has changed, especially at the very bottom. A new poverty agenda is needed for a world that is itself quite new.

America's social policies have changed. Some forms of public assistance, like housing assistance and cash welfare, have been scaled back, while others, like the Earned Income Tax Credit (EITC) and the Supplemental Nutrition Assistance Program (SNAP), have grown substantially. Large-scale changes in federal poverty policy have created new winners and losers. Households just above and below the poverty threshold receive significantly more help today than they did twenty years ago—but those far below the poverty line receive significantly less (Currie 2008; Moffitt 2015). The inequality debate focuses mainly on the growing divide between the rich and the middle class. But there is a growing divide *below* the poverty line as well, between the stable, typically working poor, who benefit significantly from today's safety net, and the unstable, typically nonworking poor, who receive fewer benefits or who are even disconnected, as was the case for the women with whom Kristen Seefeldt and Heather Sandstrom spoke.

The growing rift between the working and nonworking poor is driven almost entirely by public policy priorities, not rising security or wages in the workplace. The last three decades have been marked by impressive economic growth, but increases in productivity have not translated into broad social uplift. At the bottom of the labor market, compensation has stagnated in both the private and public sectors, while the economy has expanded. By one estimate, the federal minimum wage in 2013 would have been $18.30 (not $7.25) if it had increased at the rate of productivity (Cooper 2013). "When it comes to an economy that is working for working families," write Lawrence Mishel, Jared Bernstein, and Sylvia Allegretto (2005, 34), "growth in and of itself is a necessary but not a sufficient condition. The growth has to reach the people." Roughly 30 percent of the American workforce labors for "poverty wages," and most low-wage workers are not teenagers but adults, including many parents. One study estimated that one in five children in America has a parent who would receive a raise if the minimum wage were increased (Cooper 2013).

Labor market policies designed to shake loose regulation and facilitate market flexibility have weakened organized labor and replaced long-term employment with temporary jobs. Today most workers are not unionized, and half of all new jobs end within the first year (Farber 2010; Western and Rosenfeld 2011). As the service sector has eclipsed manufacturing, the United States has witnessed an increase in "bad jobs" offering low pay, no benefits, and little certainty (Kalleberg 2011). Although no sector of the economy is untouched by precarious work, bad jobs are disproportionately staffed by the working poor. Scholars now speak of the "age of layoffs" (Uchitelle 2006, 124) and have begun to study new forms of instability among workers, including schedule unpredictability designed to maximize productivity. A recent study by Susan Lambert, Peter Fugiel, and Julia Henly (2014) found that 41 percent of early career hourly employees (ages twenty-six to thirty-two) learn about their work schedule one week or less in advance of the coming workweek. Those who are parents of young children report that their hours fluctuated in the previous month by an average of 40 percent, compared to normal hours.

The location of disadvantage also is shifting. Owing to rising housing costs in cities, an aging population, shifting patterns of immigration, changes in federal housing programs, and patterns of downward mobility, it is not far-fetched to imagine a future in which the poor do not live on the other side of the tracks but in entirely different municipalities and counties. Indeed, we need not imagine this: it already has become a reality as poverty has skyrocketed in American suburbs throughout the country (Kneebone and Berube 2013). Although disadvantage and violent crime are less severely concentrated in the suburbs than in many inner-city areas, these low-density neighborhoods are characterized by isolation and loneliness, especially among the elderly and nonworking poor. Access to key institutions—social services, grocery stores, hospitals and health clinics, schools—also is a key issue for poor suburban families, as is the growing distance to employment centers. Increasingly, the suburban poor are either living their lives on buses and trains or on foot, enduring long commutes, or enduring life alone in neighborhoods never designed for community (Murphy and Wallace 2010; Murphy, forthcoming).

The severely deprived today also pass through different institutions than they did in previous generations. The prison, for one, has become a major poverty institution, especially in the lives of poor black and Hispanic men (Pettit 2012; Western 2006). The violence and isolation of incarceration, as well as the mark of a criminal record, have steep consequences for mental health, employment, family life, and social mobility (Pager 2007; Travis, Western, and Redburn 2014). And many disadvantaged minority neighborhoods are today characterized by heightened surveillance and police presence, which has altered everyday life and the community fabric. A generation ago, poverty scholars would not have needed such a sharp focus on the nexus between punishment and poverty. The articles by John Hagan and Holly Foster and by Bryan Sykes and Becky Pettit demonstrate that a comprehensive picture of inner-city poverty is incomplete without a serious consideration of the police and incarceration—and the millions of people released from prison each year.

The family has changed. The number of American children living in single-parent homes nearly doubled between 1960 and 2010. In 1970 only 12 percent of children lived with one parent. Today one-third of all American children are not being raised by two parents, and the majority of them live in single-mother households (Federal Interagency Forum on Child and Family Statistics 2013). Family complexity has increased, especially within low-income communities, and as a result, children are being raised by multiple parent figures and the family safety net is fraying (Cancian, Meyer, and Cook 2011; Cherlin and Seltzer 2014). During the first years of the War on Poverty, destitute families often relied on extended kin networks to get by. But the family may no longer serve as a reliable source of support (Desmond 2012; Stack 1974). Understanding why is crucial for understanding the texture of severe deprivation as well as for building effective policy.

A new poverty agenda also entails returning to problems long ago considered ameliorated: elderly poverty, for example. Large-scale programs have led to a significant decrease in poverty among the aged. And politicians long ago learned that their constituents hated the idea of senior housing a lot less than the idea of public housing intended for poor families. When public housing construction for low-income households ceased, it continued for the aged: high-rises originally built for the poor have been converted for elderly use (Schwartz 2014; Vale 2009). And yet, as Helen Levy's and LaShawnDa Pittman's articles show, the elderly may not be as shielded from deprivation as is largely presumed. Their vulnerability snaps into sharpest view after new hardship measures sensitive to the lived experience of poverty in old age are applied.

It is important to notice, too, what is not in this issue—that is, what we do not write about. We have not written about poor people's politics or social movements. A generation ago, these issues were central to the study of poverty (Drake and Cayton 1945; Piven and Cloward 1993 [1971]). With some exceptions in the fields of sociology (Oliver 2008), history (Katz 2012), and political science (Burch 2013), the political sociology or political science of poverty remains severely underdeveloped, even as Robert Sampson's (2012) novel work on "collective efficacy" in disadvantaged communities has laid a solid foundation on which to build a new research agenda. Basic questions about inequality within the civil sphere, political nihilism and capability, and uneven resistance to marginality remain unanswered. The vast majority of poverty researchers take as their audience policymakers, not publics. Do we still believe, I wonder, in the political capabilities of low-income communities? Is a revised civil rights movement or refashioned labor movement possible? And if so, what should the roll of intellectuals be?

We also do not talk about exploitation—the fact that some people make a good living off the poor. Crystal's landlord, for example, owned thirty-six units squarely in the inner city, rented exclusively to tenants below the poverty line, and netted roughly $10,000 a month, more than what Crystal took home in a year (Desmond 2016). Poverty research today pivots on the concept of a *lack*. Structural accounts emphasize the inner city's lack of jobs, lack of social services, or lack of organizations. Cultural accounts emphasize the inner city's lack of role models, lack of custodial fathers, or lack of middle-class values (Satter 2009). In fixating on what poor people lack, we have neglected to notice the powerful ways in which exploitation contributes to the reproduction of urban poverty. In several realms, public-private partnerships have been championed as an effective vehicle through which to address social problems. But this approach not only leaves the relationship between poverty and profit intact but also relies on the American taxpayer to shoulder the burden when employers refuse to provide workers with a living wage or when landlords drive up rent to maximize their rate of return. Inequality and poverty march together in lockstep. Addressing one without paying attention to the other results in a watered-down, inefficient antipoverty policy at best. Our policies should view exploitation as a serious impediment to saving, social mobility, decent housing, and self-reliance. But what might a public policy that effectively addresses exploitation look like?

PUBLIC POLICY AND MORAL URGENCY

What does the severe deprivation perspective mean for public policy? By way of conclusion, let me offer three policy implications that correspond to the three components of severe deprivation.

Acute Hardship

The severe deprivation perspective calls attention to what might be called "policy skimming": simultaneously increasing aid for working families and withdrawing some forms of support for the very poor.[3] In 2012 the federal government spent $54 billion on the Earned Income Tax Credit and $17 billion on Temporary Assistance for Needy Families (TANF) (Aron, Jacobson, and Turner 2013). Many analysts associated with the political left have pronounced that a broad retrenchment of aid to the needy has occurred since the 1980s. But the evidence tells quite a different story. Per capita spending on means-tested programs—even excluding Medicaid—almost doubled between 1986 and 2007. Spending on welfare programs for the poor has increased substantially, but the beneficiaries of this spending have been the working poor and families just above or just below the federal poverty line. Three decades ago, the poorest families in America received most (56 percent) of the transfers going to families with private incomes below 200 percent of the federal poverty threshold; in recent years, those families received less than one-third (32 percent) of the transfers (Moffitt 2015). Today the distinction between the "deserving" and "undeserving"

---

3. When President Johnson set out to see American poverty, he visited coal miners—workers. Today, to see the neediest cases, a lawmaker seeking to launch a renewed war on poverty would visit families on welfare or SSI, or the disconnected.

poor carries with it a real cash value. Some parts of the safety net have been patched with cloth taken from other parts.

The question, then, becomes not, *how* do we solve poverty, but *whose* poverty are we solving? And why? This rephrasing helps us adjudicate between our need to emphasize how effective the safety net truly is (and has been) and the fact that so many people are falling through its holes (Bailey and Danziger 2013; Edelman 2012). As Liana Fox and her coauthors demonstrate in their article, in the absence of programs, things would be considerably worse. And yet, ours remains a country beset by severe deprivation.

Compounded Hardship
Our perspective is decidedly anti-silver-bullet. If severe deprivation is by definition the clustering of multiple disadvantages, then going singularly after one thing would be inefficient at best. We can give a working single mother a tax credit and see returns, but what about her abusive boyfriend? We can plant a charter school in a low-income neighborhood, but will the poorest children benefit when landlords respond by raising the rent? The desire to somehow outsmart poverty with a new innovation—to discover a cure—is strong both within and outside the academy. But the severe deprivation perspective gestures more toward an "all hands on deck" approach. This is easier said than done.

For one thing, budgetary allocations encourage policymakers, especially at the federal level, to emphasize the importance of their pet issue rather than the necessity of cross-system collaboration. Changes in resource allocation that slacken competition between offices and incentivize interdepartmental policy design are fundamental to building a more holistic antipoverty policy. Second, the complexity of poverty is extremely difficult to communicate. Findings from a randomized control trial that evaluate a program intervention on a particular outcome—such as a study showing that a jobs program decreases youth violence (Heller 2014)—are beautiful and powerful in their simplicity, and the policy implication seems clear. But when the focus moves to the gnarled problems of poverty, the sell to policymakers and the public requires a new kind of language and framing.

A third challenge is one of scale. Interventions that adopt a multidimensional approach to deprivation tend to pour an enormous amount of resources into bounded neighborhoods. For example, President Barack Obama's Promise Zone initiative promotes job creation, economic growth, educational opportunity, and safety in twenty neighborhoods around the country. Can such an approach reach beyond those twenty neighborhoods? Can we—should we—imagine a multidimensional poverty agenda that is not rooted in poverty places? Whatever the challenges, considering the compounded nature of severe deprivation allows us to see the problem and its solutions in a new light and to rethink the ends for which our nation should strive.

Persistent Hardship
"Persistent" is another way of saying "generational," which is another way of saying "historical," which trains our attention on past wrongs: from systemic racism and the bleeding of black wealth to the rise of "tough on crime" policies (see, for example, Oliver and Shapiro 1997; Western 2006). Any hard look at past wrongs and their lingering effects reveals that addressing poverty is not only a matter of effective policy design and expanded economic opportunities but also a matter of justice and fairness. In policy circles, however, emphasis on what *can* be done supersedes what *should* be done. A spirit of pragmatism prevails. Researchers in a previous era used their skills to build a case for visionary change encapsulated in landmark rulings (for example, *Brown v. Board of Education*) or major pieces of legislation (the Great Society). Today many seem satisfied to advocate for "nudges" and incremental change. Fundamental reforms, from the New Deal to the Civil Rights Act, were advanced by normative arguments about what was right, not by cost-benefit analyses. As the sociologist David Grusky (2014) recently said, "If we're serious about winning a second War on Poverty . . . we need to shake off the shackles of the seemingly realistic." Somewhere along the way, being a hard-nosed, rigor-

ous, data-driven researcher became linked with being disinterested and "realistic." The normative impulse of social science was scrubbed out. But as a National Academies report on mass incarceration recently recognized (Travis, Western, and Redburn 2014, 320), some of our most pressing policy questions "cannot be resolved by reference to evidence" or "by weighing narrowly quantifiable costs against benefits."

The severe deprivation approach engages in an empirically driven values conversation about poverty in America, one that is transparent about the moral principles undergirding research and policy, that specifies and reimagines desirable ends, and that rigorously assesses whether we are living up to our professed values. Bearing witness to severe deprivation in one of the richest countries on the planet and chronicling the lives of the poor in their full complexity and humanity requires both intellectual and normative commitments.[4] The articles in this volume demonstrate that we can hold ourselves to the highest scientific standards and still inflect our work with a spirit of moral urgency.

This volume is a collective attempt to model a different way of doing poverty research, one that embraces the full complexity of poverty (realizing that the noise sometimes is the signal), advances a research agenda that subscribes fully to both the scientific and the normative project, and looks squarely at the trauma of poverty, its sadness, without reducing people to their hardships alone.

One day when homeless, Crystal and Vanetta were eating lunch at a McDonald's and a boy walked in. He was maybe nine or ten, in dirty clothes and with unkempt hair. One side of his face was swollen. The boy didn't approach the counter. Instead, he wandered slowly through the tables, looking for scraps.

Crystal and Vanetta noticed him at the same time. "What you got?" Crystal asked, riffling through her pockets. The women pooled what they had to buy the boy dinner. Staring up at the menu, Crystal wrapped her arm around the boy like she was his auntie or big sister. She made sure he was okay, handed him the food, and sent him on his way with a hug.

"Reminds me of when we was kids," Vanetta said, shaken.

Crystal watched the boy dash across the street. "I wish I had me a house. I would take him in."

REFERENCES

Alkire, Sabina, and James Foster. 2011. "Counting and Multidimensional Poverty Measurement." *Journal of Public Economics* 95: 476–87.

Aron, Laudan, Wendy Jacobson, and Margery Austin Turner. 2013. *Addressing Deep and Persistent Poverty: A Framework for Philanthropic Planning and Investment*. Washington, D.C.: Urban Institute.

Bailey, Martha, and Sheldon Danziger, eds. 2013. *Legacies of the War on Poverty*. New York: Russell Sage Foundation.

Brady, David. 2003. "Rethinking the Sociological Measurement of Poverty." *Social Forces* 81: 715–51.

Brooks-Gunn, Jeanne, and Greg Duncan. 1997. "The Effects of Poverty on Children." *The Future of Children* 7: 55–71.

Burch, Traci. 2013. *Trading Democracy for Justice: Criminal Convictions and the Decline of Neighborhood Political Participation*. Chicago: University of Chicago Press.

Cancian, Maria, Daniel Meyer, and Steven Cook. 2011. "The Evolution of Family Complexity from the Perspective of Nonmarital Children." *Demography* 48: 957–82.

Cherlin, Andrew, and Judith Seltzer. 2014. "Family Complexity, the Family Safety Net, and Public Policy." *ANNALS of the American Academy of Political and Social Science* 654: 231–39.

Cooper, David. 2013. "Raising the Federal Minimum Wage to $10.10 Would Lift Wages for Millions and Provide a Modest Economic Boost." Washington, D.C.: Economic Policy Institute.

Currie, Janet. 2008. *The Invisible Safety Net: Protecting the Nation's Poor Children and Families*. Princeton, N.J.: Princeton University Press.

---

4. The same is true for the most ostensibly disinterested, scientific study barren of empathy. Normative commitments invade. We might as well be transparent and intellectually serious about them.

DeParle, Jason. 2010. "Living on Nothing but Food Stamps." *New York Times,* January 2.

Desmond, Matthew. 2012. "Disposable Ties and the Urban Poor." *American Journal of Sociology* 117: 1295–1335.

———. 2014. "Relational Ethnography." *Theory and Society* 43: 547–79.

———. 2016. *Evicted: Poverty and Profit in the American City.* New York: Crown.

Drake, St. Clair, and Horace Cayton. 1945. *Black Metropolis: A Study of Negro Life in a Northern City.* New York: Harcourt, Brace, and World.

Edelman, Peter. 2012. *So Rich, So Poor: Why It's So Hard to End Poverty in America.* New York: New Press.

Farber, Henry. 2010. "Job Loss and the Decline in Job Security in the United States." In *Labor in the New Economy,* edited by Katharine G. Abraham, James R. Spletzer, and Michael Harper. Chicago: University of Chicago Press.

Federal Interagency Forum on Child and Family Statistics. 2013. *America's Children: Key National Indicators of Well-Being, 2013.* Washington: Federal Interagency Forum on Child and Family Statistics.

Gans, Herbert. 1995. *The War Against the Poor: The Underclass and Antipoverty Policy.* New York: Basic Books.

———. 2014. "Studying the Bottom of American Society." *Du Bois Review: Social Science Research on Race* 11: 195–204.

Grusky, David. 2014. "Four Myths About Poverty." *Chronicle of Higher Education,* February 24, B11–14.

Halle, David. 1984. *America's Working Man: Work, Home, and Politics Among Blue-Collar Property Owners.* Chicago: University of Chicago Press.

Heller, Sara. 2014. "Summer Jobs Reduce Violence Among Disadvantaged Youth." *Science* 346: 1219–23.

Jencks, Christopher. 1992. *Rethinking Social Policy: Race, Poverty, and the Underclass.* New York: HarperPerennial.

Kalleberg, Arne. 2011. *Good Jobs, Bad Jobs: The Rise of Polarized and Precarious Employment Systems in the United States, 1970s to 2000s.* New York: Russell Sage Foundation.

Katz, Michael. 2012. *Why Don't American Cities Burn?* Philadelphia: University of Pennsylvania Press.

Kneebone, Elizabeth, and Alan Berube. 2013. *Confronting Suburban Poverty in America.* Washington, D.C.: Brookings Institution Press.

Lambert, Susan J., Peter J. Fugiel, and Julia R. Henly. 2014. "Precarious Work Schedules Among Early-Career Employees in the U.S.: A National Snapshot." Research brief. Chicago: University of Chicago, Employment Instability, Family Well-Being, and Social Policy Network (EINet).

Lamont, Michel, and Mario Luis Small. 2008. "How Culture Matters: Enriching Our Understanding of Poverty." In *The Colors of Poverty: Why Racial and Ethnic Disparities Persist,* edited by David Harris and Ann Lin. New York: Russell Sage Foundation.

Meyer, Bruce, and James Sullivan. 2012. "Identifying the Disadvantaged: Official Poverty, Consumption Poverty, and the New Supplemental Poverty Measure." *Journal of Economic Perspectives* 26: 111–35.

Mishel, Lawrence, Jared Bernstein, and Sylvia Allegretto. 2005. *The State of Working America, 2004–2005.* Ithaca, N.Y.: ILR Press.

Moffitt, Robert. 2015. "The Deserving Poor, the Family, and the U.S. Welfare System." *Demography* 52(3): 729–49.

Murphy, Alexandra. Forthcoming. *When the Sidewalks End: Poverty in an American Suburb.* New York: Oxford University Press.

Murphy, Alexandra, and Danielle Wallace. 2010. "Opportunities for Making Ends Meet and Upward Mobility: Differences in Organizational Deprivation Across Urban and Suburban Poor Neighborhoods." *Social Science Quarterly* 91: 1164–86.

Myrdal, Gunnar. 1963. *Challenge to Affluence.* New York: Pantheon.

O'Connor, Alice. 2009. *Poverty Knowledge: Social Science, Social Policy, and the Poor in Twentieth-Century U.S. History.* Princeton, N.J.: Princeton University Press.

Oliver, Melvin, and Thomas Shapiro. 1997. *Black Wealth/White Wealth: A New Perspective on Racial Inequality.* New York: Routledge.

Oliver, Pamela. 2008. "Repression and Crime Control: Why Social Movement Scholars Should Pay Attention to Mass Incarceration as a Form of Repression." *Mobilization: An International Quarterly* 13: 1–24.

Pager, Devah. 2007. *Marked: Race, Crime, and Finding Work in an Era of Mass Incarceration.* Chicago: University of Chicago Press.

Patterson, Orlando, ed. 2015. *The Cultural Matrix: Understanding Black Youth.* Cambridge, Mass: Harvard University Press.

Pettit, Becky. 2012. *Invisible Men: Mass Incarceration*

and the Myth of Black Progress. New York: Russell Sage Foundation.

Piven, Frances Fox, and Richard Cloward. 1993 [1971]. Regulating the Poor: The Functions of Public Welfare, 2nd ed. New York: Vintage.

Sampson, Robert. 2012. Great American City: Chicago and the Enduring Neighborhood Effect. Chicago: University of Chicago Press.

———. 2014. "Criminal Justice Processing and the Social Matrix of Adversity." ANNALS of the American Academy of Political and Social Science 651: 296–301.

Satter, Beryl. 2009. Family Properties: How the Struggle over Race and Real Estate Transformed Chicago and Urban America. New York: Metropolitan Books.

Schwartz, Alex. 2014. Housing Policy in the United States, 3rd ed. London: Routledge.

Sen, Amartya. 1976. "Poverty: An Ordinal Approach to Measurement." Econometrica: Journal of the Econometric Society 44(2): 219–31.

———. 1999. Development as Freedom. New York: Anchor Books.

Shaefer, H. Luke, and Kathryn Edin. 2013. "Rising Extreme Poverty in the United States and the Response of Federal Means-Tested Transfer Programs." Social Service Review 87: 250–68.

Sharkey, Patrick. 2013. Stuck in Place: Urban Neighborhoods and the End of Progress Toward Racial Equality. Chicago: University of Chicago Press.

Shonkoff, Jack, et al. 2012. "The Lifelong Effects of Early Childhood Adversity and Toxic Stress." Pediatrics 129: e232–46.

Stack, Carol. 1974. All Our Kin: Strategies for Survival in a Black Community. New York: Basic Books.

Travis, Jeremy, Bruce Western, and Steve Redburn. 2014. The Growth of Incarceration in the United States: Exploring Causes and Consequences. Washington, D.C.: National Academies Press.

Uchitelle, Louis. 2006. The Displaced American: Layoffs and Their Consequences. New York: Alfred A. Knopf.

Vale, Lawrence. 2009. From the Puritans to the Projects: Public Housing and Public Neighbors. Cambridge, MA: Harvard University Press.

Walsh, James, Jeremy Kress, and Kurt Beyerchen. 2005. "Book Review Essay: Promises and Perils at the Bottom of the Pyramid." Administrative Science Quarterly 50(3): 473–82.

Western, Bruce. 2006. Punishment and Inequality in America. New York: Russell Sage Foundation.

Western, Bruce, and Jake Rosenfeld. 2011. "Unions, Norms, and the Rise in U.S. Wage Inequality." American Sociological Review 76: 513–37.

Wilson, William Julius. 1987. The Truly Disadvantaged: The Inner City, the Underclass, and Public Policy. Chicago: University of Chicago Press.

PART I
Severe Deprivation Among the Young and Old

Trends in Deep Poverty from 1968 to 2011: The Influence of Family Structure, Employment Patterns, and the Safety Net

LIANA FOX, CHRISTOPHER WIMER, IRWIN GARFINKEL, NEERAJ KAUSHAL, JAEHYUN NAM, AND JANE WALDFOGEL

This paper examines the changing face of deep poverty in the United States over the past fifty years and the role of family structure, employment patterns, and governmental taxes and transfers in explaining these trends. Using a newly developed historical measure of poverty based on the Census Bureau's supplemental poverty measure, we find that deep poverty rates have been fairly constant over the past fifty years, both overall and for families with children. In view of changes in family structure and government policy over this period, the intransigence of deep poverty is surprising. However, this overall stability obscures changes in the demographics of individuals and families in deep poverty, as well as the role of government policy. Governmental transfers reduce the risk of deep poverty for all subgroups examined, but the significance and the role of these programs have changed over time.

Keywords: historical Supplemental Poverty Measure (SPM), historical poverty trends, antipoverty programs

One of the primary goals of government is to provide an adequate safety net to ensure that vulnerable members of society are protected from the most severe forms of deprivation. Public policies designed to target and aid certain groups necessarily create winners and losers over time, with certain demographic groups benefiting more from government intervention than others. Accurately measuring the size and demographics of the poorest segment of the population provides important insights into the functioning of the safety net. This article uses a newly developed measure of poverty to more fully capture the experience of those at the bottom of the income distribution, focusing on those primarily subsisting on less than half the poverty threshold. This article expands our current knowledge about the role of the safety net over the past fifty years and explores how effective the

---

Liana E. Fox is postdoctoral researcher at the Swedish Institute for Social Research at Stockholm University. **Christopher Wimer** is research scientist and co-director of the Center on Poverty and Social Policy at the Columbia School of Social Work. **Irwin Garfinkel** is Mitchell I. Ginsberg Professor of Contemporary Urban Problems at the Columbia School of Social Work. **Neeraj Kaushal** is professor at the Columbia School of Social Work. **JaeHyun Nam** is a graduate student at the Columbia School of Social Work. **Jane Waldfogel** is Compton Foundation Centennial Professor for the Prevention of Children's and Youth Problems at the Columbia School of Social Work.

Direct correspondence to: Liana Fox at fox.liana@gmail.com, Swedish Institute for Social Research, Stockholm University, Universitetsvägen 10 F, Stockholm, Sweden 10691; Christopher Wimer at cw2727@columbia.edu, 1255 Amsterdam Ave., Rm. 735, New York, NY 10027; Irwin Garfinkel at ig3@columbia.edu, 1255 Amsterdam Ave., Rm. 714, New York, NY 10027; Neeraj Kaushal at nk464@columbia.edu, 1255 Amsterdam Ave., Rm. 917, New York, NY 10027; JaeHyun Nam at jn2462@columbia.edu, 1255 Amsterdam Ave., Rm. 722E, New York, NY 10027; and Jane Waldfogel at jw205@columbia.edu, 1255 Amsterdam Ave., Rm. 729, New York, NY 10027.

safety net has been at targeting vulnerable families.

Understanding historical trends in severe deprivation in America is a challenging endeavor, both conceptually and technically. Many types of measures exist, and many are defensible. Severe deprivation is most commonly measured using the "deep poverty" rate, which is generally defined as having resources that total less than half of a specified poverty threshold. Indeed, this rate is published every year by the U.S. Census Bureau in its annual publication on poverty and income in the United States (see, for example, DeNavas-Walt and Proctor 2014). If a poverty threshold is understood as the least amount of income necessary to maintain a basic minimal living standard, those with resources less than half of this standard are thought to be in the most severe state of disadvantage. While other articles in this volume concentrate on other, and sometimes more severe, definitions of disadvantage, we focus on deep poverty given our ability to examine long-term trends in deep poverty rates and composition, as well as the role of social policies in ameliorating deep poverty.

The primary challenge in understanding historical trends in severe deprivation lies in the fact that current estimates of deep poverty are typically based on a fundamentally flawed measure of official poverty. This measure fails to fully capture the role of governmental safety net programs because it excludes the value of in-kind benefits—such as the Supplemental Nutrition Assistance Program (SNAP, formerly the Food Stamp Program) and housing assistance—as well as the role of the tax system, including tax credits such as the Earned Income Tax Credit (EITC). Deep poverty rates based on official measures also rely on an outdated poverty threshold, which is based solely on the cost of food and how that figured into family budgets in the 1950s and 1960s. Rates defined with reference to such thresholds fail to take into account changing living standards: some necessities, like food, have become a smaller part of family budgets, while others, like housing, are consuming a relatively greater share.

In this article, we utilize a recently developed and more comprehensive approach to poverty measurement to reanalyze trends in deep poverty in America. Recent analyses using such a measure show that considerable progress has been made in reducing overall poverty in the past fifty years (Fox et al. 2015; Wimer et al. 2013). At the same time, despite decades of economic growth, very little has changed for the poorest segment—that is, the share of the population with income below 50 percent of the poverty line. Indeed, as we show later, the rate of deep poverty in the United States has remained relatively constant over the past fifty years, hovering around 5 percent of the population.

This article seeks to understand such trends, not only the remarkable stasis over time but also the extent to which changes in deep poverty rates among key subgroups over time and the role of the social safety net for these groups have jointly contributed to this stasis. That is, do the flat overall deep poverty rates mask changes in who is most likely to be in severe deprivation over time? Who have been the winners, and who the losers? Specifically, this article aims to investigate whether the composition of the population in deep poverty has changed and whether policy has assisted some groups more, leaving others at a higher risk of falling into deep poverty. These questions are important given the changes in family structure in recent decades and the expansions in policies aimed at reducing poverty among specific groups, including seniors (such as Social Security and Medicare), working parents (for example EITC), and children (such as the Child Tax Credit [CTC] and the School Lunch Program).

BACKGROUND

Income below a poverty line is thought to be a statistical representation of an individual or family lacking the material resources required to meet their basic necessities over the course of a year. Deep poverty, defined as having resources less than 50 percent of the poverty threshold, represents a common measure of severe deprivation—the inability to meet even half of one's annual basic necessities.

To properly measure trends in deep poverty over time as a marker of severe deprivation, we must first have an accurate measure of poverty. The United States has published official poverty rates for its population going back to 1959.

The original official poverty thresholds were based on the cost of a minimally adequate diet in the 1950s and the proportion of families' budgets devoted to food, which at that time was one-third of the total budget (Fisher 1992). Since then, these thresholds have mostly just been updated for inflation, although some other minor changes have been made along the way.

As decades of research and commentary have demonstrated, the official measure of poverty used in the United States is deeply flawed (Blank 2008; Citro and Michael 1995). First, the poverty thresholds are outdated, as food no longer comprises such a large share of families' budgets and other expenses like shelter have grown in importance (Hutto et al. 2011). This concern has led some to argue for a so-called relative or quasi-relative poverty threshold—one that changes over time as consumer expenditure patterns and living standards change (for a discussion, see Iceland 2005). Second, the American family has gone through tremendous changes over the past fifty years, with rising shares not only of single-parent families but also of cohabiting couples and cohabiting-parent families (Cancian and Reed 2009). This is problematic from a poverty measurement perspective since the official measure considers only those related by blood, marriage, or adoption as the unit sharing resources—that is, as "family" (see Provencher 2011). Third, and most important from our perspective, the official measure fails to count many of the resources devoted to alleviating poverty in the United States; these include near-cash or in-kind benefits like SNAP benefits and housing assistance as well as benefits that reach families through the tax system, like the Earned Income Tax Credit and the Child Tax Credit.

To remedy these and other deficiencies with the official measure, the National Academies of Science convened a panel of experts in the mid-1990s to recommend changes to the nation's poverty measurement system (Citro and Michael 1995). The panel's landmark report made numerous recommendations for improving the measurement of poverty, including innovations designed to reduce or eliminate the deficiencies noted here. Over the subsequent fifteen years, researchers at the U.S. Census Bureau and the Bureau of Labor Statistics (BLS) and in academia and think tanks experimented with measures based on these recommendations. In 2010 the Interagency Technical Working Group (ITWG) formed from across a number of government agencies issued a report with formal recommendations for the creation of a new Supplemental Poverty Measure (SPM) that the Census Bureau would publish each year alongside the official measure, in collaboration with the BLS and other agencies (ITWG 2010). Starting with the calendar years 2009 and 2010 (Short 2011), the Census Bureau began formally releasing the SPM in 2011, with annual releases thereafter.

As of this writing, the SPM has been released by the Census Bureau only for the calendar years 2009 through 2013, for reasons that are primarily technical: all of the data required to compute the SPM exist only for 2009 onward. This makes the SPM, for all its methodological improvements, inadequate for assessing long-term historical trends in either poverty or deep poverty. To fill this gap, in past work we have constructed an alternative time series using a newly developed measure that we call the historical Supplemental Poverty Measure, for all years between 1967 and 2012. The historical SPM time series attempts to implement the SPM in a consistent way over time to the best of our abilities given available data. In two recent papers using our historical SPM (as well as an alternative version of the historical SPM that uses an absolute or "anchored" poverty threshold) (Fox et al. 2015; Wimer et al. 2013), we have found that long-term trends in poverty as measured using the historical SPM are more favorable than official statistics would suggest. We find that much of the progress made in reducing poverty over the past fifty years, especially in recent years, is a result of government policies and programs, and especially those very programs not counted in official poverty statistics (with the notable exception of Social Security, which has reduced elderly poverty substantially and is included in the official poverty measure). We have also found that, regardless of whether we use a relative or anchored poverty threshold, deep poverty rates under our historical SPM time series have been fairly flat since the 1960s, again largely as a result of resources coming from government policies and programs.

In this article, we explore long-term trends in deep poverty in more detail, taking a particular look at changes in family structure and employment, as well as government policies and programs. Our central questions are: (1) How have deep poverty rates changed for different types of families, and in particular for families with children? (2) What would deep poverty rates among families with children look like over time absent changes in family structure and changes in employment patterns? (3) How would deep poverty rates for different family structure and employment subgroups look absent accounting for government policies and programs? (4) What do the trends imply for the changing composition of the deep poor over this period?

DATA AND METHODS

The data come from the 1968–2013 Annual Social and Economic Supplement (ASEC) to the Current Population Survey (CPS), also known as the March Supplement. It is important to note, as discussed in more detail later in the article, that this is a household-based survey of the non-institutionalized population. As such, it does not enumerate or capture some of the most severely disadvantaged individuals in American society, such as the homeless, the incarcerated, and those living in group housing in its many forms. Each survey covers income and associated topics in the prior calendar year, so these analyses cover the years 1967 to 2012. All figures are created using centered three-year moving averages, so our analysis covers the calendar years 1968 to 2011. We augment the annual CPS files to create our historical SPM series using information from the 1960–1961, 1972–1973, and 1980–2012 Consumer Expenditure (CEX) survey—a national survey tracking Americans' expenditures in a comprehensive variety of domains—as well as administrative data sources where necessary. Here we outline our approach to constructing the historical SPM time series, including the creation of poverty resource-sharing units, historical SPM poverty thresholds, and SPM resources. For a full accounting of all the methodological choices underlying our historical SPM series, see Fox et al. (2015) and its detailed technical appendix.

Poverty Units

To construct a historical SPM time series, the first step is to create a historically consistent poverty unit, which is the unit within a household deemed to be sharing resources to meet routine needs and expenses. Under the official measure, the poverty unit is the family, or anyone in the household related by blood, marriage, or adoption. The SPM makes a number of departures from this definition of the unit, in particular by including cohabiting unmarried partners together in the same unit, as well as by attaching unrelated children and foster children under the age of twenty-two to the household reference person. (For a full discussion of these issues, see Provencher 2011).

Constructing these poverty units consistently back to 1967 is challenging, in that not all unmarried partners in the household were identified in the CPS until 2007, and no unmarried partners were identified in households before 1995. In addition, foster children were not identified in the CPS until 1988. While we make no attempts to find foster children prior to 1988, given their extremely small sample size in any given year, we do attempt to identify unmarried partners and their children. To do this we use the Census Bureau's adjusted Persons of the Opposite Sex Sharing Living Quarters (POSSLQ) method. Lynne Casper, Philip Cohen, and Tavia Simmons (1999) define an adjusted POSSLQ household as one in which two unrelated adults (ages fifteen and older) of the opposite sex live together, with no other adults except relatives and foster children of the reference person or children of unrelated subfamilies. In our construction of poverty units and the poverty universe, we also exclude people living in group quarters (for example, college dormitories) in all years.

Poverty Thresholds

Under the SPM, the Bureau of Labor Statistics computes poverty thresholds on an annual basis using the most recent five years of CEX data (for details on the procedures for setting SPM thresholds in the CEX, see Garner 2011). The BLS first selects all consumer units with exactly two children and then estimates their expenditures on a core set of goods and services that includes food, clothing, shelter, and utilities (FCSU). They then find the average of the thirtieth to the thirty-sixth percentiles of expenditures on this basket for three different groups, defined by their housing status: renters, owners holding a mortgage, and owners not holding a mortgage. These figures are then multiplied by 1.2 to account for other common necessities (such as toiletries).

To estimate these thresholds historically we use historical data from the CEX. Because the CEX became an annual survey in 1980, the first year we are able to estimate a historical poverty threshold similar to the BLS threshold is 1984, covering the years 1980 to 1984. For 1980–1983, we use sequentially fewer years of data in estimating thresholds, so our 1983 threshold is based on 1980 to 1983, 1982 on 1980 to 1982, and so on. Prior to 1980, there were only two CEX surveys, one in 1960–1961 and one in 1972–1973. We thus construct a threshold in each of those years and then interpolate thresholds in intervening years using the rate of change in inflation. We also deviate from the Census Bureau and BLS in not adjusting our historical poverty thresholds for geographic differences in the cost of housing prices, given the lack of consistent and comparable data on these costs back to 1967.

To give some context, in 2012 the deep poverty SPM threshold for a two-adult, two-child family was $12,529. This was based on a typical two-adult, two-child family in deep poverty spending an average of $418 per month on food, $50 per month on clothing, $180 per month on shelter, and $187 per month on utilities.

SPM Resources

The SPM makes a number of changes to the definition of the resources available to meet the expenses deemed necessary in the poverty thresholds. First, it considers after-tax income rather than pretax income, both by subtracting federal and state income tax liabilities and payroll taxes and by adding any tax credits such as the Earned Income Tax Credit or Child Tax Credit. Second, it adds a variety of in-kind or near-cash benefits to the definition of resources: SNAP, the School Lunch Program, the Special Supplemental Nutrition Program for Women, Infants, and Children (WIC), the value of government housing assistance, and the Low-Income Home Energy Assistance Program (LIHEAP). Third, it subtracts some nondiscretionary expenses from resources, including medical out-of-pocket expenses and work and child care expenses. Following is a brief description of our approach to including these resources in the CPS.

Taxes: Census Bureau tax calculator estimates are available in the CPS back to 1980 (for the calendar year 1979). Prior to that, we rely on the TAXSIM program of the National Bureau of Economic Research (NBER) (Feenberg and Coutts 1993) to estimate taxes for 1967 to 1978. Details of the tax model can be found in Fox et al. (2015).

In-kind benefits: Of the five in-kind benefits we added to resources, only LIHEAP is measured in the CPS in all the years that the program existed. For certain years, then, we must impute benefits for the remaining four programs. For SNAP, data are not available prior to 1980 (for the calendar year 1979). We thus impute SNAP from the 1972–1973 CEX for all years between 1967 and 1978, constraining the imputation to specific percentages of households based on the percentage of households receiving SNAP in 1980 (1979) and changes in SNAP caseloads between 1967 and 1979. We then estimate values for imputed recipients using distributions of 1972–1973 values, adjusted for inflation in a given year. A similar approach is used in the imputation of the School Lunch Program (also prior to 1980 [1979]), housing assistance (prior to 1976 [1975]), and WIC (prior to 2001 [2000]). Values for school lunch are estimated in a similar manner to values for SNAP. Values for housing assistance are based on estimated household rental payments and the difference between estimated rental payments and the shelter component of the poverty threshold. Values for WIC are estimated based on annual administrative data.

Nondiscretionary expenses: Medical and child care expenses have been measured in the CPS only since 2010 (for calendar year 2009). Other work-related expenses (such as commuting costs or uniforms) are always estimated in the CPS and never directly measured, even in the Census Bureau's current SPM estimates. Thus, we impute medical and child care estimates for the entire time series and similarly estimate other work-related expenses for the entire time series using Census Bureau methods. Taking work expenses first, we estimate these as 85 percent of the median weekly work expenses calculated in the Survey of Income and Program Participation (SIPP) and then multiply by the number of weeks worked for each worker in the CPS. (Census Bureau researchers provided us with a historical table of these values going back to 1997.) We then calculate these values back to 1967, using changes in inflation. For medical expenses, we impute values from the CEX, attempting to mimic the distributions of medical expenses for key groups defined by income, number of elderly members of the poverty unit, and number of people in the poverty unit. For child care expenses, we take a similar approach, but first impute the incidence of child care expenses for units with children. Following the SPM, work and child care expenses are summed and capped at the level of the lowest-earning spouse's or partner's earnings. Because of the length of time over which we must impute and the lack of good benchmarks against which to assess them, our imputations in particular should be interpreted with caution. It is worth noting, however, that our main results are the same with or without the exclusion of medical and work and child care expenses from resources, at least in terms of the trends if not the overall levels.

Family Type, Family Structure, and Employment Status

We examine all three of the key constructs that we use to explore deep poverty trends—family type, family structure, and employment status—at the SPM-unit level. For family type, we define three mutually exclusive groups. We first identify the presence of working-age family members (ages eighteen to sixty-four) in a unit and then divide those units into families with children and those without children. The third category includes those families with no eighteen- to sixty-four-year-olds—these are elderly-only families. (The small number of SPM units with all members under the age of eighteen are dropped from the analyses.) Within these three primary family types, we define family structure by whether the unit is married, cohabiting, or single. Thus, if anyone in the SPM unit is married, we code everyone in that unit as residing in a married family. If no one is married but a cohabiting couple is part of the unit, the unit is coded as cohabiting. The remaining families are coded as single-headed families.

For employment status, we consider four mutually exclusive groups, focusing on units with at least one eighteen- to sixty-four-year-old member: units where all working-age adults are working full-time, full-year (defined as thirty-five hours or more per week for at least fifty weeks a year);[1] units where all working-age adults are working, but at least one is not working full-time, full-year; units where at least one working-age adult is working but at least one working-age adult is not working (a status that includes both unemployed workers and workers out of the labor force for any other reason); and units with eighteen- to sixty-four-year-olds present but none are working.

We first present three rates of deep poverty: (1) for the overall population, (2) by family type, and (3) among families with children for key family structure and employment subgroups. We then present a formal "decomposition" of the role of family structure and employment

---

1. Weekly hours are based on responses to the question of how many hours were usually worked per week in the preceding year. While prior to 1975 respondents were asked only about actual hours worked the previous week, not usual hours worked the previous year, they were also separately asked whether they worked full-time, part-time, or not at all in the previous year. We use the latter variable for classification for 1967–1974.

status in explaining long-term trends in deep poverty among families with children. This decomposition is followed by an assessment of the role of policies and programs in reducing poverty rates across family types and across subgroups of families with children. We conclude by documenting the changing composition of the deep poor that results from the trends that we detail. We use centered three-year moving averages for all figures.

RESULTS

Trends in Incidence of Deep Poverty

We begin by showing trends in deep poverty for the total population, with and without the inclusion of resources stemming from government policies and programs. Overall, the post-tax-and-transfer deep poverty rate in the United States has been fairly constant over the past fifty years, remaining around 5 percent of the non-institutionalized, civilian population. Over this time the role of government taxes and transfers in alleviating deep poverty has grown (see figure 1). Without these programs, the rate of deep poverty would have increased from 12.8 percent to 18.7 percent from 1968 to 2011 and also would have been more volatile over the time period.

While the overall incidence of deep poverty has been relatively unchanged over the past fifty years, different groups have experienced differing trends. Table 1 shows deep poverty rates for a number of demographic groups. This basic demographic analysis shows that the risk of falling into deep poverty has changed considerably for various subgroups over time. In 1968 elderly units and single-parent families with children were most likely to fall into deep poverty, but by 2011 working-age families without an employed adult had substantially higher deep poverty rates than any other group.

Since 1968, deep poverty rates for working-age families with or without children have been relatively constant, while for elderly families with no working-age adults present, there was a sharp decline in the deep poverty rate up until about the mid-1980s, followed by a gradual rise. Looking at rates by race-ethnicity, we can see

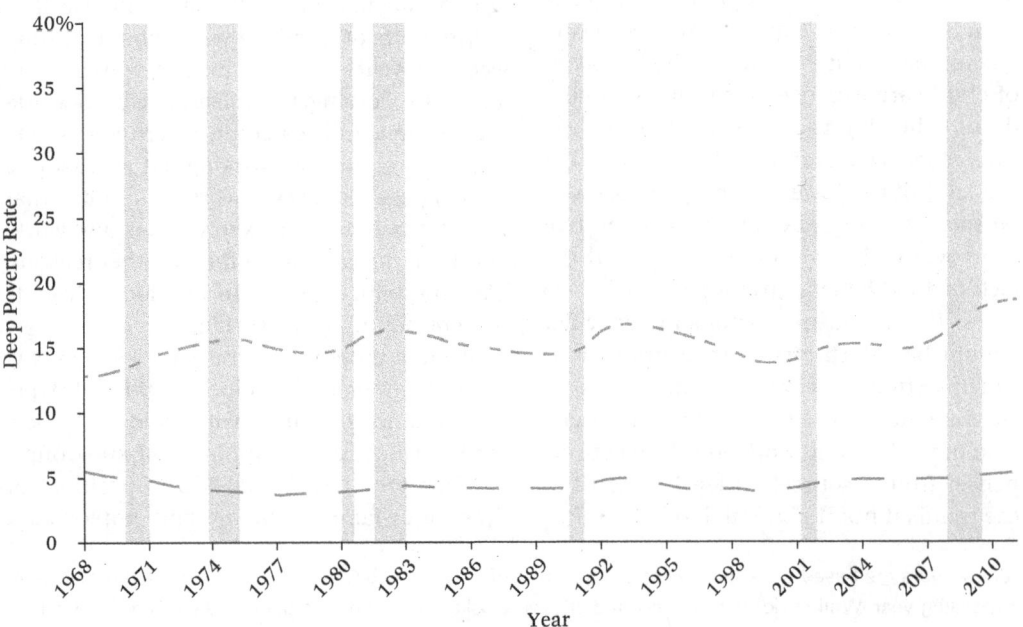

Figure 1. Overall Deep Poverty, with and Without Taxes and Transfers, 1968–2011

——— SPM Deep Poverty   - - - SPM Deep Poverty Without All Taxes and Transfers

Source: Authors' calculations from CPS ASEC, 1967–2012.

Table 1. Demographics of Deep Poverty, 1968–2011 (Using Three-Year Moving Averages)

	1968	1978	1988	1998	2008	2011	2011–1968 Percentage Point Change	2011–1968 Percentage Change
Overall	5.5%	3.8%	4.1%	4.1%	4.9%	5.3%	−0.1%	−2.2%
Family type								
Working age with children	4.8%	3.9%	4.4%	3.8%	4.3%	4.9%	0.1%	2.1%
Working age, no children	5.1%	3.3%	3.5%	4.2%	5.4%	5.9%	0.9%	16.8%
Elderly	13.2%	4.4%	4.2%	4.9%	6.2%	5.3%	−8.0%	−60.2%
Family structure								
Single	15.5%	8.9%	8.5%	9.1%	9.9%	10.7%	−4.8%	−30.8%
Cohabiting	5.5%	3.3%	4.9%	4.0%	4.8%	5.5%	0.0%	−0.4%
Married	3.7%	2.4%	2.5%	1.9%	2.6%	2.7%	−0.9%	−24.8%
Family employment status								
All adults (age 18–64) employed full-time	2.0%	1.1%	1.0%	0.8%	0.6%	0.6%	−1.4%	−71.8%
All adults (age 18–64) employed at least part-time	5.0%	3.0%	3.4%	3.1%	3.1%	3.1%	−1.9%	−37.6%
At least one adult (age 18–64) not employed	3.5%	2.9%	3.8%	3.5%	3.9%	3.9%	0.4%	10.0%
All adults (age 18–64) not employed	20.8%	16.5%	17.3%	24.5%	28.3%	29.4%	8.6%	41.5%
No adults 18–64 in unit	14.8%	4.9%	4.8%	5.5%	6.6%	5.5%	−9.3%	−62.8%
Race/ethnicity								
White	4.4%	3.2%	3.5%	3.6%	4.3%	4.7%	0.3%	−7.7%
White, non-Hispanic	—	3.0%	3.1%	3.0%	3.6%	3.9%	—	—
Black	14.2%	8.0%	7.6%	7.1%	8.1%	8.7%	−5.5%	38.9%
Asian	—	—	5.5%	5.3%	5.8%	5.8%	—	—
Hispanic	—	6.0%	8.2%	7.3%	7.6%	8.1%	—	—
Family structure (working age with children)								
Single	19.0%	12.4%	11.9%	11.2%	10.9%	12.0%	−7.0%	−36.7%
Cohabiting	5.2%	4.0%	6.6%	4.8%	5.6%	6.8%	1.6%	30.4%
Married	3.4%	2.5%	2.7%	1.8%	2.3%	2.6%	−0.9%	−25.4%
Family employment status (working age with children)								
All adults (age 18–64) employed full-time	2.2%	1.2%	1.2%	0.8%	0.5%	0.5%	−1.7%	−78.8%
All adults (age 18–64) employed at least part-time	5.0%	2.9%	3.4%	2.8%	2.3%	2.3%	−2.7%	−53.8%
At least one adult (age 18–64) not employed	3.5%	3.1%	4.2%	3.6%	3.9%	4.1%	0.6%	16.0%
All adults (age 18–64) not employed	21.6%	21.8%	21.2%	32.5%	38.4%	39.6%	18.0%	83.3%

Source: Authors' calculations from CPS ASEC, 1967–2012.
Notes: Race categories are inclusive of all ethnicities unless specified. Hispanic origin is not available until 1970 and Asian not until 1985.

that while deep poverty rates for whites have been fairly constant, there has been a considerable decline for blacks.

Focusing on families of working-age adults with children, we next examine trends in deep poverty by family structure. We find that single parents with children have experienced large declines in the likelihood of deep poverty; their deep poverty rates decreased from 19.0 percent in 1968 to 12.0 percent in 2011 (see figure 2). However, much of this decline occurred prior to 1977; deep poverty rates for this group have been relatively flat since then. Deep poverty rates for cohabiting and married families with children exhibit much less change over the period. While rates for cohabiting families with children have fluctuated a bit more than for married families, it is worth noting that this is a rather small group in the CPS, especially in the early portion of the time series.

Looking at deep poverty rates by family employment status among families with children, we find that families without an employed adult are almost twice as likely to fall into deep poverty as they were fifty years ago: the deep poverty rate increased from 21.6 percent in 1968 to 39.6 percent in 2011 (see figure 3). Meanwhile, families with all adults employed full-time, full-year, have had consistently low rates of deep poverty—between 1 and 2 percent. For families with all adults working and at least one working part-year or part-time, deep poverty rates fell over the period, from about 5 percent in 1968 to 2.3 percent in 2011. And deep poverty rates for families with some but not all members working have been essentially flat over the time period. In the next section, we examine how changes in family structure and employment have interacted to produce long-term trends in deep poverty, focusing specifically on families with children.

Decomposing Deep Poverty Trends for Families with Children

By estimating the share of individuals in families with children who would fall into deep poverty by alternately holding family structure and employment constant, we can estimate the role of each in accounting for the total change in deep poverty rates from 1968 to 2011. To estimate the rate of deep poverty

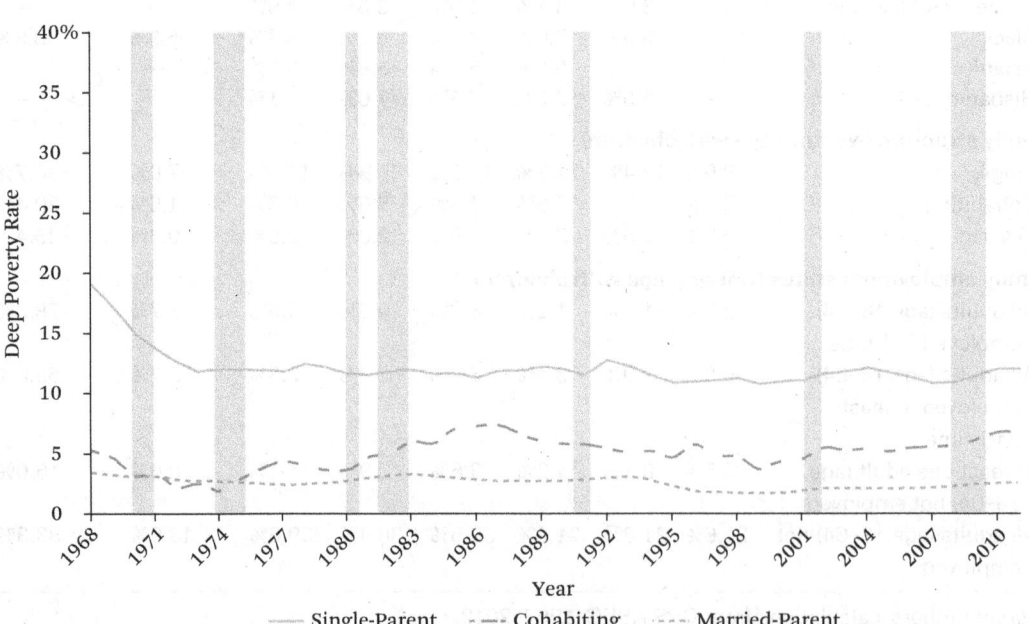

Figure 2. Deep Poverty by Family Structure Among Families with Children, 1968–2011

Source: Authors' calculations from CPS ASEC, 1967–2012.

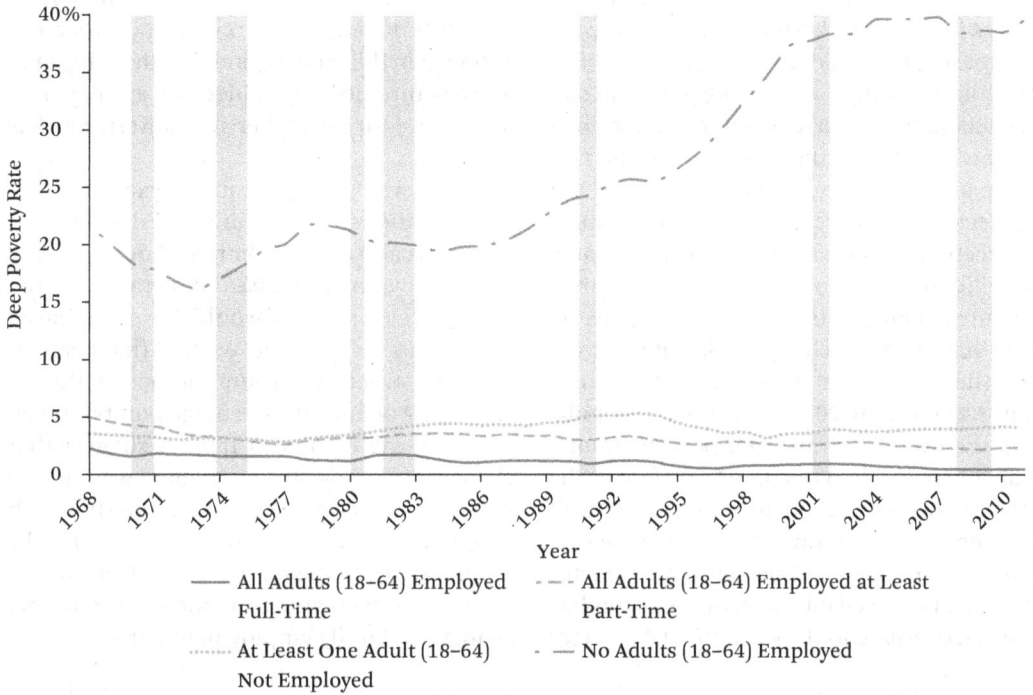

Figure 3. Deep Poverty by Family Employment Among Families with Children, 1968–2011

Source: Authors' calculations from CPS ASEC, 1967–2012.

in 2011 holding family structure constant, we use the family structure distribution (share of families with children living in single, cohabiting, or married families) from 1968 and apply this to the rates of deep poverty for each subgroup in 2011 to arrive at an estimate of what the overall deep poverty rate would have been in 2011 had the family structure of families with children stayed the same as it was in 1968 but subgroup poverty rates changed. We generate similar predicted values by estimating the impact of changing employment patterns as well as by examining corresponding predicted values in 1968 using distributions from 2011 and rates from 1968. Consider the following equation:

$$Y_j = \sum (\beta_{dj} \times \gamma_{dj}) \quad (1)$$

where Y_j is the overall deep poverty rate for working-age families with children in year j, for j equal to either 1968 or 2011; β is the share of the population in a given demographic group d (either by family type [single, cohabiting, or married] or by employment status [all employed full-time, full-year; all employed at least part-time; at least one not employed; all not employed]), and γ is the deep poverty rate for a given demographic group d.

The share of individuals who would have fallen into deep poverty in 2011 if the distribution of either family structure or employment status had remained at 1968 values can then be expressed as

$$Y_a = \sum (\beta_{d,1968} \times \gamma_{d,2011}) \quad (2)$$

and the share in deep poverty if deep poverty rates had remained constant within demographic groups would be

$$Y_b = \sum (\beta_{d,2011} \times \gamma_{d,1968}) \quad (3)$$

These counterfactuals can be compared with actual 1968 and 2011 values to indicate the role of changes in family structure or employment patterns in accounting for the total change in the rate of deep poverty from 1968 to 2011.

Table 2 details this decomposition and shows that changes in family structure, absent changes in family work patterns, would have led to increasing rates of deep poverty for families with children. If the share of individuals in single, cohabiting, or married-couple families had remained constant from 1968 to 2011, the rate of deep poverty for families with children would have declined 1.5 percentage points, from 4.8 to 3.4 percent. If, however, the employment status of families had remained constant while family structures changed, the rate of deep poverty would have been unchanged. Specifically, despite the increase in single-parent families (from 8.4 percent to 20.9 percent of the population), the overall rate of deep poverty among families with children remained constant as the share of the population in families with all adults employed full-time, full-year, increased as well (from 10.9 to 25.4 percent). A key factor here is the increased full-time, full-year employment of single parents (from 23.9 to 32.4 percent)

(see appendix figure A1). We find similar patterns if we reverse the decomposition and impose 2011 demographics on 1968 poverty rates, although in this case we find that changing family structure absent changes in employment would have led to a higher deep poverty rate (6.8 percent).

The lower panel of table 2 examines the same relationships, but instead decomposes the pretax and pretransfer rate of deep poverty. Absent government taxes and transfers, the rate of deep poverty would have increased from 8.8 to 14.3 percent. We find that changes in family structure account for most of this increase (4.2 out of 5.0 percentage points). Taken together, the results in table 2 suggest that changes in family structure alone would have increased deep poverty among families with children, but that these trends were offset by both changes in the antipoverty effects of government policies and, to a much lesser degree, changes in family employment patterns.

Table 2. Decomposition of Effect of Changing Family Structures and Employment on Likelihood of Falling into Deep Poverty

	Share in Deep Poverty	Change
Including government taxes and transfers		
Actual value, 1968 (Y_{1968})	4.8%	
Actual value, 2011 (Y_{2011})	4.9%	0.1%
Predicted value in 2011		
Holding constant family structures (Y_a)	3.4%	−1.5%
Holding constant work patterns (Y_b)	4.8%	0.1%
Predicted value in 1968		
Using 2011 family structures (Y_a)	6.8%	2.1%
Using 2011 work patterns (Y_b)	4.8%	0.0%
Pretax and pretransfer		
Actual value, 1968 (Y_{1968})	8.8%	
Actual value, 2011 (Y_{2011})	14.3%	5.5%
Predicted value in 2011		
Holding constant family structures (Y_a)	10.2%	4.2%
Holding constant work patterns (Y_b)	14.8%	−0.4%
Predicted value in 1968		
Using 2011 family structures (Y_a)	14.7%	5.9%
Using 2011 work patterns (Y_b)	9.2%	0.4%

Source: Authors' calculations from CPS ASEC, 1967–2012.

The Role of Government

The decomposition results in table 2 suggest that government policies and programs have largely offset a rise in deep poverty that would have occurred given changes in family structure over recent decades. The next set of analyses therefore focus specifically on the role of these policies and programs in reducing estimated poverty rates. Table 3 shows trends in deep poverty over time for key family types and subgroups with and without the inclusion of resources from government programs. The role of government over time operates in different ways for different groups. Overall, as we saw in figure 1, deep poverty has been flat over the period, but absent government transfers it would have actually risen by nearly six percentage points.

Looking at family type, we see that for working-age families with children, deep poverty absent government transfers would have risen by five percentage points over the period, but after including transfers the deep poverty rate in 2011 was almost the same as our estimate for 1968. A similar story is evident for working-age families without children, where we see what was about a one-percentage-point rise in deep poverty over the period but would have been a rise of about five percentage points absent government transfers. For the elderly, deep poverty rates fell both with and without government transfers, but we note that without government transfers (Social Security), deep poverty rates would have been extremely high for this group in all years.

In the third panel of table 3, we focus on working-age families with children, comparing the role of government taxes and transfers for single, cohabiting, and married-parent families. Among single-parent families, pre-tax-and-transfer deep poverty rates fell fairly consistently over time, by about 11 percentage points. After including government transfers, deep poverty rates for this group fell between 1968 and 1978, but then stayed fairly flat at between 11 and 12 percent. Thus, government programs are reducing single-parent family deep poverty less in absolute terms over time, though before government programs are taken into account, single-parent families are less likely to be falling into deep poverty today than in the past.[2] For both cohabiting and married-parent families, deep poverty would have risen more absent government taxes and transfers than we see after accounting for these, though the differences are not as substantial as they are for single-parent families.

In the last panel of table 3, we examine trends by employment status among working-age families with children. With or without government taxes and transfers, fully employed families exhibited declines in deep poverty rates over the period, though for families with not all working-age adults employed full-time, full-year, deep poverty rates would have slightly increased over the period absent accounting for transfers. More interestingly, we see the importance of the safety net in blunting the rise in deep poverty that might have occurred for families with at least one adult not employed and for families with no employed adults. For those with at least one adult not employed, deep poverty rates would have risen by about eight percentage points absent government transfers, but remained essentially flat after including those transfers. For families with no adults employed, deep poverty rates would have risen from about 60 percent to nearly 90 percent over the period, whereas after including government transfers, deep poverty rates rose by about 18 percentage points, from 21.6 percent to 39.6 percent. While this is still a large increase in deep poverty rates over time (for a group shrinking in size in relative terms), the figures in table 3 show the growing importance of government programs in ameliorating their deep poverty rates.

Figure 4 presents counterfactual estimates for the rate of deep poverty for single-parent families with children in the absence of specific programs. We focus on three major sets of antipoverty programs—cash welfare, the EITC, and nutrition programs—and examine trends in the importance of these programs in reducing deep poverty for single-parent families with children. The antipoverty role of tax credits in-

---

2. The decline in pre-tax-and-transfer single-parent poverty is largely due, of course, to increases in employment among this group, which is in turn affected by government policy.

Table 3. The Role of Government Taxes and Transfers in Alleviating Deep Poverty, 1968–2011 (Selected Years)

	1968	1978	1988	1998	2008	2011	2011–1968 Change
Overall							
SPM deep poverty	5.5%	3.8%	4.1%	4.1%	4.9%	5.3%	–0.1%
SPM deep poverty without all taxes and transfers	12.8%	14.7%	14.6%	14.6%	16.5%	18.7%	5.8%
Family type							
Working age with children							
SPM deep poverty	4.8%	3.9%	4.4%	3.8%	4.3%	4.9%	0.1%
SPM deep poverty without all taxes and transfers	8.8%	11.5%	12.7%	11.2%	12.4%	14.4%	5.5%
Working age without children							
SPM deep poverty	5.1%	3.3%	3.5%	4.2%	5.4%	5.9%	0.9%
SPM deep poverty without all taxes and transfers	11.2%	10.3%	9.2%	10.7%	13.3%	15.7%	4.5%
Elderly							
SPM deep poverty	13.2%	4.4%	4.2%	4.9%	6.2%	5.3%	–8.0%
SPM deep poverty without all taxes and transfers	63.1%	56.2%	47.1%	50.2%	52.7%	52.1%	–11.0%
Family structure (working age with children)							
Single							
SPM deep poverty	19.0%	12.4%	11.9%	11.2%	10.9%	12.0%	–7.0%
SPM deep poverty without all taxes and transfers	46.7%	44.4%	42.6%	33.6%	32.4%	35.4%	–11.4%
Cohabiting							
SPM deep poverty	5.2%	4.0%	6.6%	4.8%	5.6%	6.8%	1.6%
SPM deep poverty without all taxes and transfers	15.0%	14.1%	16.7%	12.0%	15.2%	17.9%	2.8%
Married							
SPM deep poverty	3.4%	2.5%	2.7%	1.8%	2.3%	2.6%	–0.9%
SPM deep poverty without all taxes and transfers	5.3%	5.9%	6.2%	5.1%	6.6%	7.9%	2.5%
Family employment status (working age with children)							
All adults (18–64) employed full-time							
SPM deep poverty	2.2%	1.2%	1.2%	0.8%	0.5%	0.5%	–1.7%
SPM deep poverty without all taxes and transfers	3.2%	2.1%	1.7%	2.0%	2.1%	2.3%	–1.0%
All adults (18–64) employed at least part-time							
SPM deep poverty	5.0%	2.9%	3.4%	2.8%	2.3%	2.3%	–2.7%
SPM deep poverty without all taxes and transfers	7.7%	7.1%	7.7%	8.9%	8.4%	9.4%	1.7%
At least one adult (18–64) not employed							
SPM deep poverty	3.5%	3.1%	4.2%	3.6%	3.9%	4.1%	0.6%
SPM deep poverty without all taxes and transfers	5.8%	8.3%	10.8%	11.2%	12.8%	14.2%	8.4%

Table 3. (continued)

	1968	1978	1988	1998	2008	2011	2011–1968 Change
All adults (18–64) not employed							
SPM deep poverty	21.6%	21.8%	21.2%	32.5%	38.4%	39.6%	18.0%
SPM deep poverty without all taxes and transfers	61.1%	80.3%	87.5%	88.7%	88.1%	88.3%	27.2%

Source: Authors' calculations from CPS ASEC, 1967–2012.

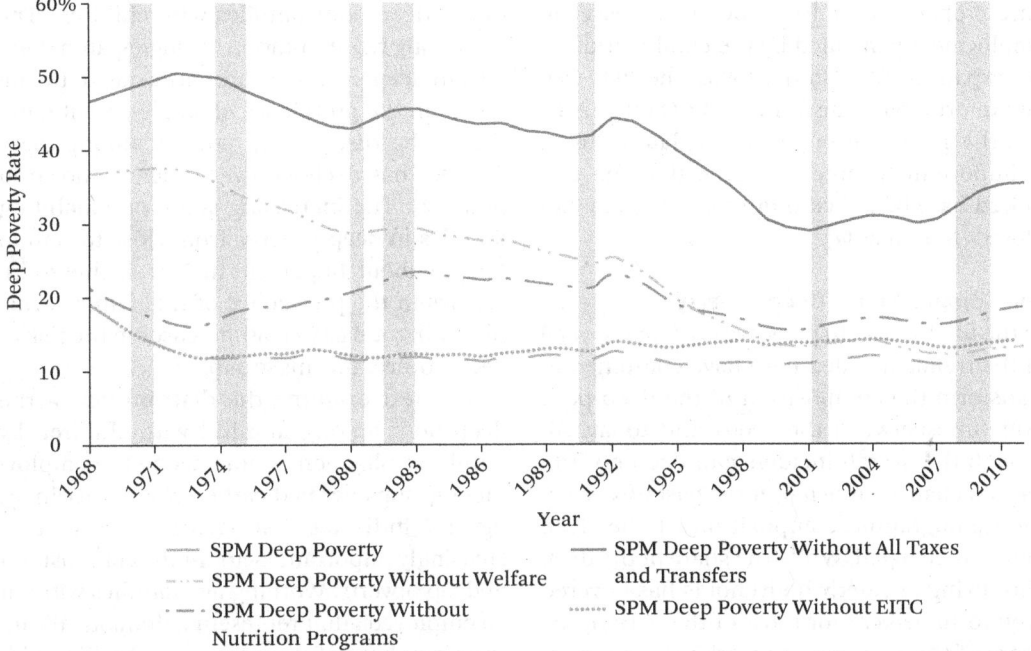

Figure 4. The Impacts of the EITC, Cash Welfare, and Nutrition Programs on Deep Poverty Among Working-Age Single-Parent Families with Children, 1968–2011

Source: Authors' calculations from CPS ASEC, 1967–2012.

creased substantially after the expansions of the EITC in the early 1990s (Grogger 2004; Hoynes 2014). Around the same time, cash welfare decreased in importance following the federal welfare reform of 1996, which time-limited the program and added work requirements. Subsequently, caseloads dropped precipitously (Blank 2002). Nutrition assistance programs like SNAP have expanded dramatically in recent years following the decline in importance of cash welfare assistance (Ganong and Liebman 2013). We focus on single-parent families with children, a particularly vulnerable group and a key group affected by these policy changes.

Figure 4 shows that, overall, taxes and transfers have a considerably smaller effect on the deep poverty rate today than they did in earlier years. In 1968 taxes and transfers decreased the deep poverty rate from 46.7 to 19.0 percent, while in 2011 the reduction was from 35.4 to 12.0 percent. Part of the reduction in the role of government can be accounted for by a decline in the rate of pre-tax-and-transfer deep poverty among single-parent families. Up until the early 1990s, cash welfare played a major role in reducing the incidence of deep poverty among single-parent families, cutting deep poverty rates by more than half in many years. However, even prior to welfare reform, the importance of cash welfare transfers had been steadily declining since the early 1970s. At the same time, the role of nutrition programs grew, peaking in importance in 1992, when it reduced deep poverty by more than ten percentage points. Since the mid-1990s, the EITC has consistently reduced deep poverty rates among individuals living in single-parent families by two to three percentage points. Overall, then, the declines in the importance of cash welfare since the 1970s have been offset by the EITC and nutrition programs, alongside greater pre-tax-and-transfer resources among single-parent families that have probably been driven by the increases in employment generated by the combination of the expanded EITC in the 1990s, the 1996 welfare reform that transformed AFDC into TANF, and the growing economy of the late 1990s. It is important to note, however, that the employed have benefited more than the non-employed (Moffitt 2014).

The Composition of Deep Poverty

In the final set of analyses, we examine how all of the trends detailed here have combined to transform the composition of the deep poor over time between the 1960s and today. Although the overall incidence of deep poverty has not changed much over the past fifty years, the demographic composition of the deep poor has changed. While the share of the deep poor living in elderly households has hovered around 10 percent for most of the period, the share of the deep poor in working-age households with or without children has varied over time, showing opposite trends: an increasing share of the deep poor are those without children, whereas the share of the deep poor with children has been declining (see appendix table A1). In 1968, 60 percent of the deep poor were in working-age families with children, 23 percent were in working-age families with no children, and about 15 percent were in elderly families. By 2011, the portrait had changed: 52 percent were in families with children, 36 percent were in working-age families with no children, and just over 10 percent were in elderly families.

Again focusing on working-age families with children, we next examine differences by family structure subgroup (single family, cohabiting family, and married family). As shown in figure 5, married families with children comprise a declining share of the deep poor families with children, whereas single-parent and cohabiting families have each been increasing in share. In 1968, the majority of deep poor families with children (about two-thirds) were married-couple families. By 2011, the largest group was single-parent families, who now make up fully half of the deep poor families with children. The increasing representation of single-parent families in deep poverty is primarily due to the increase in the prevalence of single-parent families as the risk of deep poverty among these families has declined over time (as shown in figure 2). The increasing share of cohabiting families in deep poverty, from close to zero in 1968 to about 10 percent in 2011, is due to increases in the prevalence of this family structure subgroup as well as increases in the risk of deep poverty for this group.

We next examine the distribution of the deep poor among families with children by family employment status, using the employment groups defined earlier. Not surprisingly, figure 6 indicates that having a job is an increasingly important factor in the composition of deep poverty. Working-age families without an employed adult represent a dramatically increasing share of the deep poor families with children since 1990, with the proportion at 22 percent in 1968, 34 percent in 1990, and 51 percent in 2011 (consistent with Moffitt 2014). For the group with all adults ages eighteen to sixty-four employed, the share in deep poverty steadily declined from 42 percent in 1968 to 35 percent in 1999, then rapidly declined to 17 percent by 2011.[3]

We further explore the relationship between employment and deep poverty by examining the prevalence of disability and low-wage work among the deep poor over time. First, we

---

3. Note that the composition does not sum to 100 percent owing to the omission of the group with one nonworking adult. Full details can be found in appendix table A1.

Figure 5. The Composition of Deep Poverty by Family Structure Among Families with Children, 1968–2011

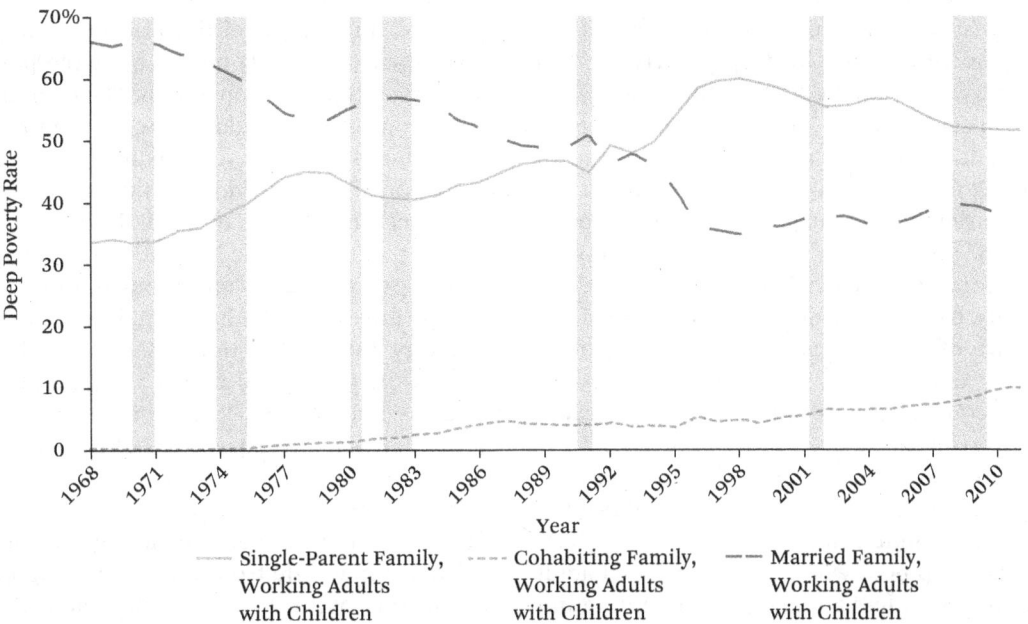

Source: Authors' calculations from CPS ASEC, 1967–2012.

Figure 6. The Composition of Deep Poverty by Employment Status Among Families with Children, 1968–2011

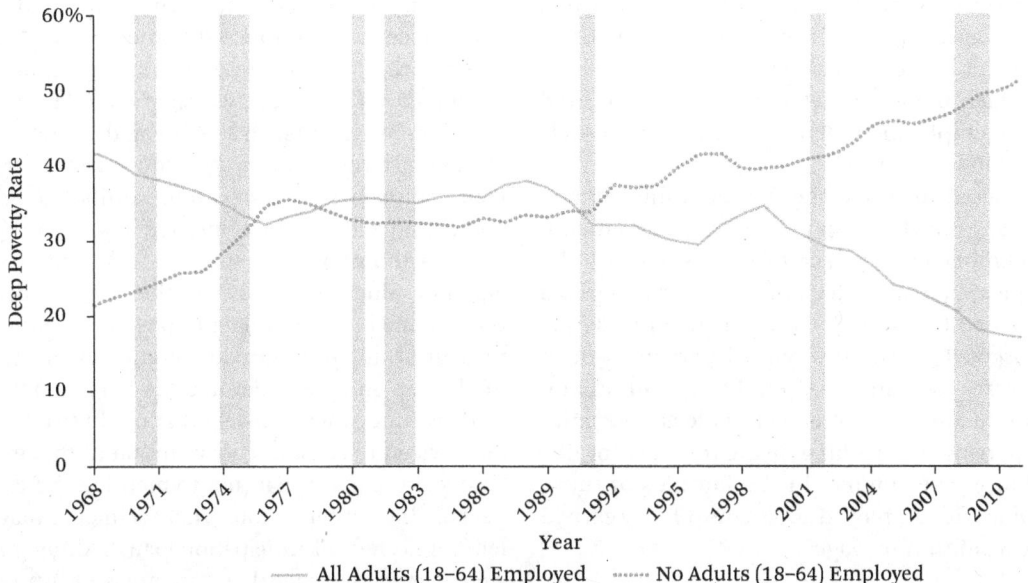

Source: Authors' calculations from CPS ASEC, 1967–2012.

look at the share of the deep poor who lived in a family with at least one member self-reporting that he or she was not employed the previous year owing to illness or disability. In 1967, 10 percent of those in deep poverty lived in such a family, and by 2012 the likelihood of living in such a family had nearly doubled, to 18 percent. During this period, the overall rate of non-employment due to illness or disability increased from 4 to 10 percent. In other words, in 1967 one in ten of the deep poor lived with someone not employed owing to illness or disability. By 2012, that share had increased to one in five of the deep poor, mimicking general trends among the non–deep poor.

Second, we looked at low-wage work by first converting annual earnings into an hourly wage rate, then identifying workers whose estimated wage rates were $1 or less above the federal minimum wage. Looking at the share of the deep poor who had an employed adult earning $1 or less above the federal minimum wage, we found that this share has actually decreased slightly over time, from 36 to 31 percent of the deep poor population from 1967 to 2012. In 2012, deep poor families were much less likely to have an employed adult than they would have been in 1967, but if they had a worker they were much more likely to have a low-wage worker (71 percent in 2012 versus 43 percent in 1967). So overall, as a growing share of deep poor families become disconnected from employment, fewer of these families rely on a low-wage worker.

Taken together, the demographic characteristics of the deep poor have changed considerably over the past fifty years. In 1967, the typical person in deep poverty was living in a married family with children and at least one worker. By 2012, the typical person in deep poverty lived in a household without an employed adult and often with at least one adult reporting not working owing to illness or disability. The workers in the families of those living with employed adults most likely earned near-minimum wage.

LIMITATIONS

Although our analyses provide a picture of deep poverty trends using a consistently and commonly measured indicator of severe deprivation in the United States, they do have a number of important limitations. First and foremost, an analysis of deep poverty using survey data necessarily misses a sizable portion of the deep poor population. The Current Population Survey is nationally representative, but it covers only the non-institutionalized population; thus, individuals living in prisons, mental institutions, and other institutional living quarters are excluded. Additionally, those living in group quarters are excluded from the poverty universe. Finally, homelessness or transitory living conditions make a sizable share of the truly disadvantaged inaccessible to a household survey. Other contributions to this volume shed considerable light on these important subpopulations.

In addition, the results presented here do not adjust for the underreporting of income. It is well known that the underreporting of benefits such as SNAP or food stamps and WIC has been growing over time (Meyer, Mok, and Sullivan 2009). Addressing this underreporting is an area of future research. In addition, income questions in the CPS focus on regular income from a variety of sources and are thus likely to miss some informal sources of support that may be critical to the severely deprived (see, for example, Edin and Lein 1997).

Following previous research on the Supplemental Poverty Measure, we value several forms of in-kind benefits (such as SNAP and the EITC) at their face value; however, doing so may overvalue some benefits for some families. One could argue that, since inefficiency is introduced with in-kind benefits and, as a result, recipients value them less than their face value, they should be discounted in a poverty resource measure. Similarly, one could argue that an annual lump sum payment like the EITC should be discounted owing to debt that might need to be serviced to smooth consumption of this income across a full year (not to mention the especially high interest rates that recipients may face for tax refund anticipation loans). Although we acknowledge that these are areas of future research, we follow current National Academy of Sciences (NAS) guidelines for the inclusion of these resources at full value in our measure.

Finally, our analyses rely heavily on imputed values, which introduce an element of uncertainty to our results. Because many components of the SPM are not measured historically in the Current Population Survey, these imputations are essential to estimating historically consistent poverty rates. Although they add some uncertainty, many of the imputed programs were quite small during the periods of imputation, and those that are more substantial do not alter our understanding of trends over time. Owing to the complexity of these , we have not been able to estimate standard errors for our poverty results, and this is an important area for future research.

In addition to these limitations, we have been unable to address several important questions. While informative about snapshots of deep poverty, this article has not examined poverty duration. We have also not examined the severity of deep poverty among those experiencing it—that is, whether their incomes are just below 50 percent of the poverty threshold or considerably lower. Such analysis is potentially feasible using the income data from the CPS, although measurement may be particularly noisy for those with very low incomes (and may be confounded by the underreporting of benefits among this population).

CONCLUSION

Our analysis has four main findings. One, we find that while trends in overall deep poverty have been relatively flat since 1968, this constancy belies considerable change in the predictors and correlates of deep poverty. Families without an employed adult were much more likely to fall into deep poverty in 2011 than in 1968, whereas single-parent families are less likely to fall into deep poverty today than in the past. Two, despite the decline in the risk of deep poverty in single-parent families, their share in the deep poverty population has steadily increased on account of the rising proportion of single-parent households in the United States. Three, results from a simple "decomposition" analysis suggest that changes in family structure since 1968 would have increased deep poverty among families with children, but that these trends were offset by both changes in the antipoverty effects of government programs and, to a lesser degree, employment patterns. Four, governmental taxes and transfers reduce the risk of deep poverty for all subgroups examined, but the significance and role of these programs has changed over time. Specifically, our analysis points to a declining role for cash welfare and a growing role for nutrition and tax programs. We also find that for families without an employed adult, the antipoverty role of taxes and transfers steadily increased from 1968 through 1988, but has been declining ever since.

Although an increase in employment has made single-parent families with children less likely to fall into deep poverty today than fifty years ago, it is not clear that these families are unambiguously better off. This analysis of poverty provides insight into one dimension of family financial well-being. Previous research has found that increases in the female labor supply have had heterogeneous effects on total hours spent with children: single mothers may have reduced the time they spend with their children, but married mothers may have been able to preserve more of this time (Fox et al. 2013). In addition, stress may reduce the quality of the time that mothers spend with their children. Additionally, depending on their family's access to quality, affordable child care, the children of working parents could experience either improvements or declines in well-being. To understand the full effect of changes in employment patterns, we would need to investigate a number of measures of child and family well-being. Finally, the shift from cash assistance to in-kind nutrition assistance and onetime tax refunds is also likely to have increased stress among mothers.

Taken together, our results suggest some fundamental shifts in the nature of deep poverty. Today fewer of the deep poor are elderly or families with children, but a growing share—now nearly 40 percent—are working-age adults without children, a group for whom the safety net is the thinnest. The makeup of deep poor families with children has also undergone striking changes. In 1968 the typical deep poor family with children was headed by a married couple and had at least one adult employed—albeit possibly part-time, part-year—but in 2011 the typical deep poor family with children was headed by a single parent or had no adult employed, reflecting the fact that these latter two subgroups are those for whom deep poverty rates are particularly high (at 12 and nearly 40 percent, respectively). The net result of these changes is one of relative stability, with deep poverty rates rarely fluctuating much below or above 5 percent. This stability is largely thanks to the role of government programs and, to a lesser extent, employment, which have held deep poverty rates at bay.

It is debatable, of course, whether the overall long-term trend of stability in deep poverty rates is good news or bad news. Given macroeconomic growth, one could argue that deep poverty should have declined instead of remaining stagnant. Conversely, it is good news that even in steep economic downturns like the double-dip recessions of the early 1980s and the recent Great Recession, the safety net has held the overall deep poverty rate down. However, as we have seen, there has also been considerable change in the composition of the deep poor underlying this stasis, and the groups that are in deep poverty today, being more isolated from society, may be more difficult to target with policy interventions than the deep poor of fifty years ago. As the deep poor become increasingly isolated from employment, child care, and school systems and experience more and more limitations due to health or disability, designing popular programs to target this population will be a challenge.

Appendix

Appendix Figure A1. Distribution of Employment Status Among Single-Parent Families with Children, 1968–2011

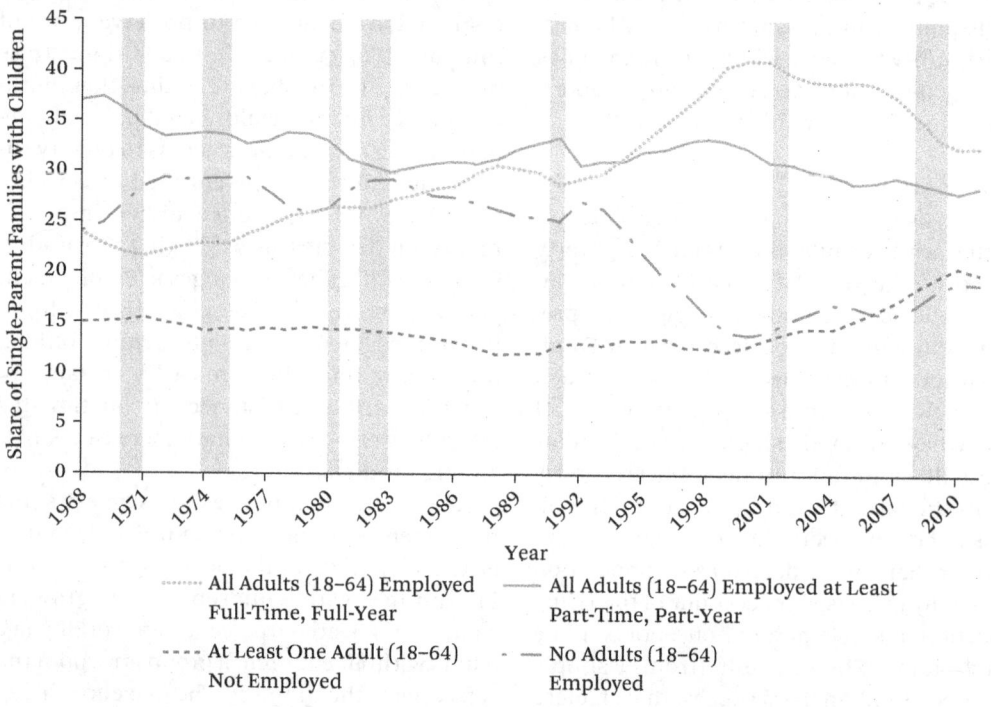

Source: Authors' calculations from CPS ASEC, 1967–2012.

Appendix Table A1. Composition of Deep Poverty, 1968–2011 (Using Three-Year Moving Averages)

	1968	1978	1988	1998	2008	2011	2011–1968 Percentage-Point Change	2011–1968 Percentage Change
Family type								
Working age with children	59.8%	63.5%	59.9%	51.6%	45.8%	46.5%	−13.2%	−22.1%
Working age, no children	23.4%	26.4%	29.6%	36.2%	41.6%	43.1%	19.7%	84.3%
Elderly	14.7%	9.0%	9.2%	10.7%	11.9%	9.9%	−4.8%	−32.9%
Family structure								
Single	43.0%	50.7%	52.6%	65.2%	60.1%	60.7%	17.7%	41.2%
Cohabiting	0.5%	1.5%	4.1%	3.7%	5.6%	6.8%	6.3%	1277.3%
Married	56.5%	47.8%	43.4%	31.1%	34.3%	32.5%	−24.0%	−42.5%
Family structure (working age with children)								
Single	33.6%	45.0%	46.3%	60.1%	52.2%	51.8%	18.3%	54.4%
Cohabiting	0.3%	1.3%	4.5%	5.0%	7.9%	10.2%	9.9%	2942.5%
Married	66.1%	53.7%	49.2%	34.9%	39.8%	38.0%	−28.1%	−42.6%
Family employment status (working age with children)								
All adults (18–64) employed full-time	4.9%	4.7%	6.3%	5.8%	3.1%	2.4%	−2.5%	−51.4%
All adults (18–64) employed at least part-time	36.7%	29.1%	31.6%	27.7%	17.5%	14.7%	−22.0%	−59.9%
At least one adult (18–64) not employed	36.7%	31.1%	28.6%	27.0%	32.0%	31.5%	−5.3%	−14.3%
All adults (18–64) not employed	21.6%	35.0%	33.5%	39.5%	47.4%	51.4%	29.8%	137.7%

Source: Authors' calculations from CPS ASEC, 1967–2012.

REFERENCES

Blank, Rebecca M. 2002. "Evaluating Welfare Reform in the United States." *Journal of Economic Literature* 40(4): 1–43.

———. 2008. "Presidential Address: How to Improve Poverty Measurement in the United States." *Journal of Policy Analysis and Management* 27(2): 233–54.

Cancian, Maria, and Deborah Reed. 2009. "Family Structure, Childbearing, and Parental Employment: Implications for the Level and Trend in Poverty." In *Changing Poverty, Changing Policies*, edited by Maria Cancian and Sheldon Danziger. New York: Russell Sage Foundation.

Casper, Lynne M., Philip N. Cohen, and Tavia Simons. 1999. "How Does POSSLQ Measure Up? Historical Estimates of Cohabitation." Working Paper 36. Washington: U.S. Census Bureau, Population Division.

Citro, Constance, and Robert Michael, eds. 1995. *Measuring Poverty: A New Approach.* Washington, D.C.: National Academies Press.

DeNavas-Walt, Carmen, and Bernadette D. Proctor. 2014. "Income and Poverty in the United States: 2013." Current Population Reports, series P60, no. 249. Washington: U.S. Government Printing Office for U.S. Census Bureau. Available at: http://www.census.gov/content/dam/Census/library/publications/2014/demo/p60-249.pdf (accessed October 1, 2015).

Edin, Kathryn, and Laura Lein. 1997. *Making Ends Meet: How Single Mothers Survive Welfare and*

Low-Wage Work. New York: Russell Sage Foundation.

Feenberg, Daniel, and Elisabeth Coutts. 1993. "An Introduction to the TAXSIM Model." *Journal of Policy Analysis and Management* 12: 189–94.

Fisher, Gordon M. 1992. "The Development of the Orshansky Poverty Thresholds and Their Subsequent History as the Official U.S. Poverty Measure." *Experimental Poverty Measures* Working Paper. Washington: U.S. Census Bureau. Available at: http://www.census.gov/hhes/povmeas/publications/orshansky.html (accessed October 1, 2015).

Fox, Liana, Irwin Garfinkel, Neeraj Kaushal, Jane Waldfogel, and Christopher Wimer. 2015. "Waging War on Poverty: Poverty Trends Using a Historical Supplemental Poverty Measure." *Journal of Policy Analysis and Management* 34(3): 567–92. doi:10.1002/pam.21833.

Fox, Liana, Wen-Jui Han, Christopher Ruhm, and Jane Waldfogel. 2013. "Time for Children: Trends in the Employment Patterns of Parents, 1967–2009." *Demography* 50(1): 25–49.

Ganong, Peter, and Jeffrey B. Liebman. 2013. "The Decline, Rebound, and Further Rise in SNAP Enrollment: Disentangling Business Cycle Fluctuations and Policy Changes." Working Paper 19363. Cambridge, Mass.: National Bureau of Economic Research.

Garner, Thesia I. 2011. "Developing Thresholds for the Supplemental Poverty Measure." Paper presented at the Annual Meeting of the Allied Social Science Associations (ASSA), Society of Government Economists Session (SGE). Denver, Colo. (January 3, 2011).

Grogger, Jeffrey. 2004. "Welfare Transitions in the 1990s: The Economy, Welfare Policy, and the EITC." *Journal of Policy Analysis and Management* 23(4): 671–95.

Hoynes, Hilary W. 2012. "Comment on Meyer and Sullivan." *Brookings Papers on Economic Activity* (Fall): 184–89.

——. 2014. "A Revolution in Poverty Policy: The Earned Income Tax Credit and the Well-Being of American Families." *Pathways*, Summer 2014, 23–27. Available at: http://www.web.stanford.edu/group/scspi/_media/pdf/pathways/summer_2014/Pathways_Summer_2014.pdf (accessed October 1, 2015).

Hutto, Nathan, Jane Waldfogel, Neeraj Kaushal, and Irwin Garfinkel. 2011. "Improving the Measurement of Poverty." *Social Service Review* 35(1): 39–74.

Iceland, John. 2005. "Measuring Poverty: Theoretical and Empirical Considerations." *Measurement: Interdisciplinary Research and Perspectives* 3(4): 199–235.

ITWG. 2010. "Observations from the Interagency Technical Working Group on Developing a Supplemental Poverty Measure." Report to the U.S. Census Bureau. Washington: U.S. Government Printing Office. Available at: http://www.census.gov/hhes/www/poverty/SPM_TWGObservations.pdf (accessed October 1, 2015).

Meyer, Bruce D., Wallace K. C. Mok, and James X. Sullivan. 2009. "The Under-Reporting of Transfers in Household Surveys: Its Nature and Consequences." Working Paper 15181. Cambridge, Mass.: National Bureau of Economic Research.

Moffitt, Robert A. 2014. "The Deserving Poor, the Family, and the U.S. Welfare System." Presidential Address to the Population Association of America. Boston (May 2).

Provencher, Ashley. 2011. "Unit of Analysis for Poverty Measurement: A Comparison of the Supplemental Poverty Measure and the Official Poverty Measure." Social, Economic, and Housing Statistics Division Working Paper 2010-14. Washington: U.S. Census Bureau.

Short, Kathleen. 2011. "The Research Supplemental Poverty Measure: 2010." Current Population Reports P60-241. Washington: U.S. Census Bureau (November).

Wimer, Christopher, Liana Fox, Irwin Garfinkel, Neeraj Kaushal, and Jane Waldfogel. 2013. "Trends in Poverty with an Anchored Supplemental Poverty Measure." *Institute for Research on Poverty (IRP)* discussion paper no. 1416-13. Madison: University of Wisconsin-Madison.

Compounded Deprivation in the Transition to Adulthood: The Intersection of Racial and Economic Inequality Among Chicagoans, 1995–2013

KRISTIN L. PERKINS AND ROBERT J. SAMPSON

This paper investigates acute, compounded, and persistent deprivation in a representative sample of Chicago adolescents transitioning to young adulthood. Our investigation, based on four waves of longitudinal data from 1995 to 2013, is motivated by three goals. First, we document the prevalence of individual and neighborhood poverty over time, especially among whites, blacks, and Latinos. Second, we explore compounded deprivation, describing the extent to which study participants are simultaneously exposed to individual and contextual forms of deprivation—including material deprivation (such as poverty) and social-organizational deprivation (for example, low collective efficacy)—for multiple phases of the life course from adolescence up to age thirty-two. Third, we isolate the characteristics that predict transitions out of compounded and persistent poverty. The results provide new evidence on the crosscutting adversities that were exacerbated by the Great Recession and on the deep connection of race to persistent and compounded deprivation in the transition to adulthood.

Key words: compounded deprivation, persistent poverty, young adulthood, Chicago

Poverty in the United States is experienced in multidimensional and intersecting forms. Problems like severe income poverty, for example, often coincide with joblessness, housing insecurity, and family instability, all of which can be mutually reinforcing. In one of the most influential accounts of such hardship, *The Truly Disadvantaged*, William Julius Wilson (2012 [1987], 3) focuses on the social transformation of the inner city in the 1970s and 1980s—especially the decline of manufacturing jobs and the outmigration of the black middle class—that disproportionately exposed poor African Americans to concentrated neighborhood disadvantage. He begins this account, however, by highlighting the "cycle of deprivation" that is generated by the concentration of poverty, female-headed families, joblessness, teenage pregnancy, and violence.

The ensuing decades have witnessed considerable research on concentrated poverty, but the nature of "compounded deprivation" has been surprisingly understudied, in three major ways. First, much research in the tradition of *The Truly Disadvantaged* has focused on trying to separate the effects of poverty from its cor-

Kristin L. Perkins is a doctoral student in sociology and social policy at Harvard University. **Robert J. Sampson** is Henry Ford II Professor of the Social Sciences and director of the Boston Area Research Initiative at the Radcliffe Institute for Advanced Study at Harvard University.

We thank Matthew Desmond, the RSF reviewers, and participants at the "Severe Deprivation in America" conference for helpful comments. This article was supported in part by a grant from the Hymen Milgrom Supporting Organization to the University of Chicago. Direct correspondence to: Kristin L. Perkins at kperkins@fas.harvard.edu, Department of Sociology, Harvard University, William James Hall, 33 Kirkland St., Cambridge, MA 02138; and Robert J. Sampson at rsampson@wjh.harvard.edu, Department of Sociology, Harvard University, William James Hall, 33 Kirkland St., Cambridge, MA 02138.

related adversities. As our review will show, the separation of individual from neighborhood poverty has animated an entire field of study. By contrast, systematic study of the intersection of individual with contextual forms of poverty—including but extending beyond material conditions like income to social forms of deprivation, such as weak social support networks or low collective efficacy—is comparatively rare.

Second, there has been a relative paucity of longitudinal studies that follow the same individuals over time so that entry into and exits from family poverty can be explicitly examined at the same time as transitions into and out of neighborhood poverty. To be sure, a burgeoning literature attempting to isolate the effect of neighborhood poverty on various outcomes does advance a temporal perspective, which we build upon. But a focus on cycles of deprivation leads to a different kind of social inquiry. More specifically, although we know that people of color are disproportionately exposed to poverty in the first place, research on continuity and change has been hard to accomplish because of the interlocking dynamics of the multiple levels of analysis required to address questions such as: What is the prevalence and timing of compounded deprivation over the life course? How does the legacy of severe initial deprivation differ by race? What factors predict an ascent from compounded deprivation? For example, can educational attainment overcome the experience of severe deprivation in childhood?

Third, there has been a new social transformation of the city. In the years since the concentration of poverty was put on the academic map by Wilson, inner cities have begun to change and diverge from how they are commonly portrayed. The dramatic drop in violence, the increase of suburban poverty, the growth of the black middle class, and large increases in immigration from around the world have reshaped cities like New York, Los Angeles, and Chicago. Indeed, New York is no longer the poster child of urban decay but rather is vibrant and growing. In addition, the Latino American population has rapidly grown around the country, and the ways in which the Great Recession altered the urban landscape—through foreclosures, losses in wealth, and increases in unemployment—are potentially just as transformative as the upheavals of the 1970s and 1980s.

This article addresses these three issues with a longitudinal analysis of compounded deprivation in a representative sample of the three largest race-ethnic groups in Chicago and American society at large—whites, African Americans, and Latino Americans—over an eighteen-year period that spans the mid to late 1990s, the 2000s, and the Great Recession era at the historical level, and the transition to adulthood at the individual level. Before describing these data in more detail, we begin with a short review of the relevant research and a discussion of how we advance prior contributions to yield new evidence on the dynamics of persistent and compounded hardship.

POVERTY'S MULTIDIMENSIONAL REACH

Social science research in the tradition of Wilson's (2012 [1987]) landmark work has made substantial progress in identifying the impact of individual poverty and neighborhood poverty on child and adolescent outcomes. In general, studies find that family poverty is associated with depression, delinquency, and drug use among adolescents, as well as decreased intellectual development among children, which is thought to operate through poverty's influence on parenting style, home environment, parental efficacy, and cognitive stimulation (Duncan and Brooks-Gunn 1997; Elder et al. 1995; Garrett, Ngandu, and Ferron 1994; Guo and Harris 2000; Lempers, Clark-Lempers, and Simons 1989). Experiencing poverty in early childhood is also linked to long-range outcomes. Using the Panel Study of Income Dynamics (PSID), for example, Greg Duncan, Kathleen Ziol-Guest, and Ariel Kalil (2010) show that family income in childhood predicts earnings and work hours at ages twenty-five to thirty-seven; they argue that the effects of family income in early childhood are stronger for measures of adult attainment than for adult health and behavior outcomes. In addition, Kelly Musick and Robert Mare (2006) find strong evidence that family poverty is transmitted over generations.

Another body of research has considered whether growing up in a high-poverty neighborhood has detrimental consequences for children and adolescents that are separate from the influences of growing up in a poor family. Reviews of this literature typically conclude that family characteristics have larger effects than neighborhood poverty on multiple problem behaviors (Ellen and Turner 1997; Jencks and Mayer 1990; Leventhal and Brooks-Gunn 2000). For example, studies in the Russell Sage volumes on neighborhood poverty (Brooks-Gunn, Duncan, and Aber 1997a, 1997b) find that proximity to middle-class or affluent neighbors is positively associated with cognitive-academic outcomes for children in disadvantaged neighborhoods, but that family poverty outweighs neighborhood poverty when both conditions are simultaneously examined.

Although the correlation between poverty and detrimental outcomes is largely undisputed, controversy has ensued over the interpretation of causality. According to one claim, the apparent effects of poverty—whether family or neighborhood—reflect instead the prior characteristics and choices of individuals. Susan Mayer (1998), for example, in an argument based on the evidence that the effect of income on children's outcomes is smaller than many scholars believe, questions the received wisdom on family income and asks if the factors that cause parents to experience low incomes also impede their children's life chances, inducing a spurious correlation. Mixed evidence from the Moving to Opportunity (MTO) experiment (Ludwig et al. 2012; Sanbonmatsu et al. 2011) has also cast doubt on the causal role of neighborhood poverty, at least with respect to adolescent outcomes and young adult achievement.

An alternative claim points to the longer-term or developmental consequences of concentrated poverty. In the MTO experiment, the average child was over ten years of age at the beginning of the voucher experiment and thus had already experienced many years of severe childhood poverty.[1] This fact is potentially decisive if concentrated disadvantage has cumulative or lagged effects on development, as suggested in research showing that setbacks in verbal learning persist years after children have been exposed to neighborhoods characterized by concentrated disadvantage (Sampson, Sharkey, and Raudenbush 2008). Also pursuing a strategy that accounts for temporal sequencing across the life course, Geoffrey Wodtke, David Harding, and Felix Elwert (2011), Wodtke (2013), and Patrick Sharkey and Elwert (2011) find that living in a disadvantaged neighborhood has negative effects on high school graduation and cognitive ability, with longer durations of exposure to concentrated disadvantage associated with more negative outcomes.[2] Moreover, new evidence from a long-term study of the MTO children finds that receiving a voucher is associated with higher adult earnings and that the magnitude of this effect declines with age, eventually flattening out to no effect among those who were adolescents at the time of treatment (Chetty, Hendren, and Katz 2015). This pattern strongly suggests that the duration and timing of exposure to concentrated poverty is important for later adult outcomes.

RESEARCH STRATEGY AND QUESTIONS

The contribution of previous research to estimating the separate effects of individual and contextual poverty on child and adolescent outcomes has been critical to advancing theory and evidence-based policies on poverty. Disentangling family from contextual poverty, however, is an attempt to tease apart what are often highly correlated adversities that co-occur in the same individuals and communi-

---

1. In the mid-1990s, MTO randomly assigned rent-subsidized vouchers to families living in public housing in high-poverty neighborhoods in five cities (Baltimore, Boston, Chicago, Los Angeles, and New York). The main findings of the experiment are based on later outcome comparisons between the group that was assigned to use the rent-subsidized vouchers in lower-poverty neighborhoods and the group that did not receive rent-subsidized vouchers.

2. Recent research also finds convergence between the MTO and observational studies when the same contexts and later outcomes are directly compared. Julia Burdick-Will and her colleagues (2011) show that concentrated disadvantage is linked to lower cognitive test scores for black children in the Chicago and Baltimore sites of the MTO, where racial segregation is higher than in Los Angeles, New York, or Boston. In Chicago the estimates are virtually equivalent to those reported in Sampson, Sharkey, and Raudenbush (2008) and from another quasi-experimental study.

ties. The piling on of multiple adversities is a substantive reality of American poverty that demands investigation in its own right, especially when it occurs in childhood or early adolescence. Indeed, durable patterns of inequality lead to the concentration in the same places and among the same people—often over long periods of time and generations (Sampson 2012; Sharkey 2013)—of correlated social adversities, such as simultaneous exposure to family- and community-level deprivation. Thus, while the causal identification of the separate effects of family and neighborhood poverty has animated much recent research, this analytic focus deflects attention from persistent, multi-stranded deprivation and its developmental course.

We also know relatively little about deprivation beyond the material realm. One can be poor and yet embedded in a rich network of social support, neighborhood cohesion, and safety. Or one can be poor and face the additional stressors of exposure to violence and neighborhood disorder (Anderson 1999), community distrust, and negative experiences with the police or prison (Pettit 2011; Pettit and Western 2004). While there is a well-known literature on social capital (Portes 1998; Putnam 2000) and a growing body of research on collective efficacy (Sampson, Raudenbush, and Earls 1997), little is known about the life-course evolution of "social-organizational deprivation" and its link to material deprivation and racial disparities. In addition to a general predilection to define deprivation economically, a major reason for this limitation is that few data sets contain direct measures of neighborhood social organization, especially over time (Prewitt, Mackie, and Habermann 2014). Studies such as the PSID provide us with rich portrayals of individual and neighborhood income trajectories, for example, but not the neighborhood contexts related to relational ties, support, efficacy, and exposure to violence. As a result, prior research has for the most part not addressed critical questions: Do the same racial or ethnic patterns in exposure to extreme economic poverty map onto compounded social-organizational deprivation? How much stability and change is there over time? Is social organization at the contextual level a key resource that helps explain escape from poverty traps (Quillian and Redd 2010) and intergenerational social mobility (Chetty and Hendren 2015)?

This article expands our knowledge of these questions by focusing on the intersection over time of individual and contextual poverty, or what we term "compounded deprivation." We also argue for a focus on the persistence of compounded material deprivation in addition to the course of compounded social deprivation and its connection to material aspects of poverty. It is only once these links are fully understood that estimating causal impacts can be meaningfully undertaken. Accordingly, our goal is to document the prevalence, developmental course, and correlates of experiencing individual and contextual deprivation, concurrently and for multiple periods. We place special emphasis on the process of climbing out of compounded deprivation.

Our data are drawn from a new follow-up of the Project on Human Development in Chicago Neighborhoods (PHDCN), a three-wave longitudinal cohort study originally conducted from 1995 to 2002. Researchers followed up a random sample of the wave 3 PHDCN participants in 2012 and 2013, as part of the Mixed-Income Project (MIP). These data yield several advantages that make them well suited for our aims.

First, because these data reflect a representative sample of Chicago families, we can examine the prevalence and timing of individual and contextual poverty in a diverse group of adolescents, in contrast to samples that are selected on the outcome of interest, such as poverty. Second, the data cover a significant part of the adolescent and young adult life course—for our focus here on the age nine, twelve, and fifteen cohorts, we have data on poverty status over approximately eighteen years. (In 2013 study participants ranged in age from twenty-six to thirty-two). A third feature is the timing of the data collection: with participants who grew up in the 1980s and 1990s and experienced their late twenties and early thirties during the Great Recession era, we can examine both pre- and post–Great Recession measures of poverty and income. Fourth, the PHDCN and the MIP followed participants wherever they moved in the United States and collected residential histories, permitting a detailed analysis of the neighborhood environment in which participants lived at every wave of data collection. Finally, unlike some of the larger nationally based studies such as the PSID, the community surveys of the PHDCN provide direct measures of factors like neighborhood social capital and efficacy; in addition, the individual sampling design of the PHDCN captures the racial and ethnic diversity of the United States and how cities have changed in recent decades. In particular, over one-third of the PHDCN sample is African American and one-third is Latino American, with a significant representation of first- and second-generation immigrants.

DATA

The Project on Human Development in Chicago Neighborhoods is a longitudinal cohort study of 6,207 children and their caregivers based on a representative sample drawn from eighty neighborhood clusters (NCs) in the city of Chicago in 1995. A two-stage sampling procedure was conducted. U.S. census data were first used to identify 343 neighborhood clusters (NCs)—groups of two to three census tracts containing approximately 8,000 people who were relatively homogeneous with respect to racial-ethnic mix, socioeconomic status, housing density, and family structure. From these, a random sample of 80 of the 343 NCs was drawn within 21 strata defined by racial-ethnic composition (seven categories) and socioeconomic status (SES; high, medium, and low). Second, within the sampled 80 NCs, children within seven age cohorts (zero [birth], three, six, nine, twelve, fifteen, and eighteen) were sampled from randomly selected households based on a screening of over 35,000 households. Dwelling units were selected systematically from a random start within enumerated blocks. Within dwelling units, all households were listed, and all age-eligible children were selected with certainty. Multiple siblings were thus interviewed within some households. At baseline, the resulting PHDCN sample was 16 percent European American, 35 percent African American, and 43 percent Latino; evenly split by gender; and representative of families living in a wide range of Chicago neighborhoods.

Extensive in-home interviews and assessments were conducted with the sampled children and their primary caregivers three times over a seven-year period, at intervals of roughly two and a half years (wave 1 in 1995–1997, wave 2 in 1997–1999, and wave 3 in 1999–2002). Participants were followed no matter where they moved in the United States. Participation at baseline and retention at wave 3 were relatively high for a contemporary urban sample, 78 percent and 75 percent, respectively. Sampling weights were derived to allow population estimates.

In 2012 and early 2013, the Mixed-Income Project located and reinterviewed randomly sampled participants who had been last contacted at wave 3 of PHDCN in the original birth cohort and the nine- to fifteen-year-old cohorts. Hereafter we define the MIP follow-up as "wave 4." These cohorts were selected to maximize variation in life-course experiences, and also because the age eighteen cohort had the highest attrition rate at wave 3 and the MIP pilot test indicated that the ages three and six cohorts were the most difficult to locate. The Chicago field operation's tracking effort was multipronged: electronic, phone-based, and in-person methods (for example, knocking on doors) were all used. The majority of interviews were carried out in person (almost 60 percent), but phone interviews were allowed if respondents preferred them or if they were easier to implement. Despite the long time that had elapsed since last contact at wave 3 and the contemporary big-city setting, MIP achieved a response rate of 63 percent of eligible cases, of which 40 percent were Latino, 37 percent black, and 19 percent white, closely matching the baseline distribution of the PHDCN sample. Ranging between ages twenty-six and thirty-two at wave 4, there were 226, 236, and 217 respondents, respectively, in the nine-, twelve-, and fifteen-year-old cohorts studied in this article.

The main survey at wave 4 was merged with the prospective waves 1 through 3 of PHDCN and several contextual databases. We first used residential histories from each wave to geo-code addresses to census tract boundaries; this allowed us to link individuals to census tract codes for each of the four waves of the combined PHDCN-MIP survey.[3] Second, we integrated census data from 1990 and 2000 (interpolated by year) and the American Community Survey (ACS) from 2008 to 2012. Third, we exploited data from the Community Surveys (CS) of the PHDCN, a multidimensional set of assessments by residents of the social-organizational characteristics of Chicago neighborhoods that was carried out at two points in time. Researchers personally interviewed 8,782 Chicago residents, representing all of the city's neighborhoods, in 1995. In 2002 a separate sample of 3,105 residents were interviewed. The basic design for the CS had three stages: at stage 1, city blocks were sampled within each neighborhood cluster; at stage 2, dwelling units were sampled within blocks; and at stage 3, one adult resident (age eighteen or older) was sampled within each selected dwelling unit. The final response rate was over 75 percent in both waves. The design yielded a representative sample of Chicago residents large enough to create reliable between-neighborhood measures at the census tract level between 1995 and 2002. The community survey data were then merged to all respondents at wave 1 and those remaining in Chicago at waves 2 and 3 (about 89 percent at wave 2 and 86 percent at wave 3).

Measures

From these merged data, we constructed measures at both the individual and neighborhood levels. Our main indicator of individual poverty is household income below a certain level at each wave. Because this analysis focuses on severe deprivation, we consider an adolescent to experience individual-level poverty if his or her household income is less than $10,000 at waves 1 to 3 and less than $15,000 at wave 4 (to account for inflation). At baseline, the value of $10,000 falls just below the first quintile of income (for example, 18 percent of adolescents lived in poverty at wave 1).[4] Income is often misreported, so for comparison we also examine individual deprivation as indexed by welfare receipt. This supplemental indicator, measured at each of the first three waves of data collection, is coded 1 if the focal adolescent's caregiver received public assistance and 0 otherwise. At wave 4 in 2012, when respondents were adults, we base the indicator on whether the participant received public assistance.[5]

We selected a set of key background variables for predicting the course of compounded poverty. So that we can make comparisons among racial-ethnic groups, in much of our

---

3. Many respondents had moved outside of Chicago. To account for the mobility of the sample we used nationally available census tracts, which were nested within the neighborhood clusters of the original PHDCN sampling design. The census tracts capture the characteristics of all the destination neighborhoods. We assigned the 2000 census tract boundaries for waves 1 to 3 and the 2010 boundaries for wave 4. This strategy reflects the most accurate measure of the characteristics of the neighborhoods in which participants were living at the time of each wave of data collection.

4. The data are weighted to account for both the sampling design and attrition. The sampling weight is designed to adjust for the original stratification of the PHDCN by neighborhood SES and racial composition, along with the age cohort selection and a poststratification of population weights to estimates of the age, gender, and race-ethnicity distribution of children in the city of Chicago in 1995. The attrition weight is defined as the inverse of the probability of being interviewed at wave 4 conditional on being in the study at wave 3. To model the probability of attrition at wave 4 we first multiply imputed missing data from waves 1 through 3 using chained regression equations. We then calculate attrition weights by estimating a logit model for the probability of attrition at wave 4 based on individual- and household-level measures of socioeconomic status and family composition, as well as neighborhood-level measures of demographic composition and social processes (such as collective efficacy and perceived violence). The inverse of each respondent's probability of response is then calculated and standardized by the mean to yield the final attrition weights. We multiply the stratification and attrition weights to produce the final weight. Although we examine results separately using the baseline sampling and attrition weights, the patterns are very similar; we thus present results based on the combined weight. We also use chained regression equations to impute missing data at wave 4, and in all models we control for interview effects on partially completed cases.

5. Adolescents in the age fifteen cohort were not surveyed with their caregiver at wave 3, so for this cohort we use the participant's own receipt of public assistance to indicate individual poverty at both waves 3 and 4.

analysis we limit our sample to those identifying as Latino (30 percent of our weighted adolescent sample), black (45 percent), or white (20 percent). We measure immigrant status with an indicator for the immigrant generation of the adolescent's caregiver (that is, the immigration context of the family of origin): first-generation (29 percent), second-generation (9 percent), or third-generation or later (62 percent). In addition to income deprivation, we account for the socioeconomic context of the adolescent's family of origin with a variable indicating whether the adolescent lived at wave 1 in a house that was owned (48 percent), whether the adolescent's caregiver was married at wave 1 (55 percent), and the educational attainment of the adolescent's caregiver. To account for nonlinearity, we measure educational attainment with a set of three dummy variables: whether the caregiver had less than a high school education (34 percent), a high school degree (15 percent), or more than a high school degree (51 percent). Finally, we include two measures of residential mobility that indicate whether an adolescent (1) moved to a new neighborhood in the city of Chicago (28 percent) or (2) moved outside of Chicago between wave 1 and wave 3 (11 percent). Our logic for these two measures derives from previous research showing large differences in outcomes and neighborhood characteristics by mover-stayer status in Chicago (Sampson 2012, 294–308).

In addition to these background variables, we take advantage of the expansive scope of the PHDCN survey and in our most complete models include components of the adolescents' households and life experiences not accounted for in many other household surveys. The first set focuses on exposure to crime at wave 1 and includes a count of the number of family members with criminal records (family criminality); the sum of forms of domestic violence to which the adolescent was exposed in the past year; the number of delinquent activities in which the adolescent was involved in the past year; and whether the adolescent had seen someone shot, shot at, or stabbed in the past year. The second set of variables comes from the Child Behavior Checklist (Achenbach 1993), administered at wave 1 of PHDCN—aggressive behavior, impulsive behavior, and anxiety or depression. Finally, we include a standardized scale of the adolescent's measured "IQ" at wave 1 based on the Wide Range Achievement Test (WRAT) and the Wechsler Intelligence Scale for Children (WISC) test (Sampson, Sharkey, and Raudenbush et al. 2008, 848), as well as a measure of final educational attainment at wave 4.

Our primary indicator of contextual poverty is the poverty rate of the census tract in which the participant lives at each wave. We define a high-poverty neighborhood as any census tract with a poverty rate of 30 percent or higher. Although any cutoff for poverty is arbitrary, we believe that this definition is justified by the distribution of neighborhood poverty rates, as neighborhoods with a poverty rate of at least 30 percent fall more than one standard deviation above the mean neighborhood poverty rate, both nationally and in the Chicago metropolitan area in 1990, 2000, and 2012. It is also common in the neighborhood effects literature to use 30 percent as a cutoff for high-poverty neighborhoods (Leventhal and Brooks-Gunn 2011; Wilson 2012 [1987], 46). Although we use the neighborhood poverty rate as our primary indicator of deprivation, we also consider unemployment rates and concentrated disadvantage as supplementary measures of contextual deprivation. Our index of concentrated disadvantage includes four tract-level characteristics: unemployment rate, share of families with children headed by a single female, poverty rate, and share of households receiving public assistance income.

We define our main indicator of compounded poverty, or deprivation, as the extent to which participants who experience poverty at the individual level (defined by household income) simultaneously experience it at the contextual level. Thus, at each wave, living in a household with an annual income less than $10,000 (waves 1 to 3) or $15,000 (wave 4) *and* living in a neighborhood with a poverty rate of 30 percent or greater is defined as compounded poverty. The advantage of this definition resides in its clear metric and straightforward interpretation.

Finally, we created a summary index to capture what we call compounded "social-organizational deprivation" at the neighborhood level. Much has been written about concepts like social capital, collective efficacy, and social (dis)order, including how to measure them and how to separate their different components (see, for example, Portes 1998; Putnam 2000; Quillian and Redd 2010; Sampson, Morenoff, and Earls 1999). Consistent with the analytic focus of this paper, however, our purpose is not to dissever but to explore the nature of compounded deprivation, in this case with respect to the nonmaterial dimensions of a neighborhood's underlying social organization. Based on theoretical grounds and prior research in Chicago (see especially Sampson 2012), we therefore selected five interrelated scales that tap a range of social-organizational conditions at each of the first three waves—from reciprocal exchange networks, collective efficacy (cohesion and social control), and organizational involvement, on the positive end of human flourishing, to perceptions of violence and disorder, on the negative end.[6]

6. We used the PHDCN community surveys matched to individual respondents living in Chicago to create an overall index of neighborhood social organization at each of the first three waves of the study. "Reciprocated exchange" is a five-item scale tapping the relative intensity of social exchange within the neighborhood on issues of consequence for children. Presented with the options of replying "never," "rarely," "sometimes," or "often," respondents were asked: (1) "About how often do you and people in your neighborhood do favors for each other? By favors we mean such things as watching each other's children, helping with shopping, lending garden or house tools, and other small acts of kindness." (2) "When a neighbor is not at home, how often do you and other neighbors watch over their property?" (3) "How often do you and people in this neighborhood have parties or other get-togethers where other people in the neighborhood are invited?" (4) "How often do you and other people in this neighborhood visit in each other's homes or on the street?" (5) "How often do you and other people in the neighborhood ask each other advice about personal things such as child-rearing or job openings?" These questions tap balanced exchange, although not necessarily intimate bonds.

"Collective efficacy" constitutes two subscales of social cohesion and shared expectations for control. Residents were asked about the likelihood that their neighbors could be counted on to take action if: (1) children were skipping school and hanging out on a street corner, (2) children were spray-painting graffiti on a local building, (3) children were showing disrespect to an adult, (4) a fight broke out in front of their house, and (5) the fire station closest to home was threatened with budget cuts. We measured social cohesion by coding whether residents agreed with the following propositions: (1) "People around here are willing to help their neighbors"; (2) "People in this neighborhood can be trusted"; (3) "This is a close-knit neighborhood"; (4) "People in this neighborhood generally get along with each other"; and (5) "People in this neighborhood share the same values." Social cohesion and social control were strongly related across neighborhoods.

"Organizational involvement" measured active involvement by residents in (1) local religious organizations, (2) neighborhood watch programs, (3) block groups, tenant associations, or community councils, (4) business or civic groups, (5) ethnic or nationality clubs, and (6) local political organizations.

The "perceived disorder" scale is made up of questions about social and physical incivilities in public. Each respondent was asked: (1) "How much graffiti do you see on buildings and walls in your neighborhood?" (2) "How many vacant or deserted houses or storefronts do you see in your neighborhood?" (3) "How often do you see people drinking in public places in your neighborhood?" and (5) "How often do you see unsupervised children hanging out on the street in your neighborhood?" These were rated as "a big problem," "somewhat of a problem," or "not a problem."

Finally, "violence" was measured based on the following items: (1) "During the past six months, how often was there a fight in this neighborhood in which a weapon was used?" (2) "During the past six months, how often was there a violent argument between neighbors?" (3) "During the past six months, how often were there gang fights?" (4) "During the past six months, how often was there sexual assault or rape?" and (5) "During the past six months, how often was there a robbery or mugging?"

We subjected each scale—corrected for measurement error through an Empirical Bayes model that adjusted for the demographic characteristics of respondents—to a principal components analysis. A single factor accounted for a substantial portion of the covariation among indicators at each wave. Disorder and violence load negatively, and exchange, collective efficacy, and organizational involvement load positively. We capture the shared covariance among measures in the form of the first principal component. We reverse-coded the index so that a high value represents compounded social-organizational deprivation.

RESULTS

Figure 1 shows the rate of individual and contextual poverty for our sample, weighted to reflect the population and accounting for potential attrition bias. We begin with our two indicators of deprivation at the individual level: income-defined and receipt of public assistance. At wave 1, in 1995, 18 percent of our sample experienced individual-level poverty as defined by having a household income less than $10,000. The rate of individual poverty declined through waves 2 and 3, to a low point of 13 percent at wave 3 in 2001. But by the fourth wave of data collection, corresponding to the aftermath of the Great Recession, 19 percent of our sample experienced individual-level poverty. When we define individual-level poverty using receipt of public assistance, 26 percent of our sample was poor at wave 1, declining to 12 percent at wave 3, then increasing again to 26 percent by wave 4. With the exception of wave 3, a bigger share of our sample is defined as poor when we use the public assistance definition than when we use the household income definition; however, both indicators follow the same temporal trend.

Contextual poverty exhibits less temporal variation but a similar overall trend. At the beginning of the study, about 27 percent of adolescents were living in a high-poverty neighborhood. The proportion living in a high-poverty neighborhood declined slightly, to 23 percent, at wave 3, and then increased again, to 28 percent, by wave 4 in 2012.

Findings from prior neighborhood-effects research both nationally and in Chicago (Sampson 2012; Sharkey 2013) lead us to expect significant racial differences in the experience of neighborhood poverty. Figure 2 supports this expectation with respect to differences in neighborhood poverty rates for the three main racial-ethnic groups in our sample: Latino, black, and white. However, consistent with our goal of examining compounded poverty, we also examine the simultaneous experience of individual-level poverty. The resulting model reveals neighborhood poverty rates for six groups at each wave. There are very few whites in our sample who had household incomes below $10,000 at waves 1 to 3 and $15,000 at wave 4, an important substantive finding in itself but one that warrants caution when comparing poverty and nonpoverty groups by racial-ethnic group.

In general, we see that blacks experienced significantly higher neighborhood poverty

Figure 1. Weighted Prevalence of Individual and Contextual Poverty

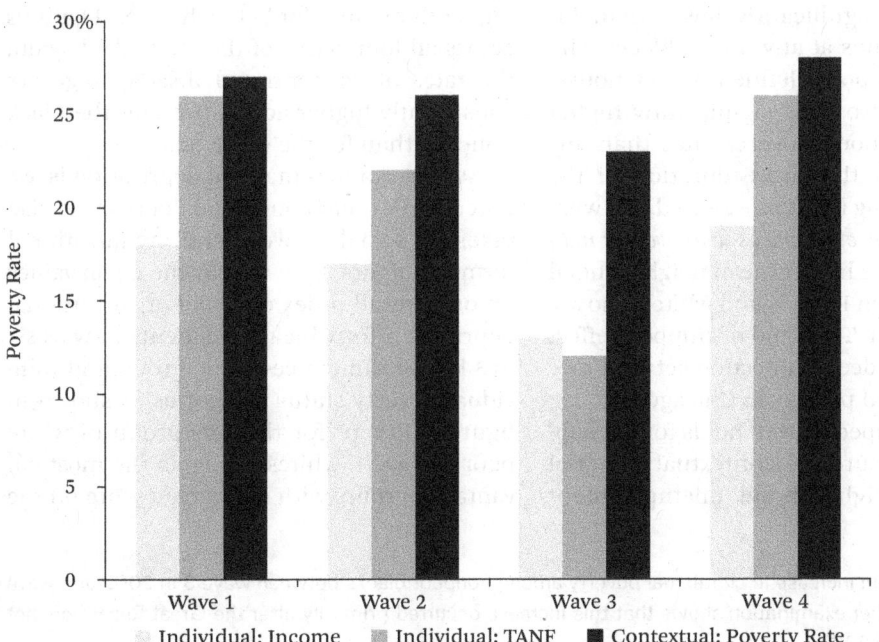

Source: Authors' calculations using data from the U.S. Census Bureau and PHDCN-MIP.

Figure 2. Mean Contextual Poverty Rate by Race-Ethnicity and Individual Poverty Status

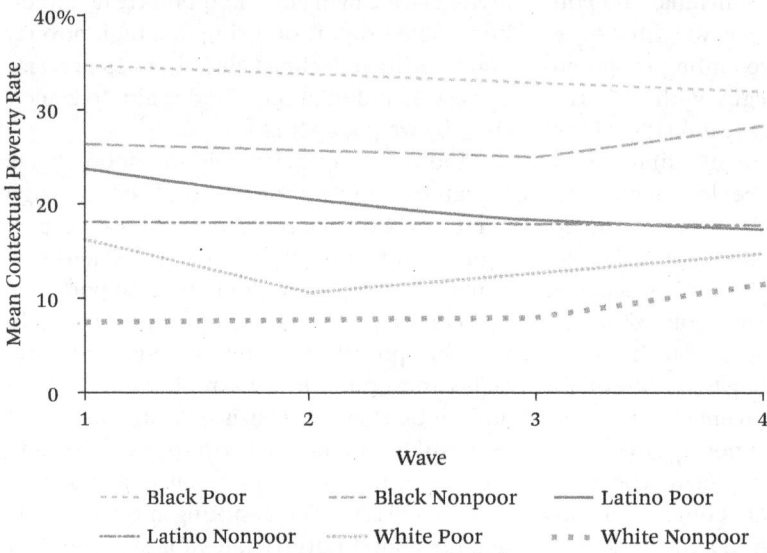

Source: Authors' calculations using data from the U.S. Census Bureau and PHDCN-MIP.

rates than Latinos or whites across the study period from 1995 to 2012. Note that the mean neighborhood poverty rates remain fairly constant and high across waves for blacks, at above 25 percent, and for Latinos, at between 17 and 24 percent. Whites experienced a slight increase in mean neighborhood poverty between waves 3 and 4, but the wave 4 (or post–Great Recession) mean for all whites, at 12 percent, was still significantly lower than for blacks and Latinos at any wave.[7] Blacks who are individually poor, defined by low household income, also have significantly higher mean neighborhood poverty rates than any other group for the entire duration of the study. This finding is not unexpected, but what is striking is that *even blacks who are not individually poor* have higher mean neighborhood poverty rates than Latinos and whites who *are* individually poor. This kind of "flipped" effect underscores the deep connection between race and concentrated poverty in Chicago.

The same flipped pattern holds for our supplemental measures of contextual material deprivation: neighborhood unemployment rate and concentrated disadvantage. The black-white ratio of mean neighborhood unemployment rates of the black *non*poor to the white poor at wave 1 is 1.86, increasing to over 2.00 by wave 3 before falling to 1.75 at wave 4. There are stark differences in neighborhood concentrated disadvantage by racial-ethnic group as well. Blacks' scores on the concentrated disadvantage index are substantially higher than those for both whites and Latinos across all four waves of the study. And again, the rates of concentrated disadvantage are consistently higher across time for the black nonpoor than for the white poor.

As important as material deprivation is, we noted earlier that contextual deprivation also takes on social network and organizational forms. In figure 3, we display the mean values on our overall index of social-organizational deprivation for Chicago residents at waves 1 to 3 by the same race-ethnic group and individual poverty status categories as shown in figure 2. Except for the tiny group of white poor at wave 1, whites are again the most advantaged group, with an average score on the

---

7. Figure 2 shows an increase in contextual poverty among nonpoor blacks between wave 3 in 2002 and wave 4 in 2013, yet further examination shows that this increase occurred primarily after the Great Recession, not between 2002 and 2007.

Figure 3. Mean Rate of Social-Organizational Deprivation by Race-Ethnicity and Individual Poverty Status

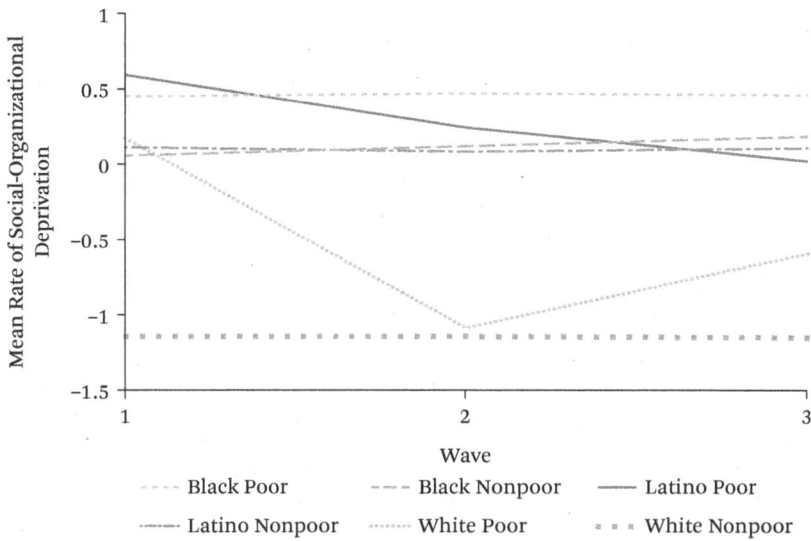

Source: Authors' calculations using data from PHDCN-MIP.

social deprivation scale well below the mean at every wave. Latinos and blacks have mean scores above 0 at each wave. But whereas blacks are decidedly more disadvantaged than Latinos in terms of neighborhood poverty rates, as shown in figure 2, figure 3 demonstrates that Latinos and blacks are *similarly disadvantaged* in terms of neighborhood social organization. Our neighborhood poverty and social-organizational measures thus capture distinct types of contextual deprivation, revealed by the differences between figures 2 and 3.

CROSS-LEVEL DEPRIVATION

One of our major goals is to explore the probability of experiencing compounded poverty—both contextual and individual—across time. Aggregate estimates mask heterogeneity by racial and ethnic group here as well, so figure 4 presents results separately for Latinos, blacks, and whites. This figure is based on a logistic panel regression model that predicts compounded poverty at each wave, controlling for demographics—racial-ethnic group, sex, and age (see model 1 in table 1). The non-overlapping social worlds of compounded deprivation are clearly seen. Blacks exhibit the highest predicted probability, at 0.17 at wave 1. This estimate declines to approximately 0.12 at wave 3, but increases a full 50 percent, to 0.18, by wave 4. Latinos and whites, by contrast, have much lower and near-zero predicted probabilities of experiencing compounded poverty; at no time period is the predicted probability more than 0.02 for Latinos or whites. The significant odds ratio of 31.04 for the black dummy variable in model 1 reflects the elevated probability of experiencing compounded poverty among blacks compared to whites. This value may appear to be unusually large, but we should reiterate the findings from our descriptive analysis that experiencing compounded poverty is particularly rare among whites: at none of the four waves did more than three white adolescents have both a household income below $10,000 (or $15,000) and live in a neighborhood with a poverty rate of at least 30 percent. Therefore, it is to be expected that the odds ratio comparing blacks to whites will be quite substantial and trend toward infinity given the "structural zero" of compounded poverty in the transition to young adulthood that reflects the reality among whites. Put differently, experiencing

Figure 4. Predicted Probability of Compounded Poverty by Race-Ethnicity

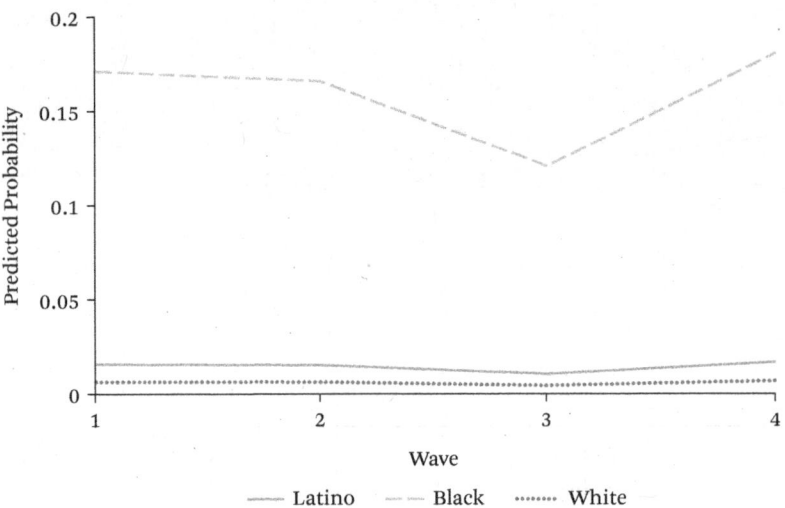

Source: Authors' calculations using data from the U.S. Census Bureau and PHDCN-MIP.

compounded poverty is a phenomenon limited almost entirely to blacks.

Having established the probability of compounded poverty in the three major racial-ethnic groups in our sample, we turn to a more expansive multivariate analysis that predicts exposure to compounded poverty using additional background characteristics. Table 1 shows the results of three additional clustered logistic models.[8] Model 2 predicts the binary outcome of compounded poverty using adolescents' age, sex, race-ethnicity, dummy variables for wave, and additional covariates that capture characteristics of their home lives at baseline and later experiences with residential mobility. Based on the descriptive analysis in figure 1, which shows poverty at its lowest level at wave 3, we define this time period as our reference category.

The results show that controlling for the additional background characteristics attenuates the odds ratio for blacks, at 15.80, compared to 31.04 in model 1. In addition to the association between compounded poverty and race, model 2 shows that having a first-generation immigrant caregiver is associated with much lower odds of compounded poverty compared to having a caregiver who is a third- or later-generation immigrant. The socioeconomic status of the adolescent's household at wave 1 is associated with compounded poverty controlling for the adolescent's age, race, and wave: living in an owned home at wave 1 is associated with lower odds of compounded poverty, and an adolescent whose caregiver has less than a high school education is nearly three times as likely to experience compounded poverty compared

---

8. We have multiple observations of exposure to compounded poverty at each wave of the study ($n = 2{,}612$) and thus a person-period model. Because our data are clustered by individual across time, we correct standard errors in the logistic regressions. We also estimate a mixed-effects logistic regression in STATA that accounts for both fixed and person effects, given by $\Pr(y_{ij} = 1 | \mathbf{x}_{ij}, \mathbf{u}_j) = H(\mathbf{x}_{ij}\beta + \mathbf{z}_{ij}\mathbf{u}_j)$, where $\mathbf{x}_{ij}$ is a vector of covariates for the fixed effects and β represents the corresponding coefficients. The vector $\mathbf{z}_{ij}$ represents the random intercepts and $\mathbf{u}_j$ represents the random effects. H is the logistic cumulative distribution function. This modeling strategy allows us to estimate whether the underlying probability of compounded poverty differs among individuals; we find that there is substantial individual heterogeneity in the propensity to experience compounded poverty, with a significant standard deviation of the individual intercept in all models estimated. Although the substantive results from the mixed-effects model are very similar to the model with clustered standard errors, the confidence intervals in the former are much larger. Table 1 presents the clustered logistic models.

Table 1. Clustered Logistic Models Predicting Compounded Poverty: Exponentiated Coefficients

	Model 1	Model 2	Model 3	Model 4
Age	1.022	0.985	0.930	0.948
	[0.916, 1.141]	[0.873, 1.112]	[0.813, 1.063]	[0.824, 1.090]
Sex (male = 1)	0.785	1.040	1.135	1.133
	[0.442, 1.392]	[0.598, 1.808]	[0.658, 1.956]	[0.656, 1.955]
Latino	2.465	1.913	1.716	1.600
	[0.728, 8.350]	[0.527, 6.945]	[0.488, 6.027]	[0.432, 5.918]
Black	31.04***	15.80***	11.48***	11.80***
	[9.896, 97.37]	[4.928, 50.66]	[3.709, 35.54]	[3.849, 36.19]
Wave 1	1.666	1.473	1.155	1.264
	[0.813, 3.415]	[0.684, 3.174]	[0.524, 2.548]	[0.545, 2.930]
Wave 2	1.536	1.458	1.283	1.350
	[0.823, 2.867]	[0.744, 2.856]	[0.645, 2.554]	[0.662, 2.749]
Wave 3	Reference	Reference	Reference	Reference
Wave 4	1.278	2.119	4.241	3.394
	[0.302, 5.412]	[0.397, 11.31]	[0.663, 27.13]	[0.504, 22.84]
Caregiver first-generation		0.323*	0.323*	0.354+
		[0.119, 0.880]	[0.111, 0.939]	[0.114, 1.097]
Caregiver second-generation		0.301	0.263	0.286
		[0.049, 1.857]	[0.038, 1.835]	[0.040, 2.040]
Homeowner wave 1		0.334**	0.387*	0.405*
		[0.153, 0.731]	[0.162, 0.927]	[0.170, 0.964]
Caregiver education: less than high school		2.978*	2.599+	2.678+
		[1.125, 7.881]	[0.881, 7.671]	[0.954, 7.513]
Caregiver education: high school degree		Reference	Reference	Reference
Caregiver education: greater than high school		0.553	0.540	0.619
		[0.207, 1.477]	[0.194, 1.500]	[0.235, 1.631]
Moved in Chicago		1.285	1.108	1.100
		[0.694, 2.377]	[0.579, 2.119]	[0.571, 2.117]
Moved outside of Chicago		0.527	0.400	0.392
		[0.163, 1.705]	[0.099, 1.616]	[0.098, 1.568]
Wave 4 educational attainment				0.835
				[0.593, 1.177]
Additional individual background characteristics[a]			Yes	Yes
Observations	2,612	2,612	2,612	2,612

Source: Authors' calculations using data from the U.S. Census Bureau and PHDCN-MIP.
Note: 95 percent confidence intervals are in brackets.
[a]Additional individual background characteristics include caregiver marital status, family criminality, domestic violence, delinquency, exposure to violence, aggression, impulsivity, anxiety or depression, and IQ, all measured at wave 1.
+$p < .10$; *$p < .05$; **$p < .01$; ***$p < .001$

to an adolescent whose caregiver has a high school degree.

Model 3 in table 1 includes all of the covariates from model 2 and adds an additional series of background characteristics from wave 1 that capture the adolescent's exposure to crime (both within the household and the neighborhood); measures of emotional and behavioral well-being; and individual differences long noted as salient in the literature on human capital attainment (Heckman 2006), including both cognitive skills (such as ability) and noncognitive skills (such as self-control). Notwithstanding these extensive additional covariates, our finding about race remains disturbingly robust. Notably, the odds ratio for blacks declines from around 16.0 in model 2 to about 11.5 but remains significant and substantial, reflecting the much greater odds of experiencing compounded poverty among blacks compared to whites. The first-generation immigrant and homeownership indicators also remain significant and negatively associated with compounded poverty independent of family criminality, exposure to violence, and any emotional or behavioral problems experienced by the adolescent, while having a caregiver with less than a high school education is associated with greater odds of experiencing compounded poverty compared to having a caregiver with more education.

Figure 5, which shows the conditional probability of experiencing compounded poverty based on model 3 shown in table 1, allows us to see temporal trends disaggregated by race. Blacks still have higher predicted probabilities of experiencing compounded poverty than Latinos and whites at all waves of the study, controlling for all of the background covariates in table 1. The predicted probability of compounded poverty for blacks declines from about 0.15 at wave 1 to 0.11 at wave 3, before increasing to 0.16 in the Great Recession era between waves 3 and 4. Although less than the unadjusted magnitude in figure 4, this is still a 45 percent increase from pre– to post–Great Recession in compounded deprivation among blacks. In contrast, the predicted probability of compounded poverty among Latinos remains below 0.02 for the duration of the study, whereas among whites it never rises above 0.01.

Our final model in table 1 presents a strict test by introducing final educational attainment. Although education has been shown to be influenced by neighborhood and family poverty (Wodtke, Harding, and Elwert 2011), our goal is to determine the persistence of the racial disadvantages that we have observed to this point. Model 4 thus controls for wave 4 educational attainment as a stand-in for the differential trajectory that adolescents may take after accounting for their background and wave 1 characteristics. Final educational attainment, however, is not independently associated with experiencing compounded poverty, and controlling for educational outcomes does not alter our main findings about the association between race and compounded poverty. Indeed, the odds ratio for blacks barely budges from model 3, and whites remain uniquely advantaged despite adjusting for the socioeconomic characteristics of the household in which they were raised and major individual differences in human capital potential and final educational attainment.

Moreover, we see similarly stark disparities when predicting social-organizational deprivation using race-ethnicity and the same covariates we use to predict compounded poverty in models 3 and 4. Controlling for caregiver, background, and other wave 1 characteristics, being black or Latino is associated with significantly higher scores on the social-organizational deprivation scale, with blacks having an average score 1.10 points above whites and Latinos 0.85 points above whites. This multivariate finding reflects the mean differences in social-organizational deprivation by racial-ethnic group shown in figure 3.

PERSISTENT AND COMPOUNDED DEPRIVATION

The models we present here have shown that racial-ethnic background and family socioeconomic characteristics strongly predict the course of compounded poverty. But how persistent or chronic is compounded poverty? In particular, conditional on background characteristics, what is the effect of being in compounded poverty at the start of the study on later compounded poverty? Equally

Figure 5. Predicted Probability of Compounded Poverty by Race-Ethnicity, Conditional on Background Characteristics and Individual Differences

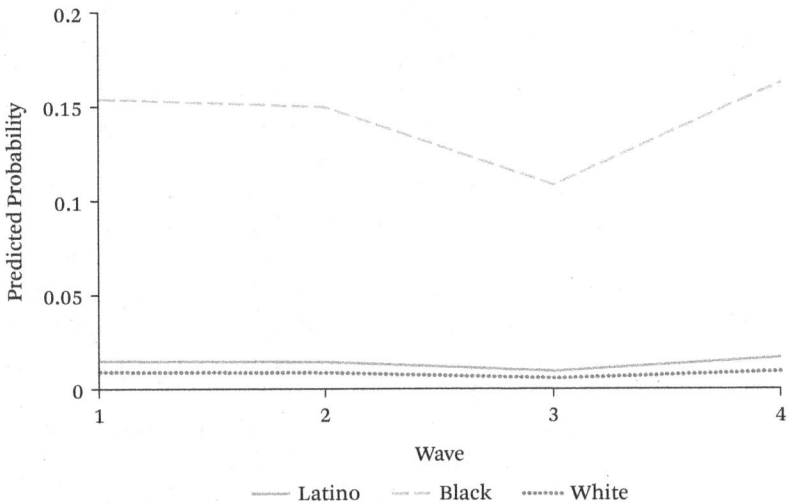

Source: Authors' calculations using data from the U.S. Census Bureau and PHDCN-MIP.

important, conditional on being in compounded poverty status at baseline, who is most likely to *transition out of* compounded poverty?

In table 2, we address these questions in the form of a basic change model that predicts compounded poverty subsequent to wave 1, conditional on compounded poverty at wave 1 and other background (racial-ethnic group, caregiver immigrant generation, caregiver education) and wave 1 (age, living in an owned home) characteristics. Our dependent variable is binary, where 1 indicates that the participant experienced compounded poverty in at least one wave of the study after wave 1: a participant receives a 1 on this variable if they experienced compounded poverty at wave 2, wave 3, wave 4, or any combination of these three waves. (Being in compounded poverty at all waves was a very rare event and confined to blacks only.) This binary outcome is estimated with logistic regression.

The results from model 1 show that persistence is substantial. The legacy of inequality is such that the odds ratio corresponding to compounded poverty at wave 1 is greater than 7, with a 95 percent confidence interval of approximately 5 to 10. We can interpret these findings to conclude that living in a low-income household in a neighborhood with a high poverty rate at wave 1 is associated with much lower odds of an adolescent escaping these conditions at later waves; the experience of compounded poverty is powerfully durable.[9]

The characteristic that is most strongly predictive of falling into compounded poverty at later waves is being black compared to being white, controlling for background and wave 1 characteristics (including exposure to compounded poverty at wave 1). This odds ratio,

---

9. We also ran the models in table 2 using compounded poverty at wave 1, 2, or 3 to predict compounded poverty at wave 4, as many of the adolescents lived with their primary caregivers during the first three waves of the study before establishing independent residences by wave 4. In model 1, compounded poverty at one of the first three waves significantly predicts compounded poverty at wave 4, holding all else constant. Once we add the additional background characteristics in model 2 and wave 4 educational attainment in model 3, compounded poverty during adolescence no longer significantly predicts compounded poverty at wave 4, though the association remains positive. Across all models, being black compared to white is strongly and positively associated with compounded poverty at wave 4.

Table 2. Logistic Models Predicting Stability and Change in Persistent Compounded Poverty, Waves 2 to 4: Exponentiated Coefficients

	Model 1	Model 2	Model 3
Compounded poverty wave 1	7.242***	10.15***	9.700***
	[5.046, 10.39]	[6.071, 16.98]	[5.833, 16.13]
Age at wave 1	0.970	0.918⁺	0.948
	[0.893, 1.053]	[0.832, 1.012]	[0.856, 1.050]
Sex (male = 1)	1.113	1.246	1.253
	[0.853, 1.452]	[0.869, 1.785]	[0.901, 1.743]
Latino	1.111	1.018	0.840
	[0.503, 2.458]	[0.438, 2.366]	[0.336, 2.099]
Black	10.41***	8.602***	8.824***
	[6.076, 17.84]	[4.294, 17.23]	[4.479, 17.38]
Caregiver first-generation	0.397*	0.312*	0.381*
	[0.182, 0.863]	[0.133, 0.734]	[0.151, 0.957]
Caregiver second-generation	0.371	0.269	0.310
	[0.089, 1.551]	[0.047, 1.528]	[0.047, 2.047]
Homeowner wave 1	0.320***	0.258***	0.268***
	[0.200, 0.511]	[0.132, 0.503]	[0.138, 0.518]
Caregiver education: less than high school	2.209*	1.683	1.688
	[1.141, 4.274]	[0.720, 3.934]	[0.717, 3.978]
Caregiver education: high school degree	Reference	Reference	Reference
Caregiver education: greater than high school	0.488*	0.442⁺	0.523
	[0.269, 0.885]	[0.195, 1.005]	[0.233, 1.178]
Wave 4 educational attainment			0.768⁺
			[0.578, 1.019]
Additional individual background characteristics[a]		Yes	Yes
Observations	653	653	653

Source: Authors' calculations using data from the U.S. Census Bureau and PHDCN-MIP.
Note: 95 percent confidence intervals are in brackets.
[a]Additional individual background characteristics include caregiver marital status, family criminality, domestic violence, delinquency, exposure to violence, aggression, impulsivity, anxiety or depression, and IQ, all measured at wave 1.
⁺$p < .10$; *$p < .05$; **$p < .01$; ***$p < .001$

too, is very large, which is consistent with earlier findings: blacks are more likely than whites and Latinos to experience individual poverty at each wave, and as we saw in figure 2, blacks also have higher mean neighborhood poverty rates than whites and Latinos. But even when we adjust for where an individual starts out, being black, compared to being white or Latino, puts one at much greater risk of later compounded poverty.

The significant odds ratio for the indicator that the adolescent's caregiver has less than a high school education suggests that adolescents who grew up in homes where their caregivers had low levels of educational attainment have higher odds of experiencing compounded poverty later in adolescence and young adulthood, holding constant racial-ethnic background, age, homeownership, and compounded poverty at wave 1. This independent association of educational attainment with compounded poverty complements other recent findings that individuals with low levels of completed education are especially disadvantaged across a number of domains, employment and incarceration in particular (Western 2006). Being black and poorly educated is a particularly powerful combination of correlated adversities.

Model 2 in table 2 parallels model 3 in table 1 by expanding the number of covariates to include additional background and wave 1 characteristics of the adolescents in our sample and their households. Even with these additional controls capturing exposure to crime and emotional or behavioral problems, the odds ratios for the early experience of compounded poverty and being black compared to white remain significant, positive, and substantial. This suggests that other background characteristics do not mediate the association between race and compounded poverty and the durability of compounded poverty. Put differently, experiencing compounded poverty is so entrenched that a black adolescent who lives in a poor household in a high-poverty neighborhood at wave 1 but who is advantaged in other respects—he or she may have educated caregivers, experience low exposure to violence, and suffer few emotional or behavioral disadvantages—still has relatively low odds of escaping compounded poverty in the transition to young adulthood.

Finally, introducing wave 4 educational attainment in model 3 once again does not change our main conclusions. The wave 4 educational attainment odds ratio of 0.768 suggests that higher educational attainment by wave 4 is associated with lower odds of experiencing compounded poverty at waves 2, 3, or 4; but this association is only marginally significant, and the odds ratios for being black and experiencing compounded poverty at wave 1 remain large, positive, and significant: the legacy of inequality is not easily erased even with advances in schooling. Our results from all three models in table 2 hold when we run the models on a sample restricted to just blacks and Latinos. Nor does adjusting for social-organizational deprivation erase the strong legacy of prior disadvantage: the odds ratios for compounded poverty at wave 1 and for being black are 8.68 and 6.29, respectively (results not shown). Although a full analysis is beyond the scope of this article, social-organizational deprivation in the adolescent's wave 1 neighborhood is nonetheless positively linked with experiencing compounded poverty at later waves, controlling for the adolescent's age, race-ethnicity, caregiver's education, caregiver's immigrant generation, and caregiver's homeownership: the more social-organizational deprivation the adolescent experiences in his wave 1 neighborhood, the greater the odds that he or she will later experience compounded poverty. Once we account for the additional covariates in model 3, the association between social-organizational deprivation at wave 1 and later compounded poverty is reduced (t ratio = –1.86).

CONCLUSION

Despite theoretical motivation stemming from assertions of the importance of "cycles of deprivation" in the classic work, the trend in poverty research in recent years has been to dissect individual components and to estimate the effects of specific dimensions of poverty. While essential, this approach overlooks how severe deprivation is experienced in the United States, especially in cities that have undergone substantial changes in immigration and demographic composition as well as the social hardships brought on by the Great Recession. To address this issue, the first goal of our article was to document core facts about severe deprivation, with a focus on the prevalence of individual and neighborhood poverty in the transition to young adulthood during the Great Recession era.

Prior research prepared us to expect that adolescents from low-income households live in neighborhoods with higher poverty rates than do adolescents who live in higher-income households. But race matters greatly for this finding, in counterintuitive ways when considered over the long run. Based on data for three cohorts of adolescents living in Chicago, we find that over the eighteen years from 1995 to 2013, blacks who were nonpoor had higher mean neighborhood poverty rates at wave 1, *and at every subsequent wave,* than Latinos and whites who were individually poor at each wave. Blacks in our study, even the nonpoor, were also decidedly more disadvantaged than whites and Latinos in terms of neighborhood unemployment rates and concentrated disadvantage. Furthermore, nonpoor blacks experienced substantially more deprivation than poor whites in dimensions of neighborhood social organization, such as low collective efficacy and exposure to violence.

Our second goal built on the first by introducing the concept of compounded poverty, or deprivation, which describes the extent of simultaneous exposure to both individual and contextual poverty during adolescence and young adulthood. Although the aggregate prevalence of this joint poverty exposure is relatively low in our sample, ranging from 6 percent to 9 percent across waves, it varies from between 11 and 18 percent of blacks across time to very low exposure for Latinos and virtually none for whites. Our measure of compounded deprivation is thus a major example of the correlated adversities to which black adolescents in our sample were differentially exposed as they transitioned into young adulthood.

Our third aim was to determine the characteristics that predict exposure to compounded poverty at any given wave and across waves, including the period of the Great Recession. Although prior literature has put forth many factors to explain poverty, whether broken homes, low parental education, large families, criminal involvement, exposure to violence, impulsivity, dropping out of school, or low IQ, these individual factors work against a backdrop of deep and persistent inequality over the life course. Indeed, despite taking account of an extensive group of such background characteristics and individual differences, we find that blacks experienced much higher odds of compounded poverty over time—over ten times greater than whites. Latinos also tended to have higher odds of experiencing compounded poverty than whites, but not nearly the same differential likelihood as blacks.

Table 2 further informed us about the persistent grip of compounded poverty, revealing that compounded deprivation is very difficult to escape. Overall, adolescents who experienced compounded poverty at wave 1 had over seven times higher odds of compounded poverty at later waves than did adolescents who were not both individually poor and living in a high-poverty neighborhood at wave 1, suggesting a kind of "poverty trap" that ensnares individuals for long periods. Despite a substantial association between compounded poverty at wave 1 and subsequent exposure to compounded poverty, whites were better able to escape early severe deprivation in the future; in a sense, they were "protected" from ongoing severe deprivation. Such is decidedly not the case for blacks, who by wave 4 had a predicted probability of compounded poverty of 0.16. This rate of compounded poverty is not only dramatically different from that for whites but also higher than the national average of individual poverty, which was 14.5 percent in 2013 (DeNavas-Walt and Proctor 2014). Perhaps more surprising, more blacks in our sample experienced compounded poverty at wave 4 than were married (11 percent), and nearly as many experienced compounded poverty as had graduated from college (21 percent).

Moreover, our analysis shows that while there were declines in individual and contextual poverty from the mid-1990s to the early 2000s, there were sharp upticks in individual poverty in the aftermath of the Great Recession. The pattern for contextual poverty follows the same general trend, with a less dramatic dip in the early 2000s. But further scrutiny of the overall pattern of compounded poverty results in rather stunning differences by race that are not explained by baseline or individual characteristics. As shown in figure 5, the probability of experiencing compounded poverty increased 45 percent from wave 3 to wave 4 among blacks, whereas among Latinos and whites it hovered near zero. Our data thus provide fresh evidence of the deep connection between race and the aftermath of the Great Recession, along with the crosscutting economic adversities that shape the transition to young adulthood and arguably into middle age.

Taken together, our results call into question common strategies to dissect or tease apart the effects of what are closely linked social realities that unfold in interconnected form over time. Likewise, our results point to a need to consider more holistic interventions that treat poverty as a package of material and social deprivations faced by children as they make the important transition to adulthood. Another important question for the future concerns the malleability of poverty traps, in particular as a function of the social-organizational features of neighborhoods (Quillian and Redd 2010) and the contextual origins of intergenerational social mobility (Chetty and Hendren 2015). Most interventions are time-constrained such that outcomes are measured in the short run. The evidence implies that we need to make durable investments in disadvantaged urban neighborhoods instead—to match the persistent nature of the social and institutional disinvestment that such neighborhoods have endured over many years (Sharkey 2013, 179). The field of poverty research will benefit from a more direct consideration of the long-term dynamics of compounded deprivation, both material and social-organizational.

REFERENCES

Achenbach, Thomas M. 1993. *The Young Adult Self-Report Revised and the Young Adult Behavior Checklist.* Burlington: University of Vermont, Department of Psychology.

Anderson, Elijah. 1999. *Code of the Street: Decency, Violence, and the Moral Life of the Inner City.* New York: W. W. Norton.

Brooks-Gunn, Jeanne, Greg J. Duncan, and J. Lawrence Aber, eds. 1997a. *Neighborhood Poverty: Context and Consequences for Children.* Vol. 1. New York: Russell Sage Foundation.

———, eds. 1997b. *Neighborhood Poverty: Policy Implications in Studying Neighborhoods.* Vol. 2. New York: Russell Sage Foundation.

Burdick-Will, Julia, Jens Ludwig, Stephen W. Raudenbush, Robert J. Sampson, Lisa Sanbonmatsu, and Patrick T. Sharkey. 2011. "Converging Evidence for Neighborhood Effects on Children's Test Scores: An Experimental, Quasi-experimental, and Observational Comparison." In *Social Inequality and Educational Disadvantage: New Evidence on How Families, Neighborhoods, and Labor Markets Affect Educational Opportunities for American Children,* edited by Greg Duncan and Richard Murnane. New York: Russell Sage Foundation.

Chetty, Raj, and Nathaniel Hendren. 2015. "The Effects of Neighborhoods on Intergenerational Mobility: Childhood Exposure Effects and County Level Estimates." Equality of Opportunity Project Working Paper. Cambridge, Mass.: Harvard University.

Chetty, Raj, Nathaniel Hendren, and Lawrence F. Katz. 2015. "The Long-Term Effects of Exposure to Better Neighborhoods: New Evidence from the Moving to Opportunity Experiment." Equality of Opportunity Project Working Paper. Cambridge, Mass.: Harvard University.

DeNavas-Walt, Carmen, and Bernadette D. Proctor. 2014. *Income and Poverty in the United States: 2013.* Report P60-249. Washington: U.S. Census Bureau.

Duncan, Greg J., and Jeanne Brooks-Gunn, eds. 1997. *Consequences of Growing Up Poor.* New York: Russell Sage Foundation.

Duncan, Greg J., Kathleen M. Ziol-Guest, and Ariel Kalil. 2010. "Early-Childhood Poverty and Adult Attainment, Behavior, and Health." *Child Development* 81(1): 306–25.

Elder, Glen H., Jr., Jacquelynne S. Eccles, Monika Ardelt, and Sarah Lord. 1995. "Inner-City Parents Under Economic Pressure: Perspectives on the Strategies of Parenting." *Journal of Marriage and the Family* 57(3): 771–84.

Ellen, Ingrid Gould, and Margery Austin Turner. 1997. "Does Neighborhood Matter? Assessing the Recent Evidence." *Housing Policy Debate* 8: 833–66.

Garrett, Patricia, Nicholas Ngandu, and John Ferron. 1994. "Poverty Experiences of Young Children and the Quality of Their Home Environments." *Child Development* 65(2): 331–45.

Guo, Guang, and Kathleen Mullan Harris. 2000. "The Mechanisms Mediating the Effects of Poverty on Children's Intellectual Development." *Demography* 37(4): 431–47.

Heckman, James J. 2006. "Skill Formation and the Economics of Investing in Disadvantaged Children." *Science* 312: 1900–1902.

Jencks, Christopher, and Susan E. Mayer. 1990. "The Social Consequences of Growing Up in a Poor Neighborhood." In *Inner-City Poverty in the United States,* edited by Lawrence Lynn and Michael McGeary. Washington, D.C.: National Academy Press.

Lempers, Jacques D., Dania Clark-Lempers, and Ronald L. Simons. 1989. "Economic Hardship, Parenting, and Distress in Adolescence." *Child Development* 60(1): 25–39.

Leventhal, Tama, and Jeanne Brooks-Gunn. 2000. "The Neighborhoods They Live In: The Effects of Neighborhood Residence on Child and Adolescent Outcomes." *Psychological Bulletin* 126: 309–37.

———. 2011. "Changes in Neighborhood Poverty from 1990 to 2000 and Youth's Problem Behaviors." *Developmental Psychology* 47(6): 1680–98.

Ludwig, Jens, Greg J. Duncan, Lisa A. Gennetian,

Lawrence F. Katz, Ronald C. Kessler, Jeffrey R. Kling, and Lisa Sanbonmatsu. 2012. "Neighborhood Effects on the Long-Term Well-Being of Low-Income Adults." *Science* 337: 1505–10.

Mayer, Susan E. 1998. *What Money Can't Buy: Family Income and Children's Life Choices*. Cambridge, Mass.: Harvard University Press.

Musick, Kelly, and Robert D. Mare. 2006. "Recent Trends in the Inheritence of Poverty and Family Structure." *Social Science Research* 35(2): 471–99.

Pettit, Becky. 2011. "Compounded Disadvantage: Race, Incarceration, and Wage Growth." *Social Problems* 58: 257–80.

Pettit, Becky, and Bruce Western. 2004. "Mass Imprisonment and the Life Course: Race and Class Inequality in U.S. Incarceration." *American Sociological Review* 69: 151–69.

Portes, Alejandro. 1998. "Social Capital: Its Origins and Applications in Modern Sociology." *Annual Review of Sociology* 24: 1–24.

Prewitt, Kenneth, Christopher Mackie, and Hermann Habermann, eds. 2014. *Civic Engagement and Social Cohesion: Measuring Dimensions of Social Capital to Inform Policy*. Washington, D.C.: National Academies Press.

Putnam, Robert. 2000. *Bowling Alone: The Collapse and Renewal of American Community*. New York: Simon & Schuster.

Quillian, Lincoln, and Rozlyn Redd. 2010. "Can Social Capital Explain Persistent Racial Poverty Gaps?" In *The Colors of Poverty: Why Racial and Ethnic Disparities Persist*, edited by Ann Chih Lin and David R. Harris. New York: Russell Sage Foundation.

Sampson, Robert J. 2012. *Great American City: Chicago and the Enduring Neighborhood Effect*. Chicago: University of Chicago Press.

Sampson, Robert J., Jeffrey D. Morenoff, and Felton Earls. 1999. "Beyond Social Capital: Spatial Dynamics of Collective Efficacy for Children." *American Sociological Review* 64(5): 633–60.

Sampson, Robert J., Stephen W. Raudenbush, and Felton Earls. 1997. "Neighborhoods and Violent Crime: A Multilevel Study of Collective Efficacy." *Science* 277: 918–24.

Sampson, Robert J., Patrick Sharkey, and Stephen W. Raudenbush. 2008. "Durable Effects of Concentrated Disadvantage on Verbal Ability Among African-American Children." *Proceedings of the National Academy of Sciences* 105(3): 845–52.

Sanbonmatsu, Lisa, Jens Ludwig, Lawrence F. Katz, Lisa A. Gennetian, Greg J. Duncan, Ronald C. Kessler, Emma Adam, Thomas W. McDade, and Stacy Tessler Lindau. 2011. *Moving to Opportunity for Fair Housing Demonstration Program: Final Impacts Evaluation*. Washington: U.S. Department of Housing and Urban Development.

Sharkey, Patrick. 2013. *Stuck in Place: Urban Neighborhoods and the End of Progress Toward Racial Equality*. Chicago: University of Chicago Press.

Sharkey, Patrick, and Felix Elwert. 2011. "The Legacy of Disadvantage: Multigenerational Neighborhood Effects on Cognitive Ability." *American Journal of Sociology* 116(6): 1934–81.

Western, Bruce. 2006. *Punishment and Inequality in America*. New York: Russell Sage Foundation.

Wilson, William Julius. 2012 [1987]. *The Truly Disadvantaged: The Inner City, the Underclass, and Public Policy*. Chicago: Chicago University Press.

Wodtke, Geoffrey T. 2013. "Duration and Timing of Exposure to Neighborhood Poverty and the Risk of Adolescent Parenthood." *Demography* 50(5): 1765–88.

Wodtke, Geoffrey T., David J. Harding, and Felix Elwert. 2011. "Neighborhood Effects in Temporal Perspective: The Impact of Long-Term Exposure to Concentrated Disadvantage on High School Graduation." *American Sociological Review* 76(5): 713–36.

Income, Poverty, and Material Hardship Among Older Americans

HELEN LEVY

Using data from the 2008 and 2010 waves of the Health and Retirement Study to analyze the determinants of material hardship among individuals ages sixty-five and older, I look at five self-reported hardships: food insecurity, skipped meals, medication cutbacks, difficulty paying bills, and dissatisfaction with one's financial situation. One-fifth of the elderly report one or more of these hardships. Although hardship is more likely for those with low incomes, most older Americans experiencing hardship are not poor. I analyze whether alternative measures of resources do a better job of predicting hardship than does income relative to the federal poverty threshold. I find that spending relative to the poverty threshold does a worse job predicting hardship than does income relative to poverty. Subtracting out-of-pocket medical spending from income yields a measure that is an even better predictor of hardship. In multivariate models, I find that self-reported health, activity limitations, and disability are significant predictors of hardship. Having reliable children (as assessed by the respondent) or an able-bodied spouse reduces the likelihood of hardship. Poor health increases hardship through three channels: by lowering income, by increasing out-of-pocket medical spending, and through its direct effect on hardship. The first two of these—lower income and higher medical spending—are much less quantitatively important than the third; in a nutshell, poor health makes it harder to get by with less.

Keywords: poverty, material hardship, food insecurity, older Americans

Social Security has enjoyed great success at reducing poverty and promoting independence among the elderly (Engelhardt, Gruber, and Perry 2005; Engelhardt and Gruber 2006). Indeed, the poverty rate among individuals age sixty-five or older was estimated at 9.5 percent in 2013, far lower than for children (19.9 percent) or for working-age adults (13.6 percent) (DeNavas-Walt and Proctor 2014). Poverty is an incomplete measure of material well-being, however, and is not synonymous with material hardship. A number of recent studies have analyzed hardship in the non-elderly population, particularly among single-mother families and former welfare recipients (Danziger et al. 2000; Iceland and Bauman 2007; Mayer and Jencks

---

Helen Levy is research associate professor at the Institute for Social Research at the University of Michigan.

I gratefully acknowledge helpful suggestions from Sanders Korenman, from Dean Lillard, from workshop participants at the Social Security Administration, Office of Research, Evaluation, and Statistics, and from participants in the Russell Sage Foundation "Severe Deprivation in America" conference. The Health and Retirement Study is sponsored by the National Institute on Aging (grant number NIA U01AG009740) and is conducted by the University of Michigan. I acknowledge financial support from the National Institute on Aging (grant number NIA K01AG034232). This project was also supported by a grant from the Social Security Administration through the Michigan Retirement Research Center. The findings and conclusions expressed are solely those of the author and do not represent the views of the Social Security Administration, any agency of the federal government, or the Michigan Retirement Research Center. Direct correspondence to: Helen Levy at hlevy@umich.edu, Institute for Social Research, University of Michigan, 426 Thompson St., Ann Arbor, MI 48104.

1989; Meyer and Sullivan 2003; Rector, Johnson, and Youssef 1999; She and Livermore 2007; Sullivan, Turner, and Danziger 2008). Much less work has analyzed hardship among the elderly, perhaps because of their lower rates of official poverty.

The distinction between poverty and material hardship may be even more important for the elderly than it is for the non-elderly. Aging-related declines in physical and cognitive ability may visit material hardship even on individuals with relatively high incomes; at the same time, some elderly individuals with low income may have substantial assets that protect them from hardship. For both of these reasons, the relationship between income and hardship among the elderly is likely to be both complex and different from that for younger individuals. The recent development of an experimental poverty measure by the U.S. Census Bureau reflects some of these concerns. For example, one criticism of the official poverty measure is that it does not take into account the burden of high out-of-pocket medical spending, which is much more likely to be a problem for elderly households (Short 2014; Short and Garner 2002). Census Bureau estimates using an alternative poverty measure proposed by the National Academy of Sciences yield elderly poverty rates that are approximately twice the current official measure.[1]

At a time when pressure on the federal budget is giving rise to discussions of how entitlement programs benefiting the elderly might be restructured, understanding economic vulnerability among the elderly takes on new importance. How should the burden of any cuts in spending be distributed? Spending cuts can affect beneficiaries (for example, changing the formula for calculating Social Security cost-of-living increases; increasing beneficiary cost-sharing under Medicare), or they can affect health care providers (for example, cuts in Medicare reimbursement rates). For cuts that are borne by beneficiaries, policymakers must decide which beneficiaries will bear the brunt of these cuts and how to protect those who are most vulnerable.

In this article, I use data from the 2008 and 2010 Health and Retirement Study (HRS) to document patterns of material hardship among the elderly. I use five different measures of material hardship: food insecurity, skipped meals, cutting back on medications because of cost, difficulty paying bills, and dissatisfaction with one's financial situation. Overall, 21 percent of the elderly report one or more of these hardships. Among individuals in the lowest income quintile, the fraction is 37 percent, and even among those in the top income quintile, 11 percent report some hardship. Most elderly individuals who experience hardship are not poor. One alternative measure of resources that might be expected to predict hardship among older Americans better than income does, household spending, actually performs worse than income. To paint a fuller picture of why older individuals, including some with quite high incomes, experience hardship, I estimate multivariate models predicting hardship as a function of income and other characteristics, including health and cognition. In multivariate models, health status is a highly significant predictor of hardship: individuals who report being in worse health or who report more limitations on physical activity are much more likely to experience hardship. This result is robust to the inclusion of controls for income and out-of-pocket health spending, suggesting that poor health directly increases the risk of hardship, rather than only through its indirect effects on income or out-of-pocket medical spending. I also find that the risk of hardship is mitigated by having an able-bodied spouse; the risk of hardship is elevated for those with disabled spouses or very unreliable children.

These findings have important implications for public policy. First, since most of the elderly experiencing hardship are in fact not poor and therefore not eligible for means-

---

1. U.S. Census Bureau, "Poverty: Experimental Measures," available at: http://www.census.gov/hhes/www/povmeas/tables.html (last revised October 16, 2014). Another proposed measure of poverty based on data from the Luxembourg Income Study (LIS) would also yield higher poverty rates for the elderly (Brady 2004). Barbara Butrica, Dan Murphy, and Sheila Zedlewski (2010) demonstrate that a range of alternative measures of poverty yield higher poverty rates for the elderly.

tested transfer programs, increasing outreach with the goal of enrolling more eligible elderly in these programs has limited potential to reduce hardship. Similar logic suggests that while increasing benefit levels might reduce hardship among those who are already receiving benefits, its potential to reduce hardship is limited since transfer program recipients make up only about one-quarter of the elderly who experience hardship. Second, poor health's direct effect on hardship suggests that policy interventions that provide in-kind benefits—for example, congregate meal programs—could alleviate hardship more effectively than those that simply transfer cash.

PREVIOUS RESEARCH

A large literature considers the adequacy or optimality of retirement savings. A traditional approach to assessing the adequacy of retirement savings is to compare the income stream that would result from annuitizing wealth at the time of retirement to pre-retirement income (Mitchell and Moore 1998; Poterba, Venti, and Wise 2012). Retirement wealth is considered adequate if it yields an income stream that is not too much below one's income before retirement—regardless of how low this level may be. Numerous studies have noted that it is smooth *consumption*, rather than income, that reflects optimality, and a number of papers have tested this proposition (Engen et al. 1999; Hurd and Rohwedder 2006a, 2006b, 2008a, 2008b, 2011; Scholz, Seshadri, and Khitatrakun 2006). Again, the focus here is on smoothness over time rather than on the level of consumption; in particular, very low levels of consumption (so low as to result in food insecurity with hunger, for example) are not inconsistent with optimality in the economic sense.

A second relevant set of papers focuses on poverty among the elderly. Some of these extend the traditional approach to the adequacy of retirement wealth by comparing annuitized income streams to the poverty level or some other threshold level of expenditure required to meet basic needs; others compare actual income to the poverty level, while still others compare actual consumption to the poverty level (Brady 2010; Fisher et al. 2009; Haveman et al. 2003; Haveman et al. 2006; Haveman et al. 2007; Hungerford 2001; Johnson and Mermin 2009; Love, Smith, and McNair 2008; VanDerhei and Copeland 2010). An important subset of these papers focus on the high rate of poverty among elderly widows (Bound et al. 1991; Gillen and Kim 2009; McGarry 1995; McGarry and Schoeni 2005; Sevak, Weir, and Willis 2003; Weir and Willis 2000; Zick and Holden 2000).

An alternative approach to evaluating the economic well-being of the elderly is to analyze material hardship directly. Material hardship is operationalized in many different ways, depending on the population studied and the available data, and these methods are reviewed elsewhere (Beverly 2001; Federman et al. 1996; Ouellette et al. 2004). Some version of this approach has been applied to the non-elderly population, particularly to single-mother families and former welfare recipients (Danziger et al. 2000; Iceland and Bauman 2007; Mayer and Jencks 1989; Meyer and Sullivan 2003; Rector et al. 1999; She and Livermore 2007; Sullivan et al. 2008). Only one such study focuses on the elderly (Charles et al. 2006).

Finally, several studies have analyzed the determinants among the elderly of the two important outcomes that are treated as measures of hardship in the current analysis—food insecurity and medication cutbacks. One study using data from the Third National Health and Nutrition Examination Survey (1988–1994) and a much smaller 1994 survey of the elderly in New York State finds that low income, functional limitations, Hispanic ethnicity, younger age, and use of food stamps significantly predict food insecurity among the elderly (Lee and Frongillo 2001). In a related study, in-depth interviews were conducted with fifty-three elderly respondents about the causes of their food insecurity; this study concludes that, "although money is a major cause of food insecurity, elders sometimes have enough money for food but are not able to access food because of transportation or functional limitations, or are not able to use food (that is, not able to prepare or eat available food) because of functional impairments and health problems" (Wolfe, Frongillo, and Valois 2003, 2762).

A study of medication cutbacks among the elderly looked at medication restriction among seniors by using data on the approximately

5,000 respondents age seventy and older in the 1995–1996 wave of the HRS (the so-called AHEAD cohort) who regularly used prescription drugs (Steinman, Sands, and Covinsky 2001). This study finds that among the 1,911 of these respondents who had no drug coverage, poor health, nonwhite race-ethnicity, low education, low income, and high out-of-pocket drug costs are all significant predictors of medication restrictions. Finally, two studies of approximately 4,000 individuals age fifty and older with chronic illness find that younger age, lower income, and higher out-of-pocket costs all significantly predict medication restrictions (Heisler, Wagner, and Piette 2005; Piette, Heisler, and Wagner 2004).

This analysis updates and extends these studies by (1) looking at both types of cutbacks (medications and food) as well as two other self-reported measures of hardship in a common empirical framework; (2) linking the results to the more general literature on poverty; (3) using more recent data; (4) including more covariates; and (5) estimating individual fixed-effects models that eliminate time-invariant sources of unobserved heterogeneity.

DATA

Data for the analysis come from the Health and Retirement Study, a longitudinal study that has interviewed older adults since 1992. The HRS sample is described in detail elsewhere (Sonnega et al. 2014). Briefly, the HRS sample began with a cohort of approximately 12,600 respondents between the ages of fifty-one and sixty-one living in 7,700 households. Over time, the sample has been expanded and refreshed so that it is now nationally representative of the U.S. population over the age of fifty. Core interviews are conducted every two years either in person or over the phone with the full sample of respondents, querying them about their health, cognition, labor force status, income, and assets. For married couples, each member of the couple reports on his or her health, cognition, and labor force status, while household-level information, such as assets and income, are reported by a "financial respondent" on behalf of the household. Among married couples in our sample, husbands served as the financial respondent about two-thirds of the time. However, because single women outnumber single men in this age range, about half of all the financial respondents in our sample (including both singles and married couples) are female. Supplemental interviews on special topics are administered periodically to subsets of respondents. As described in more detail later in this article, this analysis relies on data from the 2008 and 2010 core surveys; from "leave-behind" surveys of psychosocial characteristics that were administered to half the sample in 2008 and the other half in 2010; and from the 2007 and 2009 waves of the Consumption and Activities Mailer Survey (CAMS), a supplemental survey of household spending patterns and time use administered to a random subsample of respondents.

Variables

The different variables used in the analyses are constructed as follows:

Measures of Hardship

The core HRS survey includes three yes or no questions that I use as measures of material hardship; individuals responding "yes" are coded as experiencing the hardship:

1. *Food insecurity:* "(Since your last interview/in the last two years), have you always had enough money to buy the food you need?"
2. *Skipped meals:* "At any time (since your last interview/in the last two years), have you skipped meals or eaten less than you felt you should because there was not enough food in the house?"
3. *Medication cutbacks:* "At any time (since your last interview/in the last two years) have you ended up taking less medication than was prescribed for you because of the cost?"

In addition, the psychosocial leave-behind questionnaire includes two questions about the respondent's financial situation:

1. *Difficulty with bills:* "How difficult is it for (you/your family) to meet monthly payments on (your/your family's) bills?" Response options are: "not at all difficult," "not very dif-

ficult," "somewhat difficult," "very difficult," and "completely difficult." I code respondents as experiencing this hardship if they chose either "very difficult" or "completely difficult."

2. *Dissatisfaction with finances:* "How satisfied are you with your present financial situation?" Response options are: "completely satisfied," "very satisfied," "somewhat satisfied," "not very satisfied," and "not at all satisfied." I code respondents as experiencing this hardship if they chose either "not very satisfied" or "not at all satisfied."

Economic Status

I use measures of family income and total household assets from the RAND HRS data file (version N, October 2014). A comparison of poverty rates among the elderly and near-elderly in HRS 2010 using this variable shows that they benchmark reasonably well to poverty rates for a similarly defined sample using data from the March 2010 Current Population Survey (CPS).[2] Both income and assets are inflated to real 2010 values using the Consumer Price Index for All Urban Consumers (CPI-U) from the Bureau of Labor Statistics (BLS).

Total household spending: Information is available on total household spending for the subset of respondents included in the CAMS. I use the imputed version of this variable for 2007 and 2009 from the RAND data file (RAND CAMS, version D2, April 2015) and convert to real 2010 dollars using the CPI-U.

Out-of-pocket medical spending: I use measures of out-of-pocket medical spending for the respondent and spouse from the RAND HRS data file (version N, October 2014). The RAND measure is based on a question about respondents' expenses during the previous two years. I convert this measure to 2010 dollars using the CPI-U and divide by two to get a measure of real annual out-of-pocket spending, which I subtract from annual income in some analyses.

Health: Respondents reported their overall assessment of their own health as "excellent," "very good," "good," "fair," or "or poor."

Physical (Nagi) limitations: The HRS asks respondents whether they have difficulty because of a health problem with twelve different activities: walking several blocks, jogging a mile, walking a mile, sitting for two hours, getting up from a chair, climbing several flights of stairs, climbing a single flight of stairs, stooping, raising their arms above shoulder level, pulling or pushing large objects (the size of a living room chair), lifting or carrying weights over ten pounds (like a heavy bag of groceries), and picking up a dime from a table. From these responses I create an index of physical limitations by summing the number of positive responses to these items; the index takes on values from 0 (the healthiest, with no limitations) to 12 (the sickest, with the most limitations) (Fonda and Herzog 2004).

Number of medications taken regularly: The HRS asks respondents whether they take medications regularly for twelve different conditions: high blood pressure, diabetes, chronic lung disease, heart problems, conditions related to stroke, emotional, nervous, or psychiatric conditions, joint or muscle pain, asthma or allergies, stomach problems, sleep problems, anxiety, or depression. I use the number of medications taken regularly as a measure of the complexity of the respondent's medication regimen.

Cognitive ability: In the HRS core survey, interviewers read a list of ten words to respondents, who then recall as many words as they can. They are asked to recall the words immediately after hearing the list and also several minutes later. I use the sum of these from the 2006 survey, ranging from zero to twenty, as one indicator of cognitive ability. I also use respondents' scores on the "Serial Sevens" test, in which they are asked to count backward from 100 by sevens up to five times. The score is the number of correct subtractions (from zero

---

2. Poverty rates for individuals ages fifty-six to sixty-four are 10.8 percent in HRS and 10.4 percent in CPS; for individuals ages sixty-five and older, the rates are 9.0 percent in HRS and 9.1 percent in CPS.

to five). Many respondents who have difficulty with these tasks refuse to complete them; I categorize those with missing data (about 15 percent for word recall and 7 percent for Serial Sevens) into the lowest performance category on each of these cognitive tests. Additional documentation on the HRS cognition measures is available elsewhere (Ofstedal, Fisher, and Herzog 2005).

Program use: I create dummy variables reflecting participation in three means-tested transfer programs: Medicaid, Supplemental Security Income (SSI), and food stamps. The Medicaid dummy indicates whether the individual reported having had Medicaid coverage at all during the two years since the previous interview. The SSI and food stamp dummies indicate whether the respondent—and spouse for married respondents—received any income from this source during the previous calendar year.

Labor force status: The core survey asks all respondents: "Are you working now, temporarily laid off, unemployed and looking for work, disabled and unable to work, retired, a homemaker, or what?" I use the responses to this question to create a labor force status indicator; the categories used in the multivariate analysis are "working," "unemployed," and "disabled," with a residual category that includes retirees, homemakers, and respondents reporting "other" labor force status.

Demographics, education, and marital status: The analysis also includes controls for respondent age, race (white non-Hispanic, African American non-Hispanic, other non-Hispanic), ethnicity (Hispanic, not Hispanic), marital status, gender, and years of education.

The Sample

Because not all individuals are asked each question in each wave, the sample depends on the variables that are being analyzed. In 2008, 10,891 community-dwelling individuals ages sixty-five and older completed core interviews; in 2010, 10,423 did so. (The full HRS sample in each year, including individuals under the age of sixty-five, is around 17,000.) In 2008 and 2010, approximately 40 percent of the sample completed a leave-behind questionnaire, including two of my hardship measures (difficulty with bills and financial dissatisfaction) in each year. For the main analyses, which include the outcomes from the leave-behind questionnaire, this yields a sample of 8,738 individuals, with the data almost evenly split between those whose data are from 2008 and those whose data are from 2010. For panel analyses, which are possible only for outcomes from the core survey (food insecurity, skipped meals, and medication cutbacks), I have a sample of 9,078 respondents who are, for the most part, the same respondents in the sample used for the main analysis. Finally, for analyses including total spending *and* the leave-behind variables, I have a much smaller sample of 2,106 observations. All analyses use sampling weights unless noted otherwise.

RESULTS

Basic Descriptive Statistics

Table 1 presents basic descriptive statistics for the full sample and also by family income relative to poverty (less than 100 percent of the federal poverty level, 100 to 199 percent, 200 to 299 percent, 300 to 399 percent, 400 to 499 percent, and 500 percent or higher). Overall, 21 percent of the elderly reported some hardship; considering only the four hardships other than financial dissatisfaction (food insecurity, skipped meals, medication cutbacks, or difficulty paying bills), this figure is 13 percent. Seven percent reported medication cutbacks, 4 percent reported food cutbacks, and 2 percent reported skipping meals; 5 percent had difficulty paying bills, and 14 percent were dissatisfied with their financial situation. Among those who did experience some hardship, lower-income households were more likely to experience more than one hardship. Seven percent of the sample lived in poverty, and nearly one-quarter lived in a family with income less than 175 percent of the federal poverty level. Ten percent of the elderly reported using Medicaid, food stamps, SSI, or some combination of the three programs, with

Table 1. Material Hardship and Sociodemographic Characteristics of Americans Age Sixty-Five and Older: Sample Means

	Income as a Percentage of the Federal Poverty Level						
	Full Sample	Less Than 100%	100–199%	200–299%	300–399%	400–499%	500% or Higher
Any hardship	0.210	0.443	0.317	0.213	0.181	0.134	0.109
Any hardship other than dissatisfaction	0.125	0.301	0.191	0.131	0.097	0.063	0.060
Food insecurity	0.044	0.168	0.066	0.035	0.026	0.017	0.018
Skipped meals	0.021	0.110	0.033	0.014	0.010	0.002	0.005
Medication cutbacks	0.067	0.123	0.105	0.081	0.057	0.032	0.031
Difficulty paying bills	0.051	0.155	0.084	0.051	0.033	0.022	0.018
Dissatisfied with financial situation	0.142	0.307	0.215	0.142	0.129	0.096	0.067
Mean number of hardships, if greater than 0	1.4	1.7	1.5	1.5	1.4	1.2	1.2
Age	74.5	75.5	76.5	75.5	74.1	73.6	72.7
Unmarried male	0.100	0.132	0.118	0.105	0.085	0.112	0.077
Unmarried female	0.297	0.642	0.459	0.305	0.221	0.185	0.159
Married male	0.339	0.133	0.226	0.320	0.383	0.386	0.453
Married female	0.264	0.094	0.198	0.270	0.311	0.318	0.311
White non-Hispanic	0.855	0.571	0.802	0.881	0.878	0.907	0.919
African American non-Hispanic	0.070	0.218	0.097	0.062	0.052	0.046	0.036
Other race non-Hispanic	0.019	0.028	0.021	0.014	0.022	0.014	0.020
Hispanic (any race)	0.056	0.182	0.080	0.042	0.048	0.034	0.026
Years of education	12.7	10.3	11.5	12.4	12.6	13.1	14.2
Memory score (0–20)	8.9	7.8	8.0	8.6	9.0	9.5	9.9
Serial Sevens score (0–4)	3.4	2.3	3.0	3.3	3.6	3.7	3.9
Self-rated health is fair or poor	0.261	0.501	0.349	0.277	0.234	0.207	0.153
Number of physical limitations (0–12)	4.2	5.7	5.1	4.5	3.9	3.7	3.2
Labor force status							
Working	0.160	0.046	0.060	0.108	0.177	0.174	0.290
Unemployed	0.009	0.012	0.008	0.006	0.002	0.015	0.011
Disabled	0.043	0.157	0.070	0.039	0.024	0.021	0.013
Retired	0.693	0.640	0.742	0.745	0.715	0.722	0.610
Homemaker	0.088	0.141	0.109	0.097	0.075	0.061	0.068
Other	0.004	0.003	0.006	0.005	0.002	0.002	0.003

(continued)

Table 1. *(continued)*

	Income as a Percentage of the Federal Poverty Level						
	Full Sample	Less Than 100%	100–199%	200–299%	300–399%	400–499%	500% or Higher
Family income	$57,359	$9,672	$18,369	$30,177	$42,662	$54,137	$128,403
Total spending[a]	$38,176	$22,078	$25,863	$33,664	$35,843	$44,918	$59,059
Wealth (including home value)	$545,913	$106,035	$199,055	$329,224	$440,648	$552,270	$1,137,306
Any transfer program use	0.097	0.499	0.169	0.050	0.051	0.035	0.016
Medicaid	0.074	0.395	0.124	0.043	0.034	0.028	0.011
Food stamps	0.051	0.316	0.082	0.023	0.024	0.013	0.005
SSI	0.030	0.197	0.047	0.010	0.013	0.007	0.005
Unweighted sample size	8,737	686	1,898	1,729	1,276	915	2,234
Weighted sample fraction in this column	100%	7.1%	21.4%	19.0%	14.6%	10.6%	27.3%

Source: Health and Retirement Study, 2008 and 2010.
Note: Overall unweighted sample size is 8,738.
[a]Sample sizes for this variable are 182, 532, 382, 313, 224, and 473 across the six columns, respectively.

a much higher prevalence, not surprisingly, among lower-income households; half of all households in poverty reported some program use, while fewer than 2 percent of households with income higher than five times the poverty level (corresponding to approximately the top quartile of the income distribution) did. Most (84 percent) of the sample members were no longer working, and 26 percent reported that their health was only fair or poor.

How Well Does Income Explain Hardship Among the Elderly?

The prevalence of hardship declines as income increases, as shown in figure 1 (the data used to create this figure are in appendix table A1). There is a strong relationship between income and hardship: in the lowest income category—households with income below 75 percent of the poverty threshold, which account for about 3.4 percent of older Americans—38.5 percent experienced hardship. The prevalence of hardship increases slightly in the next income category, then declines slowly as income increases. At a certain point, which varies depending on which hardship is being analyzed, the relationship flattens out; additional income above this level does nothing to reduce hardship.

The nonlinear relationship between income and hardship is not particularly surprising; what *is* surprising is how high income must be before additional income is no longer associated with lower hardship. Income must be about five times the poverty level before its effect on the probability of reporting any hardship fades out. This persistence of hardship is driven mostly by medication cutbacks, difficulty paying bills, and financial dissatisfaction; the income gradients associated with food insecurity and skipped meals fade out earlier, at about twice the poverty level. Also surprising is the fact that even at the highest levels of income, the prevalence of hardship is not zero. In families with incomes greater than five times the poverty level, about 5 percent of elderly individuals experienced some hardship. Hardship at higher levels of income con-

Figure 1. Hardship Among Americans Age Sixty-Five and Older by Income

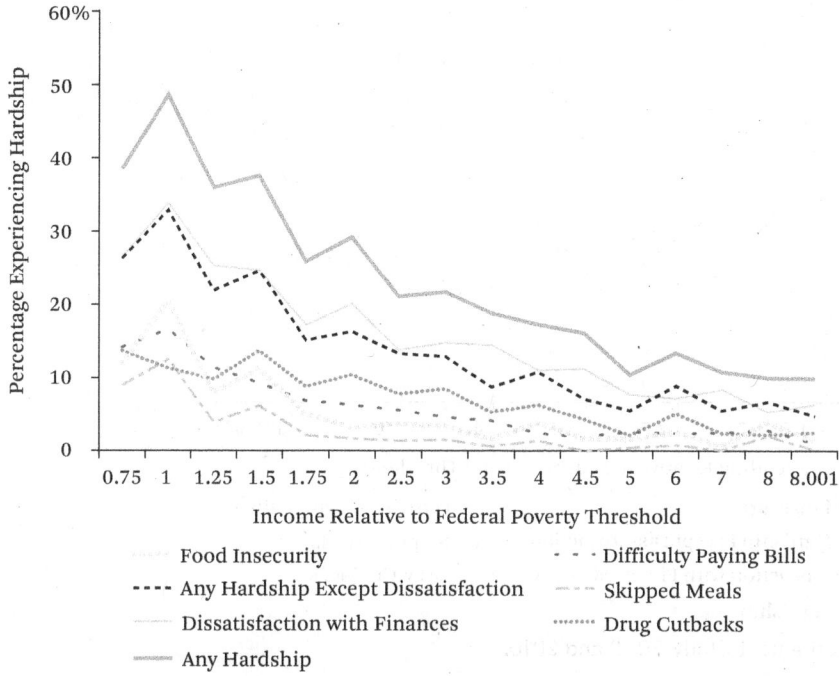

Source: Health and Retirement Study, 2008 and 2010.

sists mostly of medication cutbacks and dissatisfaction; only 1 or 2 percent of these individuals reported food insecurity or difficulty paying bills, and skipping meals was essentially unknown among families with income greater than three times the poverty level.

Would Alternative Measures of Resources Predict Hardship Among the Elderly More Accurately than Income Does?

As already noted, other resource measures, such as consumption and disposable income, may target hardship more accurately than income does, particularly for the elderly. To test this possibility, I explore two other measures of resources: (1) total spending, using the subset of respondents for whom CAMS data are available, and (2) income minus household out-of-pocket medical spending. Figures 2 and 3 replicate figure 1 using these two alternative measures of resources. Figure 2 shows that total spending does not seem to do a better job than income of discriminating between those households that are likely to experience hardship and those that are not. This echoes the conclusion reached by Kerwin Kofi Charles and his colleagues (2006), who use somewhat different methods. In contrast, repeating the same tabulation using a measure of household income net of out-of-pocket medical spending (figure 3) does a somewhat better job than does income alone of identifying households at risk of hardship. That is, there is more mass in the left tail in figure 3 than in figures 1 or 2, and the probability of hardship declines more smoothly.

While this eyeball test makes sense, it is not obvious how we could quantify the accuracy with which a resource measure identifies hardship. One way of doing this is to calculate how high up the resource distribution it is necessary to go before we have identified half (or some other chosen fraction) of those in hardship. Table 2 operationalizes this concept by calculating the median value of different resource measures for individuals experiencing each kind of hardship. A resource mea-

Figure 2. Hardship Among Americans Age Sixty-Five and Older by Spending

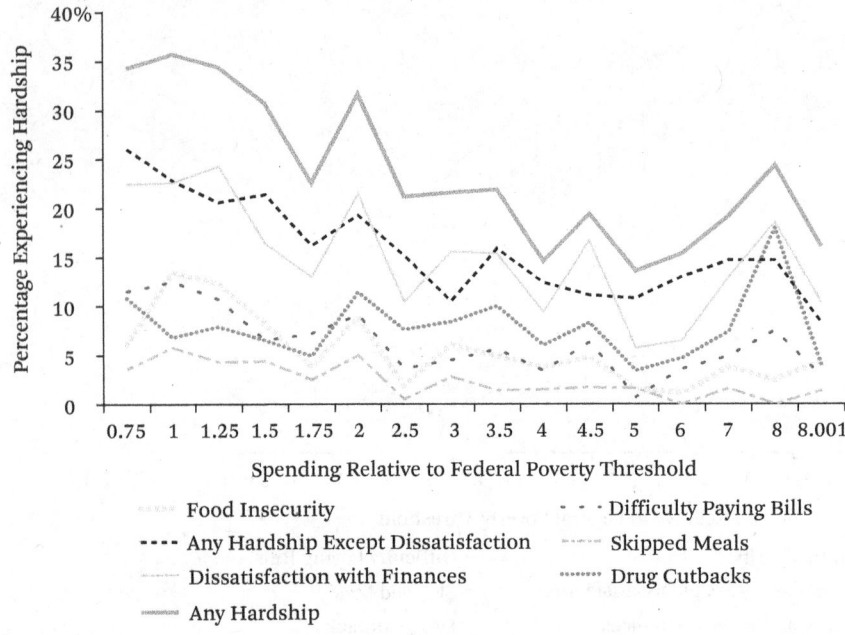

Source: Health and Retirement Study, 2008 and 2010.

Figure 3. Hardship Among Americans Age Sixty-Five and Older by Income Minus Out-of-Pocket Medical Spending

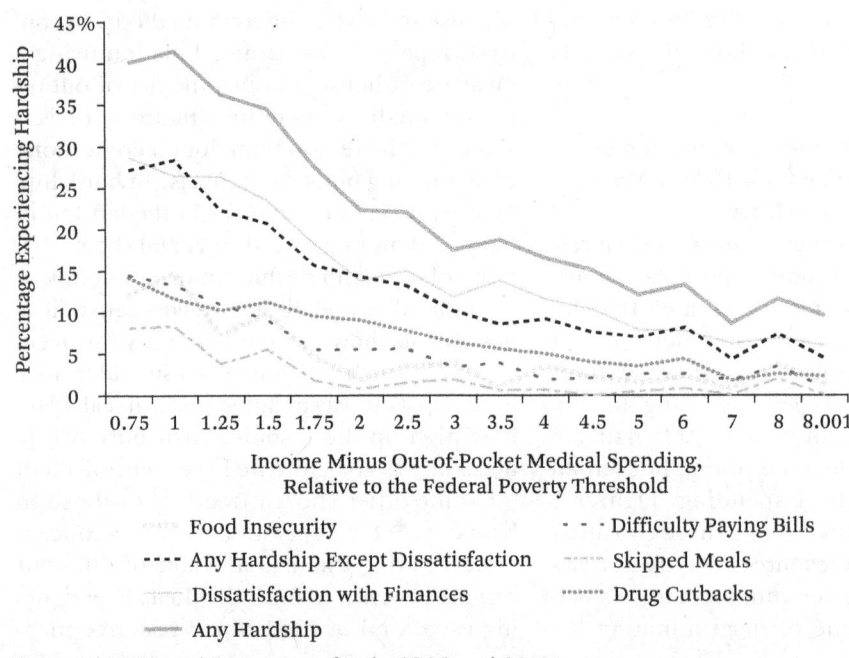

Source: Health and Retirement Study, 2008 and 2010.

Table 2. Median Resources Among Americans Age Sixty-Five and Older Who Experience Hardship

	Food Insecurity	Skipped Meals	Medication Cutbacks	Difficulty Paying Bills	Dissatisfaction with Finances	Any Hardship	Any Hardship Except Dissatisfaction
Alternative measures of resources							
Income							
Full sample	$17,260	$15,766	$25,467	$19,397	$22,742	$23,444	$21,828
Sample with spending data only	$14,636	$13,620	$25,068	$17,062	$19,563	$20,296	$19,198
Spending	$21,355	$18,228	$29,003	$20,887	$24,742	$24,751	$24,230
Income minus medical spending	$15,326	$13,861	$22,377	$16,964	$20,075	$20,780	$19,197
Alternative measures of resources/needs							
Income/needs							
Full sample	1.51	1.32	2.19	1.67	1.99	2.05	1.96
Sample with spending data only	1.47	1.29	2.12	1.47	1.82	1.85	1.77
Spending/needs	2.00	1.80	2.55	1.94	2.24	2.24	2.26
Income minus medical spending/needs	1.38	1.22	1.92	1.46	1.78	1.84	1.73
Unweighted sample size							
Full sample	408	184	616	479	1,280	1,917	1,171
Sample with spending data only	105	41	159	123	324	483	305

Source: Health and Retirement Study, 2008 and 2010.

sure that more accurately identifies hardship will have lower values in table 2; that is, more of the population with hardship will be clustered at low resource levels. Table 2 confirms the intuition of figures 1, 2, and 3: total spending is inferior to income for targeting hardship, while income net of out-of-pocket medical spending is superior. There is still a lot of hardship, however, that is not explained by subtracting out-of-pocket medical spending from income; half of individuals reporting hardship were in households with income net of out-of-pocket medical spending greater than 170 percent of their federal poverty threshold.

Is Hardship Related to Failure to Take Up Transfer Programs?

The role of transfer programs is particularly interesting because the existing literature mostly shows that hardships are *more* likely among recipients than among eligible nonrecipients. In particular, a number of studies find that food insecurity is more prevalent among food stamp recipients than among nonrecipients (Haider, Jacknowitz, and Schoeni 2003; Wilde and Nord 2005), presumably because the timing of enrollment, conditional on having income low enough to be eligible, is not random: people enroll in these programs when they have fallen on tough times. As a result, the partial correlation between program use and hardship reflects both self-selection into program use and any causal effect of program use on hardship, two factors that are likely to go in different directions (Haider, Jacknowitz, and Schoeni 2003; Wilde and Nord 2005). More recent studies relying on plausibly exogenous variation in program use to identify the effect of food stamps find mixed effects, which is probably related to variation in the validity of the instrumental variables strategy (Greenhalgh-Stanley and Fitzpatrick 2013; Schmidt, Shore-Sheppard, and Watson 2013).

Because I have no exogenous variation in program use, and also because public program use is not well measured in surveys (Meyer, Mok, and Sullivan 2009), I do not attempt to draw any causal inference about the relationship between take-up and hardship. Rather, my goal is to document how many of those experiencing hardship are not taking up public programs for which they may be eligible, in order to understand how much scope there is for reducing hardship by, for example, improving program outreach. Figure 4 (based on the data presented in appendix table A2) explores the relationship between hardship and transfer program use by categorizing the elderly experiencing hardship by income (collapsed into two categories: greater than or less than 175 percent of poverty) and the use of transfer programs (food stamps, Medicaid, and SSI). As already noted, about half of those experiencing hardship fell into the higher income category; about 10 percent of these (or 5 percent of the total) were programs users. In the lower-income group, most but by no means all of the elderly who experienced food insecurity or skipped meals were already using public programs. About half of low-income elders who had difficulty paying bills used public programs. For the other hardships—medication cutbacks and financial dissatisfaction—most of the elderly who experienced them did not use SSI,

Figure 4. Distribution of Americans Age Sixty-Five and Older Experiencing Hardship by Family Income and Use of Transfer Programs

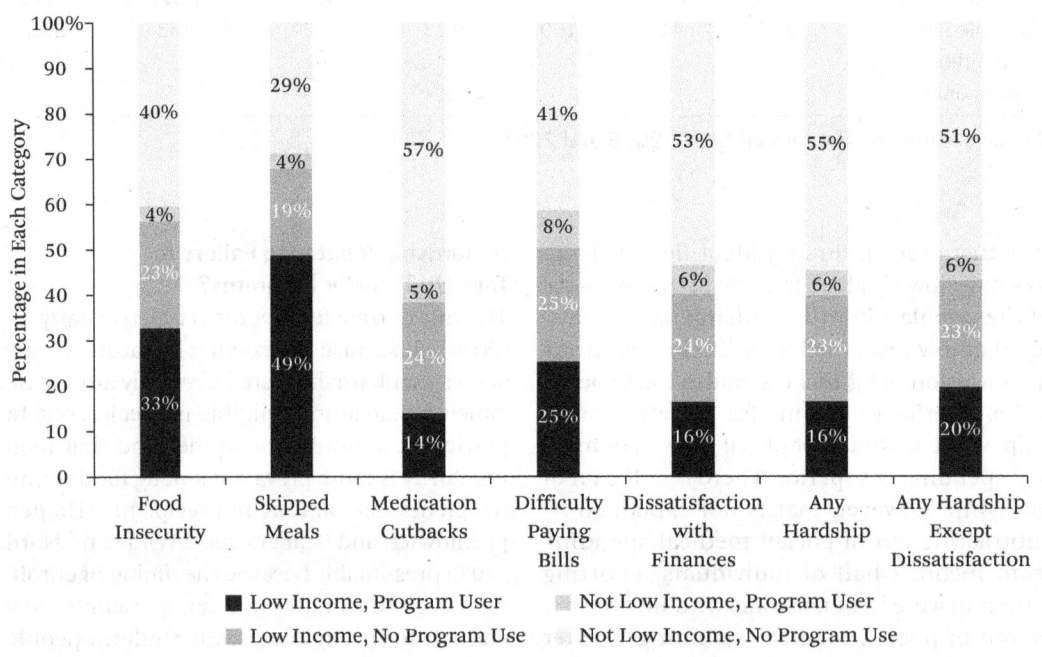

Source: Health and Retirement Study, 2008 and 2010.

Medicaid, or food stamps. The fact that, overall, only 23 percent of those experiencing hardship were low-income individuals failing to take up any public programs suggests that improving outreach alone, without also expanding eligibility or increasing benefits, would have a limited effect in mitigating hardship.

Multivariate Results

The main result from this descriptive analysis is that while hardship is more likely among those with lower incomes, most of the elderly experiencing hardship are not poor. Why are so many nonpoor elderly experiencing hardship? To understand the determinants of hardship in a multivariate context, I estimate linear probability models predicting hardship as a function of economic resources, demographic characteristics, health, and cognition. I estimate the model separately for five hardships—(1) food insecurity, (2) skipped meals, (3) medication cutbacks, (4) difficulty paying bills, and (5) dissatisfaction with one's financial situation—and for two summary outcomes: (6) any of the above five hardships, and (7) any of the above five hardships except dissatisfaction with one's financial situation.

All models include controls for the natural log of real income net of out-of-pocket medical spending; the natural log of total real wealth; age; an indicator for fair or poor self-rated health; the number of Nagi limitations; the number of medications the respondent takes regularly (0 to 12); memory score (0 to 20); Serial Sevens score (0 to 5); gender and marital status dummies; an indicator for education less than high school; and race and ethnicity dummies. Regressions also include indicators of labor force status at the time of the interview (working, unemployed, or disabled), with the omitted group consisting mostly of respondents who were out of the labor force (homemakers, retirees) and a small number of respondents who reported "other" labor force status. The models reported here are parsimonious ones in which most variables (for example, education, cognition, and health status) are entered linearly or as a single dummy variable. More flexible models that include these variables as vectors of categorical dummies yield results that are very similar to the parsimonious models. Additional specification checks are discussed later.

Table 3 presents the basic multivariate results. Income and assets both significantly reduce the probability of all kinds of hardship. The coefficients imply that a 1 percent increase in income or assets translates, on average, into about a one-percentage-point reduction in the probability of food insecurity and about a two-percentage-point reduction in the probability of any of the hardships.

Other than income and assets, the most striking predictors of hardship are measures of poor health, consistent with earlier studies (Lee and Frongillo 2001; She and Livermore 2007). Being in fair or poor health, having a greater number of Nagi limitations, or reporting one's work status as "disabled" all increase the probability of hardship substantially. Why is health so important? There are three plausible mechanisms through which poor health or disability may lead to hardship. First, poor health may reduce income directly by making it harder to work. Second, poor health may increase out-of-pocket medical spending, tying up income that could be used to meet other basic needs such as food. Third, poor health may affect one's ability to make do, as suggested by earlier qualitative work (Wolfe, Frongillo, and Valois 2003).

To test the importance of the first hypothesis, I reestimated the regressions both without any income controls and with more extensive controls for income (a set of fifteen dummies reflecting categories of income-to-needs). If income is an important channel through which poor health affects material hardship, dropping the income controls ought to increase the coefficient on the measures of poor health (self-reported health, Nagi limitations, number of medications taken regularly, and disability status). In fact, these coefficients are essentially unchanged by the exclusion of income controls or the inclusion of more detailed income controls. I conclude that, among the elderly at least, income is not the primary channel through which poor health translates into hardship.

The second channel through which health may affect hardship is through out-of-pocket

Table 3. Multivariate Models Predicting Hardship Among Americans Age Sixty-Five and Older: Full Sample, OLS Estimates

	(1) Food Insecurity	(2) Skipped Meals	(3) Medication Cutbacks	(4) Difficulty Paying Bills	(5) Financial Dissatisfaction	(6) Any Hardship	(7) Any Hardship Except Financial Dissatisfaction
Ln(income-out-of-pocket spending)	−0.015 (0.002)**	−0.010 (0.002)**	−0.018 (0.003)**	−0.011 (0.003)**	−0.028 (0.004)**	−0.040 (0.005)**	−0.026 (0.004)**
Ln(wealth)	−0.008 (0.001)**	−0.006 (0.001)**	−0.006 (0.001)**	−0.011 (0.001)**	−0.019 (0.001)**	−0.025 (0.001)**	−0.017 (0.001)**
Age	−0.002 (0.000)**	−0.001 (0.000)**	−0.003 (0.000)**	−0.002 (0.000)**	−0.005 (0.001)**	−0.006 (0.001)**	−0.004 (0.001)**
Health is fair or poor	−0.000 (0.006)	0.001 (0.004)	0.014 (0.007)*	0.009 (0.006)	0.057 (0.010)**	0.059 (0.011)**	0.018 (0.009)*
Nagi limitations (0–12)	0.002 (0.001)**	0.001 (0.001)*	0.003 (0.001)**	0.004 (0.001)**	0.007 (0.001)**	0.007 (0.002)**	0.005 (0.001)**
Number of medications taken regularly (0–12)	0.003 (0.001)*	0.003 (0.001)**	0.011 (0.002)**	0.005 (0.001)**	0.006 (0.002)**	0.013 (0.002)**	0.015 (0.002)**
Memory score (0–20)	0.002 (0.001)*	0.002 (0.000)**	0.003 (0.001)**	0.002 (0.001)*	0.004 (0.001)**	0.004 (0.001)**	0.001 (0.001)
Serial Sevens score (0–4)	−0.004 (0.001)*	−0.002 (0.001)*	−0.002 (0.002)	−0.004 (0.002)**	−0.005 (0.002)*	−0.007 (0.003)**	−0.003 (0.002)
Education high school or less	0.000 (0.004)	0.006 (0.003)	−0.006 (0.005)	−0.007 (0.005)	−0.004 (0.007)	−0.011 (0.009)	−0.013 (0.007)
Female	0.025 (0.008)**	0.011 (0.006)*	0.017 (0.010)	0.025 (0.008)**	0.010 (0.013)	0.012 (0.015)	0.035 (0.012)**
Married	0.028 (0.008)**	0.016 (0.005)**	0.013 (0.010)	0.011 (0.008)	0.000 (0.013)	0.003 (0.015)	0.024 (0.012)*
Married* female	−0.040 (0.010)**	−0.024 (0.007)**	−0.008 (0.012)	−0.023 (0.010)*	−0.033 (0.016)*	−0.026 (0.018)	−0.029 (0.015)
African American non-Hispanic	0.048 (0.009)**	0.017 (0.006)**	0.025 (0.011)*	0.017 (0.009)	0.013 (0.015)	0.058 (0.017)**	0.064 (0.014)**
Other race, non-Hispanic	0.007 (0.015)	0.016 (0.011)	0.012 (0.019)	−0.037 (0.017)*	−0.034 (0.026)	0.004 (0.030)	0.003 (0.024)
Hispanic (any race)	−0.013 (0.010)	−0.009 (0.007)	−0.012 (0.012)	0.003 (0.011)	−0.010 (0.017)	−0.010 (0.019)	0.004 (0.016)
Working	0.019 (0.006)**	0.014 (0.004)**	0.009 (0.008)	0.036 (0.007)**	0.073 (0.010)**	0.074 (0.012)**	0.038 (0.010)**
Unemployed	0.046 (0.023)*	0.062 (0.016)**	0.067 (0.028)*	0.158 (0.024)**	0.306 (0.038)**	0.302 (0.044)**	0.167 (0.036)**
Disabled	0.085 (0.011)**	0.064 (0.008)**	0.051 (0.014)**	0.065 (0.012)**	0.040 (0.019)*	0.106 (0.022)**	0.112 (0.018)**
Observations	8,738	8,738	8,738	8,738	8,738	8,738	8,738
R-squared	0.07	0.07	0.06	0.09	0.11	0.15	0.12

Source: Health and Retirement Study, 2008 and 2010.
Notes: Regressions also include dummies for region (ten categories). Standard errors are in parentheses.
*$p < .05$; **$p < .01$

medical spending. As already discussed in the context of figures 1 through 3 and table 2, out-of-pocket spending does seem to explain at least partly why apparently high-income individuals experience hardship. But reestimating the models in table 1 using income minus out-of-pocket spending rather than income changes the coefficients on the health variables very little. Thus, the regression results suggest that out-of-pocket medical spending explains relatively little of the effect of poor health on hardship; health has a strong independent effect on hardship regardless of income or out-of-pocket medical spending.

This leaves the third reason for why poor health could mean more hardship: it is simply harder to get by for someone who is in poor health, and it is especially difficult to make do with less. For example, an elderly person with activity limitations might have to purchase (more expensive) prepared meals, rather than cook from scratch, or have to shop at expensive convenience stores, being unable to shop around for lower prices.

Two supplemental analyses lend support to this story. The first explores the role of spouses and their physical limitations. It is evident from the results of the multivariate models in table 3 that being married may actually increase the risk of some hardships for men, while being married reduces hardship across the board for women. Table 4 presents

Table 4. Effects of a Spouse's Physical Limitations on Experiences of Hardship Among Americans Age Sixty-Five and Older

	Food Insecurity	Skipped Meals	Medication Cutbacks	Difficulty Paying Bills	Financial Dissatisfaction	Any Hardship	Any Hardship Except Dissatisfaction
Men (n = 3,741)							
Number of wife's physical limitations							
None	-0.023	-0.006	-0.026	-0.013	-0.032	-0.078	-0.059
	(0.014)	(0.010)	(0.017)	(0.014)	(0.024)	(0.028)**	(0.022)**
One to two	0.018	0.017	0.019	0.003	-0.040	-0.034	0.021
	(0.009)	(0.006)**	(0.011)	(0.009)	(0.016)*	(0.019)	(0.015)
Three to five	0.012	0.005	0.009	0.019	0.001	-0.011	0.020
	(0.009)	(0.006)	(0.011)	(0.009)*	(0.016)	(0.018)	(0.014)
Six to twelve	0.027	0.013	0.007	0.016	0.003	0.020	0.035
	(0.009)**	(0.006)*	(0.011)	(0.009)	(0.016)	(0.018)	(0.014)*
Women (n = 4,997)							
Number of husband's physical limitations							
None	-0.041	-0.020	-0.028	-0.036	-0.109	-0.120	-0.069
	(0.016)**	(0.011)	(0.020)	(0.017)*	(0.025)**	(0.029)**	(0.025)**
One to two	-0.016	-0.011	-0.017	-0.026	-0.074	-0.074	-0.034
	(0.009)	(0.006)	(0.011)	(0.010)**	(0.014)**	(0.017)**	(0.014)*
Three to five	-0.025	-0.021	-0.007	-0.025	-0.058	-0.043	-0.022
	(0.009)**	(0.007)**	(0.012)	(0.010)*	(0.015)**	(0.017)*	(0.015)
Six to twelve	-0.024	-0.018	0.003	-0.005	-0.004	-0.007	-0.012
	(0.010)*	(0.007)**	(0.013)	(0.011)	(0.016)	(0.018)	(0.016)

Source: Health and Retirement Study, 2008 and 2010.
Notes: Table contains selected coefficients (standard errors) from multivariate models similar to those in table 1. Models are estimated separately for men and women, and the married and married*female dummies have been replaced with a full set of indicators for husbands' (wives') physical (Nagi) limitations, as described in the text.
*$p < .05$; **$p < .01$

coefficients from multivariate models that are the same as those presented in table 3 except that (1) the models are estimated separately for men and women, and (2) marital status is now measured using a complete set of dummies representing the spouse's level of physical limitations using the Nagi measures described earlier. The results for men in the top panel of table 4 show that having an able-bodied wife reduces the risk of hardship somewhat, but that having a disabled wife significantly *increases* the risk of food insecurity. For women, having a husband reduces the risk of hardship across the board, while having a husband with no physical limitations reduces hardship the most.

The second supplemental analysis focuses on children. The top row of table 5 reports the coefficients from models similar to those in table 3 but augmented with a dummy for whether or not the respondent had children. Having children does not, on average, affect hardship, but this lack of an effect masks heterogeneity in the nature of the respondent's relationship with his or her children. The psychosocial leave-behind questionnaire asks respondents with children: "How much can you rely on them if you have a serious problem?" Possible responses are "a lot," "some," "a little," and "not at all"; a small fraction of respondents with children (1 percent) did not respond to this question, and these nonresponses are treated as a separate category. When I estimate models similar to those in table 3 but augmented with a set of variables distinguishing between reliable and unreli-

Table 5. Effects of the Presence and "Quality" of Their Children on Hardship Among Americans Age Sixty-Five and Older

	Food Insecurity	Skipped Meals	Medication Cutbacks	Difficulty Paying Bills	Financial Dissatisfaction	Any Hardship	Any Hardship Except Dissatisfaction
Dummy variable indicating whether or not respondent has children							
Kids = 1	−0.009	−0.001	−0.003	0.013	0.006	0.002	0.011
	(0.013)	(0.007)	(0.005)	(0.008)	(0.007)	(0.011)	(0.013)
Full set of dummies indicating how much respondent says he or she can rely on children							
Reliability of kids missing	0.062	0.045	0.054	0.005	0.060	0.061	0.040
	(0.028)*	(0.019)*	(0.034)	(0.029)	(0.046)	(0.053)	(0.044)
Not at all	0.091	0.084	0.109	0.118	0.105	0.176	0.174
	(0.014)**	(0.010)**	(0.018)**	(0.015)**	(0.024)**	(0.027)**	(0.023)**
A little	0.002	−0.001	0.026	0.032	0.069	0.060	0.029
	(0.010)	(0.007)	(0.013)*	(0.011)**	(0.017)**	(0.020)**	(0.016)
Some	−0.001	−0.002	0.025	0.008	0.020	0.033	0.019
	(0.008)	(0.006)	(0.010)*	(0.009)	(0.013)	(0.015)*	(0.013)
A lot	−0.007	−0.008	0.003	−0.003	−0.016	−0.008	0.001
	(0.007)	(0.005)	(0.008)	(0.007)	(0.011)	(0.013)	(0.011)

Source: Health and Retirement Study, 2008 and 2010.
Notes: Table contains selected coefficients (standard errors) from multivariate models similar to those in table 1. Models are augmented with a dummy variable indicating that the respondent had children (top panel) or with a set of dummies indicating the respondent's report of how much they could rely on their children (bottom panel), as described in the text.
*$p < .05$; **$p < .01$

able children, it is clear that the lack of an effect on average masks a significant increase of hardship among those with very unreliable children. (Fortunately, this type of children were quite rare: only 3 percent of parents reported having them. This explains the lack of any significant effect in the models with a simple indicator for whether or not the respondent had children.)[3]

Turning back to table 3 to look at other predictors of hardship, we see that better memory actually *increases* the probability of hardship slightly, possibly because these respondents were more likely to know or more likely to report that they had a problem. Respondents with higher scores on the Serial Sevens test, in contrast, were significantly less likely to report difficulty paying bills or financial dissatisfaction. Education is not a significant predictor of hardship in these models, since it is highly correlated with age, income, education, and cognition. In all models, older individuals were less likely to report hardship. Steven Haider, Alison Jacknowitz, and Robert Schoeni (2003) report a similar finding for food-related hardship (skipped meals) and speculate that the well-established fact that caloric needs decline with age may be responsible. On the other hand, a similar story cannot explain why medication cutbacks also decline with age, since medication use *increases* with age.

African Americans had significantly higher rates of food insecurity and medication cutbacks; rates for other nonwhites and Hispanics were similar to those for white non-Hispanics (the omitted group). Unmarried women, three-quarters of whom are widows, reported significantly higher rates of hardship than did single men, married men, or married women; much of this effect is due to their lower incomes. As already noted, the effect of marriage is different for men and women and depends, for men, on how healthy their wife is.

Individual Fixed-Effects Estimates

To address at least partially the concern that unmeasured individual-level factors correlated with the explanatory variables may actually be causing hardship, I also estimate models with an individual fixed effect (FE) using data from the 2008 and 2010 surveys. I cannot use fixed-effects models to analyze difficulty paying bills or financial dissatisfaction, since questions about these hardships are not asked every wave. Therefore, the FE models focus on food insecurity, skipped meals, and medication cutbacks. The FE models reported in table 6 confirm the central finding of the ordinary least squares (OLS) models reported in table 3: health measured using either Nagi limitations or self-reported disability status is an important predictor of hardship. Poor self-reported health status has a small and insignificant negative effect on hardship in the FE models. Income and assets remain significant predictors for some outcomes but not for others, and with smaller magnitudes than in the OLS models. Other explanatory variables that were significant in the OLS models, such as cognition, are no longer significant in the FE models, although it is difficult to say with certainty whether this is because these variables truly do not matter in determining hardship or because there was not much change in these characteristics over the two-year window from 2008 to 2010.

DISCUSSION

The empirical analysis in this article yields two important results with implications for public policy and future research. First, I find that while hardship is more likely among poor individuals than among those with higher incomes, most older Americans experiencing hardship are neither poor nor using any transfer programs. Thus, the impact of efforts to reduce hardship by increasing outreach and enrollment among eligible nonparticipants, or

---

3. I also estimate models that distinguish between respondents with children who were coresident, who lived nearby (within ten miles), and who lived farther away. These models show higher rates of hardship among families with coresident children—almost certainly driven by selection into coresidence—and no differential effect of non-coresident children based on whether or not they lived nearby.

Table 6. Multivariate Models Predicting Hardship Among Americans Age Sixty-Five and Older: Full Sample, Individual FE Estimates

	(1) Food Insecurity	(2) Skipped Meals	(3) Medication Cutbacks
Ln(income)	−0.004	−0.003	−0.006
	(0.002)	(0.002)	(0.003)*
Ln(wealth)	−0.003	−0.002	−0.005
	(0.001)**	(0.001)**	(0.001)**
Health is fair or poor	−0.011	−0.007	−0.007
	(0.006)	(0.004)	(0.007)
Nagi limitations (0–12)	0.004	0.002	0.004
	(0.001)**	(0.001)**	(0.001)*
Number of medications taken regularly (0–12)	0.001	0.003	0.005
	(0.002)	(0.001)**	(0.002)*
Memory score (0–20)	0.000	0.000	−0.001
	(0.001)	(0.000)	(0.001)
Serial Sevens score (0–5)	0.002	0.001	−0.001
	(0.002)	(0.001)	(0.002)
Married	0.009	0.007	−0.041
	(0.018)	(0.012)	(0.021)
Married*female	−0.007	−0.013	0.066
	(0.023)	(0.015)	(0.028)*
Working	0.001	−0.003	−0.013
	(0.008)	(0.006)	(0.010)
Unemployed	−0.011	0.018	0.049
	(0.025)	(0.017)	(0.030)
Disabled	0.045	0.026	−0.003
	(0.011)**	(0.007)**	(0.013)
Observations	18,156	18,156	18,156
Number of individuals represented	9,078	9,078	9,078

Source: Health and Retirement Study, 2008 and 2010.
Note: Standard errors in parentheses.
*$p < .05$; **$p < .01$

by increasing benefit levels for those who already participate, is inevitably limited. Finding ways to target transfer programs more precisely to those experiencing hardship—which would probably involve rewriting the eligibility rules for the programs—could also be an important component of efforts to reduce hardship among the elderly.

Second, like a number of earlier studies cited here, I find that health status is an important predictor of hardship among the elderly: individuals in worse self-reported health or who report more limitations on their physical activity are significantly more likely to experience hardship. The persistence of this effect when controlling for income or for income net of out-of-pocket medical spending suggests that poor health has direct effects on hardship, not just that it affects income or expenditures. Simply put, poor health makes it harder to make do with less. Further research is needed to understand which interventions would do the most to reduce material hardship among the elderly.

APPENDIX
Appendix Table A1. Material Hardship Among Americans Age Sixty-Five and Older

	Food Insecurity	Skipped Meals	Medication Cutbacks	Difficulty Paying Bills	Dissatisfaction with Finances	Any Hardship	Any Hardship Except Dissatisfaction
Family income/poverty threshold (data for figure 1)							
0.75 or less	0.120	0.090	0.137	0.142	0.266	0.385	0.263
0.75–1.00	0.205	0.125	0.113	0.166	0.339	0.487	0.329
1.00–1.25	0.079	0.039	0.098	0.114	0.253	0.360	0.219
1.25–1.50	0.113	0.062	0.137	0.093	0.247	0.376	0.246
1.50–1.75	0.050	0.021	0.088	0.069	0.172	0.259	0.151
1.75–2.00	0.032	0.017	0.104	0.063	0.201	0.292	0.163
2.00–2.50	0.037	0.014	0.078	0.056	0.138	0.211	0.133
2.50–3.00	0.034	0.015	0.085	0.046	0.148	0.217	0.129
3.00–3.50	0.016	0.006	0.053	0.041	0.145	0.188	0.087
3.50–4.00	0.038	0.014	0.063	0.024	0.111	0.173	0.108
4.00–4.50	0.017	0.000	0.043	0.019	0.112	0.161	0.071
4.50–5.00	0.016	0.004	0.021	0.026	0.077	0.104	0.055
5.00–6.00	0.026	0.008	0.051	0.024	0.072	0.134	0.089
6.00–7.00	0.007	0.001	0.024	0.025	0.084	0.108	0.055
7.00–8.00	0.039	0.020	0.022	0.028	0.053	0.100	0.067
8.001	0.013	0.001	0.025	0.010	0.063	0.099	0.047
Family spending/poverty threshold (data for figure 2)							
0.75 or less	0.061	0.036	0.108	0.115	0.260	0.343	0.225
0.75–1.00	0.135	0.058	0.068	0.125	0.228	0.357	0.226
1.00–1.25	0.123	0.043	0.079	0.107	0.206	0.344	0.243
1.25–1.50	0.082	0.044	0.065	0.065	0.214	0.307	0.164
1.50–1.75	0.038	0.025	0.049	0.072	0.162	0.226	0.130
1.75–2.00	0.089	0.050	0.114	0.091	0.193	0.317	0.215
2.00–2.50	0.019	0.005	0.076	0.036	0.152	0.212	0.104
2.50–3.00	0.061	0.028	0.084	0.045	0.105	0.216	0.156
3.00–3.50	0.049	0.014	0.100	0.056	0.159	0.219	0.154
3.50–4.00	0.038	0.015	0.060	0.034	0.124	0.146	0.094
4.00–4.50	0.048	0.017	0.083	0.063	0.111	0.194	0.167
4.50–5.00	0.016	0.016	0.034	0.007	0.108	0.136	0.057
5.00–6.00	0.011	0.000	0.047	0.036	0.130	0.154	0.065
6.00–7.00	0.038	0.016	0.074	0.049	0.147	0.192	0.130
7.00–8.00	0.025	0.000	0.180	0.075	0.147	0.244	0.186
8.001	0.044	0.014	0.039	0.028	0.082	0.161	0.103
Family income minus out-of-pocket medical spending/poverty threshold (data for figure 3)							
0.75 or less	0.122	0.082	0.142	0.145	0.287	0.401	0.272
0.75–1.00	0.148	0.084	0.117	0.133	0.265	0.415	0.284
1.00–1.25	0.074	0.038	0.103	0.110	0.264	0.363	0.223
1.25–1.50	0.100	0.055	0.113	0.091	0.235	0.345	0.207
1.50–1.75	0.047	0.018	0.096	0.055	0.183	0.276	0.157
1.75–2.00	0.020	0.008	0.091	0.055	0.138	0.223	0.143

(continued)

Appendix Table A1. *(continued)*

	Food Insecurity	Skipped Meals	Medication Cutbacks	Difficulty Paying Bills	Dissatisfaction with Finances	Any Hardship	Any Hardship Except Dissatisfaction
2.00–2.50	0.035	0.015	0.078	0.056	0.150	0.220	0.132
2.50–3.00	0.038	0.019	0.064	0.034	0.119	0.175	0.102
3.00–3.50	0.010	0.006	0.056	0.039	0.138	0.187	0.086
3.50–4.00	0.035	0.007	0.050	0.019	0.116	0.165	0.092
4.00–4.50	0.022	0.000	0.040	0.021	0.104	0.151	0.076
4.50–5.00	0.015	0.005	0.035	0.026	0.079	0.121	0.070
5.00–6.00	0.023	0.008	0.044	0.026	0.078	0.133	0.082
6.00–7.00	0.008	0.001	0.018	0.018	0.062	0.087	0.043
7.00–8.00	0.038	0.020	0.026	0.035	0.069	0.116	0.074
8.001	0.014	0.001	0.023	0.009	0.060	0.096	0.044

Source: Health and Retirement Study, 2008 and 2010.
Notes: Estimates use sampling weights. Unweighted sample size is 8,738 for family income/poverty threshold and family income minus out-of-pocket medical spending/poverty threshold and 2,100 for family spending/poverty threshold.

Appendix Table A2. Distribution of Americans Age Sixty-Five and Older Experiencing Hardship by Family Income and Use of Transfer Programs

	Unweighted Sample n	Low Income, Program User	Low Income, No Program Use	Not Low Income, Program User	Not Low Income, No Program Use	Total
Food insecurity	408	0.328	0.234	0.035	0.403	1.000
Skipped meals	184	0.487	0.191	0.036	0.286	1.000
Medication cutbacks	616	0.139	0.245	0.046	0.571	1.000
Difficulty paying bills	479	0.253	0.251	0.084	0.413	1.000
Dissatisfaction with finances	1,280	0.163	0.239	0.064	0.535	1.000
Any hardship	1,917	0.165	0.233	0.056	0.546	1.000
Any hardship other than dissatisfaction	1,171	0.196	0.234	0.056	0.515	1.000

Source: Health and Retirement Study, 2008 and 2010.
Notes: "Low income" is defined as having family income 175 percent or less of the poverty level. "Program use" refers to any receipt of Medicaid, food stamps, or SSI.

REFERENCES

Beverly, Sondra G. 2001. "Measures of Material Hardship: Rationale and Recommendations." *Journal of Poverty* 5(1): 23–41.

Bound, John, Greg J. Duncan, Deborah S. Laren, and Lewis Oleinick. 1991. "Poverty Dynamics in Widowhood." *Journal of Gerontology* 46(3): S115–24.

Brady, David. 2004. "Reconsidering the Divergence Between Elderly, Child, and Overall Poverty." *Research on Aging* 26(5): 487–510.

Brady, Peter J. 2010. "Measuring Retirement Resource Adequacy." *Journal of Pension Economics and Finance* 9(2): 235–62.

Butrica, Barbara A., Daniel P. Murphy, and Sheila R. Zedlewski. 2010. "How Many Struggle to Get By in Retirement?" *The Gerontologist* 50(4): 482–94.

Charles, Kerwin Kofi, Sheldon Danziger, Laurie Pounder, and Robert F. Schoeni. 2006. "Consumption, Income, and Well-Being Among the

Mature Population." Ann Arbor: University of Michigan, Gerald R. Ford School of Public Policy, National Poverty Center (April).

Danziger, Sandra, Mary Corcoran, Sheldon Danziger, and Colleen M. Heflin. 2000. "Work, Income, and Material Hardship After Welfare Reform." *Journal of Consumer Affairs* 34(1): 6–30.

DeNavas-Walt, Carmen, and Bernadette D. Proctor. 2014. *Income and Poverty in the United States: 2013*. Report P60-249. Washington: U.S. Census Bureau.

Engelhardt, Gary V., and Jonathan Gruber. 2006. "Social Security and the Evolution of Elderly Poverty." In *Public Policy and the Income Distribution*, edited by Alan J. Auerbach, David Card, and John M. Quigley. New York: Russell Sage Foundation.

Engelhardt, Gary V., Jonathan Gruber, and Cynthia D. Perry. 2005. "Social Security and Elderly Living Arrangements: Evidence from the Social Security Notch." *Journal of Human Resources* 40(2): 354–72.

Engen, Eric M., William G. Gale, Cori E. Uccello, Christopher D. Carroll, and David I. Laibson. 1999. "The Adequacy of Household Saving." *Brookings Papers on Economic Activity* 2: 65–187.

Federman, Maya, Thesia I. Garner, Kathleen Short, and W. Bornan Cutter IV. 1996. "What Does It Mean to Be Poor in America?" *Monthly Labor Review* 119: 3.

Fisher, Jonathan D., David S. Johnson, Joseph T. Marchand, Timothy M. Smeeding, and Barbara B. Torrey. 2009. "Identifying the Poorest Older Americans." *Journals of Gerontology Series B: Psychological Sciences and Social Sciences* 64(6): 758–66.

Fonda, Stephanie, and A. Regula Herzog. 2004. "Documentation of Physical Functioning Measured in the Health and Retirement Study and the Asset and Health Dynamics Among the Oldest Old Study." Ann Arbor: University of Michigan, Survey Research Center.

Gillen, Martie, and Hyungsoo Kim. 2009. "Older Women and Poverty Transition: Consequences of Income Source Changes from Widowhood." *Journal of Applied Gerontology* 28(3): 320–41.

Greenhalgh-Stanley, Nadia, and Katie Fitzpatrick. 2013. "Food Stamps, Food Sufficiency, and Diet-Related Disease Among the Elderly." Discussion Paper 1407-13. Madison: University of Wisconsin, Institute for Research on Poverty.

Haider, Steven J., Alison Jacknowitz, and Robert F. Schoeni. 2003. "Food Stamps and the Elderly: Why Is Participation So Low?" *Journal of Human Resources* 38: 1080–1111.

Haveman, Robert H., Karen Holden, Andrei Romanov, and Barbara L. Wolfe. 2007. "Assessing the Maintenance of Savings Sufficiency over the First Decade of Retirement." *International Tax and Public Finance* 14(4): 481–502.

Haveman, Robert H., Karen Holden, Kathryn Wilson, and Barbara L. Wolfe. 2003. "Social Security, Age of Retirement, and Economic Well-Being: Intertemporal and Demographic Patterns Among Retired-Worker Beneficiaries." *Demography* 40(2): 369–94.

Haveman, Robert, Karen Holden, Barbara Wolfe, and Shane M. Sherlund. 2006. "Do Newly Retired Workers in the United States Have Sufficient Resources to Maintain Well-Being?" *Economic Inquiry* 44(2): 249–64.

Heisler, Michele, Todd H. Wagner, and John D. Piette. 2005. "Patient Strategies to Cope with High Prescription Medication Costs: Who Is Cutting Back on Necessities, Increasing Debt, or Underusing Medications?" *Journal of Behavioral Medicine* 28(1): 43–51.

Hungerford, Thomas L. 2001. "The Economic Consequences of Widowhood on Elderly Women in the United States and Germany." *The Gerontologist* 41(1): 103–10.

Hurd, Michael, and Susann Rohwedder. 2006a. "Alternative Measures of Replacement Rates." Working Paper 132. Ann Arbor: University of Michigan Retirement Research Center (October).

———. 2006b. "Economic Well-Being at Older Ages: Income- and Consumption-Based Poverty Measures in the HRS." Working Paper 12680. Cambridge, Mass.: National Bureau of Economic Research (November).

———. 2008a. "Adequacy of Economic Resources in Retirement and Returns-to-Scale in Consumption." Working Paper 174. Ann Arbor: University of Michigan Retirement Research Center (May).

———. 2008b. "The Adequacy of Economic Resources in Retirement." Working Paper 184. Ann Arbor: University of Michigan Retirement Research Center (September).

———. 2011. "Economic Preparation for Retirement." Working Paper 17203. Cambridge, Mass.: National Bureau of Economic Research (July).

Iceland, John, and Kurt J. Bauman. 2007. "Income Poverty and Material Hardship: How Strong Is the Association?" *Journal of Socio-Economics* 36(3): 376–96.

Johnson, Richard W., and Gordon B. Mermin. 2009. "Financial Hardship Before and After Social Security's Eligibility Age." Washington, D.C.: Urban Institute.

Lee, Jung Sun, and Edward A. Frongillo. 2001. "Nutritional and Health Consequences Are Associated with Food Insecurity Among U.S. Elderly Persons." *Journal of Nutrition* 131(5): 1503-9.

Love, David A., Paul A. Smith, and Lucy C. McNair. 2008. "A New Look at the Wealth Adequacy of Older U.S. Households." *Review of Income and Wealth* 54(4): 616-42.

Mayer, Susan E., and Christopher Jencks. 1989. "Poverty and the Distribution of Material Hardship." *Journal of Human Resources* 24(1): 88-114.

McGarry, Kathleen. 1995. "Measurement Error and Poverty Rates of Widows." *Journal of Human Resources* 30(1): 113-34.

McGarry, Kathleen, and Robert F. Schoeni. 2005. "Widow (er) Poverty and Out-of-Pocket Medical Expenditures Near the End of Life." *Journals of Gerontology Series B: Psychological Sciences and Social Sciences* 60(3): S160-68.

Meyer, Bruce D., Wallace K. Mok, and James X. Sullivan. 2009. "The Under-Reporting of Transfers in Household Surveys: Its Nature and Consequences." Working Paper 15181. Cambridge, Mass.: National Bureau of Economic Research (July).

Meyer, Bruce D., and James X. Sullivan. 2003. "Measuring the Well-Being of the Poor Using Income and Consumption." *Journal of Human Resources* 38: 1180-1220.

Mitchell, Olivia S., and James F. Moore. 1998. "Can Americans Afford to Retire? New Evidence on Retirement Saving Adequacy." *Journal of Risk and Insurance* 65(3): 371-400.

Ofstedal, Mary Beth, Gwenith G. Fisher, and A. Regula Herzog. 2005. "HRS/AHEAD Documentation Report: Documentation of Cognitive Functioning Measures in the Health and Retirement Study." HRS Documentation Report DR-006. Ann Arbor University of Michigan, Survey Research Center (March). Available at: http://hrsonline.isr.umich.edu/sitedocs/userg/dr-006.pdf (accessed October 1, 2015).

Ouellette, Tammy, Nancy Burstein, David Long, and Erik Beecroft. 2004. *Measures of Material Hardship: Final Report*. Washington: U.S. Department of Health and Human Services, Office of the Assistant Secretary for Planning and Evaluation.

Piette, John D., Michele Heisler, and Todd H. Wagner. 2004. "Cost-Related Medication Underuse Among Chronically Ill Adults: The Treatments People Forgo, How Often, and Who Is at Risk." *American Journal of Public Health* 94(10): 1782.

Poterba, James M., Steven F. Venti, and David A. Wise. 2012. "Were They Prepared for Retirement? Financial Status at Advanced Ages in the HRS and AHEAD Cohorts." In *Investigations in the Economics of Aging* edited by David A. Wise. Chicago: University of Chicago Press.

Rector, Robert E., Kirk A. Johnson, and Sarah E. Youssef. 1999. "The Extent of Material Hardship and Poverty in the United States." *Review of Social Economy* 57(3): 351-87.

Schmidt, Lucie, Lara Shore-Sheppard, and Tara Watson. 2013. "The Effect of Safety Net Programs on Food Insecurity." Working Paper 19558. Cambridge, Mass.: National Bureau of Economic Research (October).

Scholz, John Karl, Ananth Seshadri, and Surachai Khitatrakun. 2006. "Are Americans Saving 'Optimally' for Retirement?" *Journal of Political Economy* 114(4): 607-43.

Sevak, Purvia, David R. Weir, and Robert J. Willis. 2003. "Perspectives: The Economic Consequences of a Husband's Death: Evidence from the HRS and AHEAD." *Social Security Bulletin* 65(3): 2004.

She, Peiyun, and Gina A. Livermore. 2007. "Material Hardship, Poverty, and Disability Among Working-Age Adults." *Social Science Quarterly* 88(4): 970-89.

Short, Kathleen. 2014. "The Supplemental Poverty Measure: 2013." Current Population Reports P60-251. Washington: U.S. Census Bureau (October).

Short, Kathleen, and Thesia I. Garner. 2002. "Experimental Poverty Measures: Accounting for Medical Expenditures." *Monthly Labor Review* 125: 3.

Sonnega, Amanda, Jessica D. Faul, Mary Beth Ofstedal, Kenneth M. Langa, John W. Phillips, and David R. Weir. 2014. "Cohort Profile: The Health and Retirement Study (HRS)." *International Journal of Epidemiology* 43(2): 576-85.

Steinman, Michael A., Laura P. Sands, and Kenneth E. Covinsky. 2001. "Self-Restriction of Medications Due to Cost in Seniors Without Prescription Coverage." *Journal of General Internal Medicine* 16(12): 793-99.

Sullivan, James X., Lesley Turner, and Sheldon Danziger. 2008. "The Relationship Between

Income and Material Hardship." *Journal of Policy Analysis and Management* 27(1): 63–81.

VanDerhei, Jack, and Craig Copeland. 2010. "The EBRI Retirement Readiness Rating: Retirement Income Preparation and Future Prospects." *Employment Benefit Research Institute Issue Brief* 344(July): 1–36.

Weir, David R., and Robert J. Willis. 2000. "Prospects for Widow Poverty." In *Forecasting Retirement Needs and Retirement Wealth,* edited by Olivia S. Mitchell, P. Brett Hammond, and Anna M. Rappaport. Philadelphia: University of Pennsylvania Press.

Wilde, Parke, and Mark Nord. 2005. "The Effect of Food Stamps on Food Security: A Panel Data Approach." *Applied Economic Perspectives and Policy* 27(3): 425–32.

Wolfe, Wendy S., Edward A. Frongillo, and Pascale Valois. 2003. "Understanding the Experience of Food Insecurity by Elders Suggests Ways to Improve Its Measurement." *Journal of Nutrition* 133(9): 2762–69.

Zick, Cathleen D., and Karen Holden. 2000. "An Assessment of the Wealth Holdings of Recent Widows." *Journals of Gerontology Series B: Psychological Sciences and Social Sciences* 55(2): S90–97.

How Well Does the "Safety Net" Work for Family Safety Nets? Economic Survival Strategies Among Grandmother Caregivers in Severe Deprivation

LASHAWNDA PITTMAN

Using qualitative data collected from fifty-eight African American grandmothers raising grandchildren in skipped-generation households (SGHs), I reveal how and why women in non-normative families, lacking legal protections and publicly recognized authority as parents, must negotiate risk in pursuit of resources. I demonstrate that these grandmothers struggle for economic survival while seeking simultaneously to minimize the risk of losing their grandchildren and maximize their chances of receiving public assistance. I argue that grandmothers in SGHs face significant challenges obtaining government benefits owing to policy eligibility guidelines, street-level implementation, and family dynamics. Ultimately, I illustrate how the severe deprivation experienced by these grandmothers is exacerbated by their exclusion from safety net programs that could help them support the children in their care.

Keywords: grandparent caregiving, African Americans, urban poverty, safety net, economic survival strategies

How do grandparents faced with the unexpected and sudden assumption of primary caregiving responsibility for their grandchildren cope with such a situation? How do they make room for their grandchildren, especially if they are renters, subsidized housing recipients, or homeowners anxious to relocate to publicly subsidized senior housing? What factors contribute to their underutilization of public assistance despite high levels of poverty? Finally, and perhaps most importantly, how do low-income African American custodial grandmothers overcome barriers to public support, and what are the economic implications of their caregiving?

Scholars and policymakers are increasingly considering these questions of survival and adaptation as the number of grandparent-headed households (GPHHs) in the United States continues to reach historic highs. The number of

LaShawnDa Pittman is assistant professor of American ethnic studies at the University of Washington.

I am especially grateful to the study's interviewees for their participation and candor. Support was graciously provided by the National Science Foundation (award no. 1004123) and the Office of Planning, Research, and Evaluation, Administration for Children and Families, U.S. Department of Health and Human Services (grant no. 90YE0112). Research support was provided by the West Coast Poverty Center, Center for Studies in Demography and Ecology, and Women Investigating Race, Ethnicity, and Difference (WIRED). I thank Jennie Romich, Jim Gleeson, Scott Allard, and anonymous reviewers for their comments and criticisms. Direct correspondence to: LaShawnDa Pittman at lpittman@uw.edu, Department of American Ethnic Studies, University of Washington, Box 354380, Seattle, WA 98195.

children living with a grandparent has increased 22 percent since 2000 and spiked after the onset of the Great Recession (Livingston 2013). Previous research has shown that, despite the fragile economic status of grandparents, current child welfare and kinship care policies and practices make them the primary safety net for children in need of out-of-home care. This trend, combined with insufficient government supports, has profound implications for the economic welfare of GPHHs. I suggest that, as grandparent caregivers in skipped-generation households (SGHs, defined as GPHHs with no parents present) navigate the safety net, they are challenged by family dynamics, social welfare policy eligibility criteria, and street-level implementation.

My study of the survival strategies of low-income African American custodial grandmothers providing care in informal kinship arrangements (children not involved with the public child welfare system) reveals the structural vulnerability of families that experience multiple and intersecting disadvantages compounded by non-normative family forms and a lack of legal protections and publicly recognized authority as parents. I argue that, in these women's lives, risk negotiation plays a critical role as they struggle not only to maintain the resources they need to care for themselves and their families when care shifts to them but also to obtain additional resources to cover the expenses associated with caring for their grandchildren.

I begin by providing background on the dramatic rise in GPHHs among the most marginalized populations in the United States, the limited public assistance available to these households outside of the child welfare system, and their underutilization of such resources. After outlining how I collected data for this study, I examine the impact of grandparent caregiving on caregivers' fragile resources—specifically, their housing and employment status—and reveal the barriers they face in maintaining or obtaining subsidized housing and child care. I explore the challenges these caregivers confronted as they sought assistance for the children in their care and the strategies they devised to overcome obstacles. I conclude with a discussion of how GPHHs negotiate risk as they navigate formal support systems, and I discuss the implications for policies that support GPHHs.

LITERATURE REVIEW

Grandparents are primarily responsible for over 2.9 million children in the United States today. Roughly two-thirds of these grandparents are custodial grandmothers. One-fifth of GPHHs are poor, and two-thirds live below three times the federal poverty level (FPL). SGHs suffer even worse poverty rates: one-third (32 percent) live below the FPL, which is nearly double the rates among parent-child families. SGHs headed by custodial grandmothers fare the worst, with two-thirds living at or below the FPL (U.S. Census Bureau 2010).

African Americans make up a disproportionate share of GPHHs, accounting for 24 percent of these households even though they are only 13 percent of the U.S. population. Moreover, African Americans are nearly twice as likely to live in SGHs as their white counterparts (13 versus 7 percent). Black children are twice as likely to live with grandparents or other relatives than are white and Hispanic children (Livingston and Parker 2010). There are a number of reasons why blacks disproportionately form GPHHs. While the number of these households has risen among all racial-ethnic groups, the overrepresentation of African Americans in the child welfare and criminal justice systems, coupled with changing welfare policies, has dramatically altered black parents' ability to care for their children, the demands placed on caregivers, and the availability of needed resources.

Swann and Sylvester (2006), Johnson and Waldfogel (2002), and others have found that increased female incarceration, reduced cash welfare benefits, and other state-specific characteristics and policies drove the growth in foster care caseloads from 1985 to 2000. As the number of incarcerated mothers more than tripled (Swann and Sylvester 2006, 311), caseloads more than doubled, compelling grandparents to care for as many as two-thirds of the children of incarcerated mothers (Johnson and Waldfogel 2002; Travis, McBride, and Solomon 2005). As black children went from being excluded to disproportionately included in the child welfare system, a growing number of African American grandparents provided care in order to keep them from "going into the system" (Murphy, Hunter, and Johnson 2008; Roberts 2003).

Even as punitive law enforcement policies increased African American incarcerations and lengths of stay, child welfare policy called for reducing the time children spend in foster care. The Adoption Assistance and Child Welfare Act (AACWA) of 1980 and the 1997 Adoption and Safe Families Act (ASFA) were passed to reduce foster care drift and to make placement with relatives a viable option for out-of-home care (McGowan and Walsh 2000; Murphy, Hunter, and Johnson 2008). The 1996 Personal Responsibility and Work Opportunity Reconciliation Act (PRWORA) also promoted a "relatives first" approach (Smith and Devore 2004). As a result, the number of children being raised by a grandparent more than doubled, from 3 percent in 1970 to 7 percent in 2010. The most significant increase occurred among SGHs, rising more than 50 percent between 1990 and 2005 (Gleeson 1999; Scommegna 2012).

The interrelationship between the cash welfare and foster care systems also contributes to the rise in GPHHs by decreasing the resources parents have to adequately care for their children. Children who receive or have received public assistance are overrepresented in state custody. In fact, the falling values of welfare benefits were the second-largest contributor to the growth in foster care caseloads (15 percent) (Swann and Sylvester 2006). Failing to meet the new obligations under PRWORA pulled the safety net out from under many families, often permanently. Sanctions for noncompliance could reduce or terminate a family's welfare benefits. Researchers estimate that between 33 and 52 percent of welfare recipients have been sanctioned, with African Americans and the poorly educated overrepresented (Gustafson 2009, 661). Without the resources they need to provide for their families, low-income African American parents have relied on their children's grandparents to absorb caregiving responsibilities, contributing to the dramatic rise in GPHHs.

At the same time that certain public policies have led to higher rates of GPHHs, others have affected the supports available to these households. Most legislation in the last twenty years has focused on GPHHs *within* the child welfare system (Beltran 2014b). While federal and state legislation on behalf of relatives providing care *outside* of the child welfare system has consisted largely of budget-neutral policies, such as educational and health care consent laws that enable caregivers in seventeen and twenty-five states, respectively, to access education and health care for children in their care without the need for legal custody or guardianship (Beltran 2014b).

These factors both increase the number of GPHHs among African Americans and exacerbate the severe deprivation experienced by caregiving relatives. By almost every available measure, the level of need experienced by GPHHs is not reflected in their overall benefit receipt patterns (Baker, Silverstein, and Putney 2008; Copen 2006; Park 2005). Fewer than 12 percent of kinship families receive Temporary Assistance for Needy Families (TANF) assistance, and only 6 percent of children living with relatives receive TANF child-only payments, even though nearly all are eligible (Beltran 2014a). Moreover, because most kinship caregivers fail to receive TANF, they miss opportunities to connect to other critical safety net programs. TANF can be an important gateway program for low-income households because it often entails categorical eligibility for other programs. For example, only 17 percent of low-income working kinship caregivers receive childcare assistance and only 15 percent receive housing assistance. Less than half (42 percent) receive assistance from SNAP, although most report food insecurity (Annie E. Casey Foundation 2012).

State discretion to design welfare programs shapes caregivers' public assistance experiences.[1] Grandparent caregivers applying for

---

1. Under AFDC, all relatives caring for a child could receive child-only payments, but under TANF such entitlement no longer exists, although states may provide cash assistance to kinship caregivers. Currently, all states except Alabama provide TANF child-only payments to kinship caregivers who seek assistance (Mullen and Einhorn 2000; see also Park 2005).

TANF family grants must participate in work activities no later than twenty-four months after receiving assistance (Smith and Beltran 2003). Under Aid to Families with Dependent Children (AFDC), older grandparents benefited from federally mandated age exemptions, but with TANF states now have discretion regarding these exemptions. Studies have found that grandparent caregivers experience additional complications, including fulfilling their own work requirements, which may explain their difficulty in accessing full grant benefits (Baker, Silverstein, and Putney 2008; Copen 2006; Park 2005). They may also be ineligible because they timed out of the system while raising their own children (Baker, Silverstein, and Putney 2008). Most GPHHs are eligible to receive the TANF child-only grant. Adult income and assets are excluded from TANF child-only grants, and most states impose no work, income, or benefit time limits. Child-only cases have increased dramatically since the passage of PRWORA, rising from only 10 percent of the overall caseload in 1988 to 41 percent in 2009 (Falk 2014), but the overwhelming majority of GPHHs fail to utilize this resource (Annie E. Casey Foundation 2012). On top of formal policy restrictions, studies identify four main reasons for the lack of program participation among GPHHs: (1) a structural gap between non-normative family forms and social welfare policies (Baker, Silverstein, and Putney 2008); (2) lack of awareness of available rights and resources (Fuller-Thomson and Minkler 2003, 92); (3) misinformation about eligibility criteria; and (4) fear of drawing attention (Cox 2003).

The African American grandparents who are the most economically disadvantaged and who have the fewest resources to draw upon are the most likely to assume the primary caregiving role. Not surprisingly, the highest poverty rates for GPHHs occur among African American grandparents (Minkler and Fuller-Thomson 2005). These grandparents are also more likely than grandparents from other racial-ethnic groups to be caring for more grandchildren, for longer periods of time, and to be managing additional caregiving responsibilities. Insofar as their race, gender, class, and age increase their likelihood of providing care, that likelihood also shapes and is shaped by other important aspects of their lives, including their family dynamics; their employment, housing, and health status; and their access to formal and informal support systems. Thus, low-income black grandmothers contend not only with the economic burdens of primary caregiving but also with integrating the sudden and unexpected onset of caregiving responsibilities into an array of competing demands, without adequate resources.

This being the case for so many GPHHs, perhaps we should conceptualize their safety net experiences more broadly—beyond grandmothers' caregiving for their grandchildren—to add greater complexity to our understanding of their economic survival strategies and outcomes. Previous research as well as the results described here suggest that GPHHs survive using a number of strategies to weigh and negotiate relative risks.

DATA AND METHODS

Data come from a 2007–2011 qualitative study that I conducted on the coping strategies used by low-income African American grandmothers in Chicago to manage the day-to-day needs of the grandchildren they were parenting. The study population was selected because of its disproportionate rates of SGH and high rates of poverty. Data were collected through in-depth, semistructured interviews and participant observation sessions with seventy-seven custodial grandmothers between the ages of thirty-eight and eighty-three living in the greater Chicago metropolitan area; this group was small enough for in-depth analysis to be conducted but large enough to provide the analytic depth necessary to generate clear response patterns. Fourteen participant observation sessions were conducted at guardianship hearings, school or doctor visits, public aid office visits, caseworker appointments, child care centers, and so on. Respondent and institution names have been changed to protect confidentiality, per approval by the Northwestern University institutional review board.

Potential participants were alerted to the study through Chicago-area social service agencies, flyers posted in targeted communities, and word of mouth. Per guidelines for research involving human subjects, prospective participants were informed of the voluntary nature of the study and the potential risks of participating, and informed consent was obtained from each participant. Subjects were recruited to reflect diverse care arrangements, from informal care to adoption, underscoring the importance of differentiating public assistance by type. In a second wave of data collection, subjects were recruited to reflect variations in types of child care utilized, whether involving family, friends, or neighbors (FFN) or formal arrangements. This captured the intersection of custodial grandparents' resources with their access to child care. Although research was conducted in predominantly poor African American urban neighborhoods, it spilled over into additional Chicago South Side neighborhoods.

All seventy-seven participants self-identified as U.S.-born black women with an average age of fifty-four years. All study participants were primary caregivers to at least one grandchild or great-grandchild under the age of eighteen, with no parents living in the home. Study participants had 3.2 children on average. Seventeen were married, twelve were divorced, three were engaged, and eight were widows. (The rest were single.) All but twenty reported yearly household incomes of less than $15,000.[2] Of the twenty women who reported household incomes higher than $15,000, seventeen had incomes approximately one and a half times the FPL, and three had income twice the FPL. Twenty-eight of the women were working at the time of recruitment, twelve were retired, and thirty-seven were unemployed.

Study participants were raising an average of 2.37 grandchildren for an average of 5.25 years. Twenty-five grandmothers provided care informally, thirty-three were legal guardians, twelve were kinship foster care providers, three were subsidized guardians, and four had adopted their grandchildren. This paper focuses on fifty-eight of the seventy-seven caregivers who were *not* providing care under the auspices of the child welfare system (which provides higher levels of assistance).

In accordance with grounded theory, interviews were tape-recorded, transcribed, and coded in two stages using Dedoose data analysis software. Transcripts were first coded following themes identified in the guide, including codes related to the caregiving role, parental involvement, community and institutional experiences, care-work demands, stressors, and coping. The data revealed how grandmothers combined their own resources with public assistance to minimize severe deprivation; interview data were subsequently recoded using a new set of emergent codes, thereby unpacking the role played by each in shaping how the grandmothers responded to the economic demands of caregiving. What emerged was an understanding of how negotiating risk and uncertainty enters into utilizing public assistance and the mismatch between the GPHH family form and social welfare policy. Coding was cross-checked with all research assistants to ensure reliability.

FINDINGS

Grandparent caregivers must negotiate both real and perceived risks when seeking resources. These caregivers try to maintain their own public assistance even as their grandparent caregiving role undermines their efforts and eligibility. They must gauge whether they can obtain public support for the grandchildren in their care without losing custody or jeopardizing their own fragile financial status. Based on my data, GPHHs develop several risk negotiation strategies to compensate for their lack of legal protections and limited parental authority within their non-normative family form. These range from allowing parents to maintain control over scarce resources, to brokering deals with parents to share resources intended for children, to sidestepping parental authority by becoming legal guardians. GPHHs also are highly likely to accept the stigma and misinformation they receive from institutional agents. Lastly, while most struggled to satisfy eligibility criteria, others bypassed bureaucratic regulations.

---

2. The FPL during the years of data collection for families of two, three, four, and eight was $13,690, $17,170, $20,650, and $34,570, respectively.

Barriers to and Strategies for Accessing Safety Net Programs

In this section, I explore these risk negotiation strategies in three policy settings critical to GPHHs and low-income households broadly: subsidized housing, subsidized child care, and cash assistance. Table 1 outlines the eligibility criteria of the safety net programs available to informal kinship care providers in Illinois at the time of the study (2007–2011), the barriers faced by study participants trying to access public support, and the number of respondents receiving benefits as well as the number eligible for benefits.

Subsidized Housing

Some grandparents thrust into the primary caregiving role begin by determining whether their housing adequately accommodates their grandchildren. Nineteen of the fifty-eight grandmothers in the study already received some form of housing assistance (see table 2 for respondents' household sources of income).

When forty-one-year-old Ms. Boyd's twenty-one-year-old daughter left her to raise her two-year-old daughter, Ms. Boyd was using a housing choice voucher (HCV) after being displaced from Robert Taylor Homes, where she had raised two of her four children to adulthood. Ms. Francois, who'd been displaced from Cabrini-Green Homes after residing there with her four children, also relied on an HCV. Ms. Randolph and her husband were HCV recipients as well. They'd been displaced from Robert Taylor Homes, and although both were disabled, they cared for their five teenage grandchildren when the mother would not.

Study participants also included Section 8 and public housing recipients. Subsidized housing regulations prevent the housing expenditures of recipients from exceeding 30 percent of household income; unfortunately, few of the participants were employed. Although most lived on Supplemental Security Income (SSI), some, like Ms. Boyd, had no income. Ms. Cooper, a thirty-eight-year-old mother of three,

Table 1. Safety Net Programs Available to Informal Kinship Care Providers in Illinois from 2007–2011: Eligibility Criteria, Respondents Receiving Benefits and Eligible for Benefits, and Barriers to Receiving Benefits

Safety Net Programs	Eligibility Criteria	Respondents Receiving Benefits/ Respondents Eligible for Benefits[a]	Barriers to Receiving Benefits
TANF child-only grant ($107 per month for one child, $211 for two, $261 for three)	(1) Grandparent's income and assets are not counted in child's eligibility; (2) grandparent is exempt from work and time limits; (3) legal guardianship not required	13/36	(1) Misinformation from street-level bureaucrats about eligibility criteria (for example, about legal guardianship); (2) family dynamics; (3) stigma and discrimination
TANF family grant ($292 per month for a family of two, $396 for a family of three, $435 for a family of four)	(1) Income-eligible grandparents are included in assistance unit; (2) subject to work participation and five-year time limit; (3) age exemption for grandparents age sixty or older; (4) legal guardianship not required	2/13	(1) Misinformation from street-level bureaucrats about eligibility criteria (for example, about legal guardianship); (2) family dynamics; (3) inability to satisfy work, education, or training requirements

(continued)

Table 1. *(continued)*

Safety Net Programs	Eligibility Criteria	Respondents Receiving Benefits/ Respondents Eligible for Benefits[a]	Barriers to Receiving Benefits
Subsidized housing (housing expense limited to 30 percent of income)	(1) GPHH income may not exceed 50 percent of median income of area or 80 percent for those displaced by rental rehabilitation; (2) assets cannot be in excess of limitation set by the Chicago Housing Authority (CHA); (3) physical custody of child required, not legal custody; (4) limited to a subset of eligible households owing to funding restrictions	19/0	(1) Misinformation regarding legal guardianship; (2) family dynamics
Subsidized child care (no cost or copayment for formal child care)	(1) Grandparent must be income-eligible for Illinois Child Care Assistance Program; (2) employed grandparents receiving a child-only grant are eligible for day care assistance; (3) subject to work, education, and training requirements; (4) limited to a subset of eligible households owing to funding restrictions	5/0	(1) Misinformation about income eligibility requirements for employed grandparents who receive a TANF child-only grant; (2) family dynamics
Supplemental Security Income (SSI)	(1) Either grandparent or grandchild must meet disability guidelines, including countable income less than benefit amount and individual assets less than $2,000; (2) guardianship required	15/0	Family dynamics (such as conflict over legal custody)
SNAP ($189 per month maximum for one person, $347 maximum for two, $497 maximum for three, $632 maximum for four)	(1) Net household income does not exceed 130 percent of FPL; (2) grandchildren counted when determining the grant amount; (3) exempt from employment and training requirements; (4) guardianship required	30/8	Family dynamics (such as conflict over legal custody)

Source: Author's calculations.

[a]N = 58. Eligibility is defined as being income-eligible for safety net programs but *not* receiving benefits. Respondents eligible for TANF family grants are not receiving SSI or Social Security Disability Insurance (SSDI) and have not timed out of the TANF program.

Table 2. Household Income Sources of Study Participants

Income Package	Respondent Number	Income Package	Respondent Number
Housing subsidy, SNAP	N1	Housing subsidy, TANF family grant, SNAP	N33
Housing subsidy, SNAP	N2		
SSI, housing subsidy, TANF child-only grant, SNAP	N3	Child care subsidy only	N34
		SSDI only	N35
Earnings, housing subsidy, TANF child-only grant	N4	Earnings, child care subsidy, TANF child-only grant	N36
SSDI only	N5		
SSI, child care subsidy, SNAP	N6	SSI, SNAP	N37
SSI, housing subsidy, SNAP	N7	SSI, housing subsidy, SNAP	N38
Earnings, TANF child-only grant	N8		
Earnings, TANF child-only grant	N9	Housing subsidy, SNAP	N39
SSI, housing subsidy, TANF child-only grant, SNAP	N10	Earnings only	N40
		SSDI, SNAP	N41
Earnings, TANF child-only grant	N11	Earnings, SNAP	N42
SSI, housing subsidy, SNAP	N12	Earnings only	N43
Earnings, SNAP	N13	SSDI, SNAP	N44
None	N14	Earnings, housing subsidy	N45
SSDI, SNAP	N15	SSI only	N46
SSDI, pension, SNAP	N16	SSDI, earnings, housing subsidy, TANF child-only grant, SNAP	N47
Earnings only	N17		
SSDI only	N18		
SSI, earnings, SNAP	N19		
SSDI, pension, TANF child-only grant	N20	Earnings only	N48
		SSDI, housing subsidy, SNAP	N49
None	N21		
SSI only	N22	SNAP only	N50
Earnings only	N23	SSDI	N51
Earnings, TANF child-only grant	N24	None	N52
SSI, TANF child-only grant, SNAP	N25	SSDI, SNAP	N53
		SSDI, housing subsidy, SNAP	N54
Earnings, SSI	N26		
SSI, housing subsidy, SNAP	N27	Earnings, housing subsidy, SNAP	N55
SSI, SNAP	N28		
SSI, housing subsidy, TANF child-only grant, SNAP	N29	Earnings only	N56
		Earnings, housing subsidy, child care subsidy, TANF family grant	N57
SSDI, SNAP	N30		
SSI only	N31		
Housing subsidy, TANF child-only grant, SNAP	N32	Earnings, child care subsidy	N58

Source: Author's calculations.

cared for her two teenage daughters and her infant granddaughter while living in public housing. Both grandmother and mother were battling recent HIV/AIDS diagnoses. Forty-nine-year-old Ms. Alston "inherited" her mother's Chicago Housing Authority (CHA) subsidized apartment after her death and lived in it with the grandson she had raised since he was a newborn. Now four years old, his grieving mother had been unable to care for him as she battled depression after the murder of his father.

The eligibility criteria and barriers to subsidized housing receipt are presented in table 1. Because it was not uncommon for children to leave study participants' homes to reunite temporarily with their parents, then return owing to parental resistance or reluctance (Letiecq, Bailey, and Porterfield 2008), most study participants simply refused to divulge their housing composition. Ms. Jean's response when I asked whether her grandson lived with her represents the use of this risk negotiation strategy: "Uh, yes. Technically he don't, but he came back in. He's not on the lease." Ms. Jean had lived in subsidized housing for eleven years, but she had been caring for her grandson for only four. When she assumed care, the relationship between Ms. Jean and her daughter suffered because of Ms. Jean's alcoholic second husband. She and her daughter would "fall out" because Ms. Jean felt that she was disrespectful to her mate. Although she had nowhere to go, her daughter would take her baby when Ms. Jean forced her to leave their home. When the grandson told his grandmother that he and his mother had slept on a train one night, Ms. Jean called child protective services and arranged to assume legal guardianship. Although she did not add him to her lease—so as not to jeopardize her subsidized housing—the once-unemployed grandmother got a full-time job so that she could provide for him. She also divorced her second husband.

Although the Fair Housing Act (FHA) protects grandparent caregivers, state and local housing authorities may not. According to the FHA, "familial status" includes grandparents and other relatives who lack legal custody of the children they care for, if a parent or other custodial individual so designates them (Fuller-Thomson and Minkler 2003). Yet some housing authorities unlawfully require relatives to have legal custody or guardianship of grandchildren to qualify as "families" living in assisted housing. When housing authority officials and landlords of privately operated subsidized housing required grandparent caregivers to demonstrate proof of guardianship or custody, it often led to family conflict. For instance, the daughter of fifty-eight-year-old Ms. Price lived with her mother in a multigenerational household when she became pregnant with her first child.

According to Ms. Price, when she met the father of her second child, she then "started just having kids, having kids, having kids, having kids." When her daughter would not enroll the children in school or give Ms. Price guardianship so that she could do so, Ms. Price was clear—the children could stay, but her daughter and her new beau had to go. Unfortunately, she was told by housing authority officials that she had to have legal guardianship to add her grandchildren to her lease: "You have to put them on your lease that they actually stay here. . . . You have to legally have them." Ms. Price side-stepped parental authority by devising a plan to get legal guardianship of her grandchildren without her daughter's consent. This risk negotiation strategy enabled her to both keep her grandchildren in her care and maintain her housing subsidy.

Misinformation about the issue of legal guardianship or custody was a barrier to grandmothers trying to both utilize and access subsidized housing. For example, Ms. Bell obtained legal guardianship of the three grandchildren who had been in her care so that she could apply for Section 8 status. When I asked, "What made you decide to go through with the guardianship?" she replied, "Like I said, we had put in our application for Section 8. . . . I wanted a house because with three kids an apartment just ain't gonna get it. . . . 'Cause they told me I couldn't . . . unless I had guardianship papers." Despite misinformation given by street-level bureaucrats, Ms. Bell and her disabled husband tried to hold on to the grandchildren in their care *and* obtain subsidized housing by satisfying eligibility criteria. When care was transferred to her, she was working full-time, but her hours were cut during the Great Recession, causing additional financial strain.

Ms. Bell's application for subsidized housing outside of the city of Chicago exemplifies a tactic for accessing housing during the freeze on Section 8 in that city. Although she applied for Section 8 in the suburbs, the distance from the city proved prohibitive: "That's what made me opt for putting in for an application in the suburbs. . . . We didn't have transportation to get out there to search for an apartment or a house because my husband's disabled, and then by me working there was really no time to really look like I wanted to." Thus, they spent half of their income paying private market rent.

In spite of these struggles with misinformation about legal guardianship, many caseworkers, housing authority officials, and landlords not only adhered correctly to the federal statue but also advocated for these vulnerable families. For instance, when Ms. Charles's low-wage work could not cover child care, she stopped working: "I was staying with my son . . . because I wasn't making too much money. . . . I wasn't getting Social Security. I was getting like $377 a month." Ms. Charles maximized her family's public assistance by satisfying eligibility criteria for many of the programs in which she was enrolled by her caseworker, which ultimately played a key role in helping her to secure Section 8 status. Ms. Charles explained: "I had a real nice caseworker. And she seen that I was struggling, and I went through all these different programs they had me go to. She put my name in." Ms. Charles's experience, however, was more the exception than the rule for the custodial grandmothers participating in this study.

Grandmothers lacking institutional support devised other strategies to both keep their grandchildren in their care and access and utilize subsidized housing. While most adhered to CHA rules and regulations, some ignored bureaucratic strictures. For example, Ms. Jena allowed a friend to use her Section 8 voucher until she could use it herself. The gravity of her family problems kept her co-residing with her developmentally disabled daughter as well as her son and grandchildren. She explained her transition from helping her teenage daughter enter adulthood and raising her grandchildren in a multigenerational household to her present intergenerational housing arrangement with her fifteen-year-old grandson Daweed: "It's where I first utilized my Section 8. And I say 'utilized it' because I didn't actually live there. . . . Someone else did. . . . I was still livin' in [her former house]. . . . I was so desperate because I didn't want to lose that subsidy for future purposes."

Many grandmothers strategized in yet other ways to obtain public assistance or to make the most of a housing subsidy. For instance, sixty-two-year-old Ms. Mizell was losing her housing when I interviewed her. When her oldest daughter entered a battered women's shelter, the Department of Children and Family Services (DCFS) gave Ms. Mizell the three children. Ms. Mizell and another daughter then pooled their resources to rent an apartment, but the owner was selling the roach-infested, dilapidated building. She had only her Social Security income of $623 per month to care for her teenage son and grandchildren. She was contemplating moving to a shelter in lieu of other options:

"I turned it [an eviction notice] in to the [DCFS]. They wanna know from me how is my rent $600 and my income $623. I say, "I keep telling y'all I need help. Why won't y'all listen to me?" And this time when we leave here because she's selling the building I might just go to a shelter. . . . They won't give me subsidized housing. I can't go into senior housing . . . you can't take no children.

Previous studies indicate that some grandparents in similar situations have lived in senior housing with their grandchildren anyway, risking eviction, the loss of housing subsidies, and the loss of their grandchildren (Fuller-Thomson and Minkler 2003). Senior housing that did not permit children was an issue for renters *and* homeowners participating in this study who qualified for and wanted to take advantage of publicly subsidized senior housing. They all wanted to give up the homes in which they had raised their children and retire to senior housing to accommodate changes in their economic and health status.

Subsidized Child Care
Although maintaining or securing housing was critical to these grandmothers thrust into the primary caregiving role, so too was maintaining or securing employment. Caregiving for their grandchildren could push economically vulnerable caregivers into acute poverty by preventing them from participating in the labor market. Most of the employed grandmothers I studied combined paid work and care work by decreasing or increasing their work hours, changing occupations, or altering their work schedules. However, grandmothers caring for non-school-

age children faced unique challenges, and some were forced either to quit their job or to forgo seeking employment.

Grandmothers seeking subsidized child care were impeded by family dynamics as well as by programmatic barriers (see table 1 for eligibility criteria and barriers to subsidized child care). Forty-three-year-old Ms. Francois was forced to quit her job because she could not obtain child care. When Ms. Francois's granddaughter Sierra was born developmentally delayed, Myesha, the child's mother, would do nothing for or with the baby. Ms. Francois immediately stepped in to care for her granddaughter, using her own income, although she asked Myesha to care for her daughter while she worked. But Myesha was ashamed of her daughter's disability and sometimes feigned being away when her mother would attempt to drop Sierra off before work. "I used to work at [her former employer]. I used to have Myesha to watch her for me at times while I worked. . . . A lot of times she wouldn't let us in. . . . I had no one else to watch her." Ms. Francois eventually lost her job and was forced to rely on unemployment income and her personal network.

While Ms. Francois was forced to quit her job because she was unable to afford formal child care, qualify for subsidized child care, or find reliable informal child care, Ms. Boyd was unable to seek employment for the same reasons. "I need to get a job. Then that's another thing, how can I get a job with *her* [her granddaughter]?" When I asked how long she had been unemployed, she responded, "Two years [the child's age]. . . . I will need to go through the proper thing because I can't afford day care. Because you know they will pay child care. . . . But then it'd have to be in her momma name. So, then I'm dealing with that!"

What Ms. Boyd and others in her predicament meant by "that" was the tug-of-war between parents and grandparents over legal guardianship. To apply for subsidized child care Ms. Boyd would have had to be the representative payee for her granddaughter's TANF assistance. Yet this would have risked losing the child and jeopardizing her safety because the child's mother could have taken the child from Ms. Boyd to keep her public aid benefits. So Ms. Boyd allowed the mother to maintain control over the child's public assistance, forgoing child care assistance and her own employment opportunities in the process.

Family dynamics was not the only impediment that study participants faced in applying for subsidized child care. Most of them also found the Illinois Child Care Assistance Program (ICCAP) difficult to access owing to work, education or training, and income eligibility criteria. The ICCAP work and school requirements were especially difficult for low-income families (Butts, Thang, and Yeo, n.d.). They collectively questioned the logic of the program by asking, "How do I find or keep a job if I have no child care so that I can find or keep a job?"

Ms. King had difficulty finding work because of her inability to afford formal child care or qualify for subsidized child care. When her twenty-four-year-old daughter died of childbirth complications, Ms. King was left to care for a newborn and a toddler. Shortly thereafter, she lost her high-earning job. "I worked all my life. So I have never been in the system and never had to have any public assistance or anything." She needed a job to pay for child care, and she needed child care to work, but when she turned to public aid, she was faced with policies that were ill suited to her circumstances. "You cry, 'Oh why should I need child care? [*laughs*] Because you're not working or you ain't in school. I said, 'Well, how do you think I'm gonna get a job if I don't have any child care? I can't go for a job interview.' . . . I got infants. I can't go anywhere, and I can't leave them, and no one can babysit because everybody else works." She also had difficulty meeting the ICCAP school requirement. She had a bachelor's degree, and advanced degrees did not fall under the program's eligibility criteria. Eventually, Ms. King pursued a certification that satisfied the school requirement, and she was enrolling the children in formal child care at the time the interview was conducted.

The income eligibility requirement also confounded some study participants. Although many worked in low-wage jobs, they had done so long enough to earn somewhat more than was allowed by this means-tested program. Forty-eight-year-old Ms. Kelley was furious when she did not qualify for the IC-

CAP: "What's the purpose of applying for it if y'all gonna tell me I'm not approved for it because I make too much?'" She was already struggling to provide for her daughter when her son became a father. Her grandson's mother was mentally ill, however, and declared unfit, while her son was struggling with a crack cocaine addiction. Ms. Kelley had a job in social services, but "believe me," she declared, "social service make the least money, almost less than the poverty level." She paid nearly $700 a month for her grandson's child care until two months before the interview was conducted. When she could no longer afford to pay his child care fees, she took him out of formal child care and left him with one of her nieces while she worked.

While most study participants who failed to satisfy eligibility criteria either paid for or forswore formal child care, some responded by trying to bypass bureaucratic regulations. For instance, forty-eight-year-old Ms. Baker, who was married but did not report her marital status, was also told that she earned too much to qualify. "They told me I make too much money. Even though I did some illegal stuff, they still wouldn't give it to me. [*laughs*] I'll tell 'em I was a single parent." When she and her husband went to Wisconsin to rescue their grandsons from foster care, they were initially made kinship foster care providers, but later they became the children's legal guardians. They could not become subsidized guardians because they did not go through the Illinois system, so they paid out of pocket ($800 a month) for their two grandsons' child care costs. "'Cause, they told me I was ninety dollars over . . . and the discount that [the child care provider] gives me is because the kids have been with them so long." The Bakers were not the only study participants who struggled to pay for child care themselves so that they could maintain their employment.

TANF

Although this research focuses on SGHs in which parents are not living in the homes with grandmothers and grandchildren, many parents were peripherally involved in their children's lives (Baker, Silverstein, and Putney 2008). Nevertheless, in spite of a wide range of peripheral parental involvement, grandmothers excluded certain parents from assisting them, especially those who were addicted to drugs and alcohol or who had more children and were trying to maintain their own households.

The grandmothers asked the drug-free parents with no economic responsibilities beyond caring for themselves to make regular financial contributions, to fill certain specific needs, and to step in when the grandmothers and their charges needed them urgently. Parents contributed financially by paying utility bills, purchasing food, or handing over a portion of the child's monthly public assistance, such as food stamps, TANF, or Social Security payments, to the grandmother's household. Yet even though grandmothers insisted that parents who were able to contribute financially do so, the majority did not. Thus, parental contact often failed to translate into shared parental responsibility.

When a parent received TANF child-only benefits for a child, the grandparent would be disqualified from receiving such public assistance. Table 1 details this and other barriers to TANF receipt. When Ms. Boyd's daughter left her mother with her two-year-old daughter *without* transferring the child's public assistance, Ms. Boyd ended up caring for her granddaughter without either formal support or an income rather than risk her granddaughter's safety by demanding that the mother relinquish TANF payments or take care of her own child: "A lot of people say, 'You let her do it, you ain't saying nothing.' They don't understand! I'm not gonna make her take my grandbaby nowhere that it ain't safe at just so I can say she with her mommy."

Ms. Boyd was not alone: several grandmothers who were eligible for TANF child-only grants did not receive them because they let the parents receive the public assistance rather than risk parents retaliating by taking the child (Letiecq, Bailey, and Proterfield 2008). Away from the grandmother, the child might be subjected to abuse, neglect, homelessness, a dangerous environment, or abusive or negligent partners (Pittman 2014). Some grandmothers were prevented from receiving the only form of cash assistance for which they were eligible when they made the complicated and often coerced decision to forgo resources to protect their grandchildren.

Forty-seven-year-old Ms. Martin had been caring for her son's child, seven-year-old Kwan Jr., known as KJ, off and on since he was three months old, since his mother Tonya, age sixteen when he was born, had proved unreliable as a parent. As KJ's stays became less sporadic over the years he eventually was cared for solely by Ms. Martin and his father, Kwan Sr., who had been seventeen when he was born. When asked how she ultimately ended up with KJ in a SGH, Ms. Martin replied, "I had lost my job, so I had to give up my place and I was living with my sister. . . . Kwan was living there with me and a couple of my other children. And she [Tonya] just . . . told me she didn't want him anymore. . . . Then my son, he took the baby. . . . But he was only seventeen."

Parents could apply their parental rights to take children from grandmothers who lacked custody or legal guardianship (Perez-Porter and Flint 2000). Parents often removed or tried to remove children from a grandmother's care to receive the resources the child received or could potentially receive. Ms. Martin could not stop KJ's mother from using him to try to get Section 8 status. She could not prevent Tonya from resuming parenting even though "she didn't want him." So she continued to say no when Tonya attempted to resume parenting to access resources for herself: "She trying to get Section 8 and she trying to get an apartment. . . . But like I told her, 'I don't care about you putting him on the lease because they ain't gonna do nothing to me with you putting him on the lease. . . . He gonna stay right here where he is, and he's gonna stay in the school he's at.'"

While some grandmothers wanted public assistance to buttress their fragile financial status, others were willing to forgo these resources so that their financially struggling daughters could keep them. For example, Ms. Cooper allowed her daughter to receive the child's public assistance in the hope that it would help her get on the right track; she asked her daughter only to keep her granddaughter clothed, which for the most part she did. She and others expressed that this risk negotiation strategy was a small price to pay for ensuring the safety and well-being of their grandchildren. Ms. White also brokered a deal with her thirty-year-old daughter Khadeja. The fifty-two-year-old had raised Khadeja's five children for much of their lives. Initially, they all ended up in her care for the same reason: Khadeja was unwilling to even *try* to raise them. "When [her grandson] was born, she was running the streets with the baby's father. . . . I had to take care of him because she wouldn't do it. . . . She won't come down here and sign no papers to get no money for him, for him to get his shots and for him to get food stamps. I couldn't make her do this."

This pattern continued with her other children, although Khadeja's negligence escalated as she started also taking the children's resources:

> When she had [another grandson], the same thing happened. She would get his little check, she would come home for two or three days before the checks would come and clean the baby up. The day the check would come she would go to the currency exchange to get the check, and then she was gone. . . . She wouldn't come home and give me no money, she wouldn't buy the baby no clothes, and I could do it at the time because I was working as a bartender, but I just got tired of it!

It soon became clear to Ms. White that in order to get things done for the children, several of whom had learning and developmental disabilities, she would need legal guardianship. She was able to receive public assistance after becoming the children's legal guardian. However, once her daughter entered recovery, Ms. White allowed her to receive assistance for her youngest child. "I got the Link card. She got the cash card. . . . She give me $150 a month to help around here." Ms. White and her daughter had devised a system for sharing public assistance that worked.

Some grandmothers in the study strategized to procure the public assistance received by parents intended for their grandchildren rather than accommodate or negotiate with the parents. When Ms. Francois lost her job because of her caregiving responsibilities, she collected unemployment. However, when her unemployment benefits ended, Ms. Francois resorted to trickery to get her daughter Myesha to sign the necessary legal guardianship documentation: "I let [Myesha] get [her granddaughter's] Social Security check. . . . So, once my unemployment ran out, I told Myesha I had to have the check. And she didn't wanna give it to me . . . because she didn't want the baby, but she just wanted the check. So I had to go to court and file a petition so I could get legal guardianship. . . . I had to . . . tell her it was something pertaining to school with Sierra and that I needed her signature." At the time of the interview, Ms. Francois and Sierra lived solely on Sierra's SSI benefit.

Another grandmother, sixty-three-year-old Ms. Harris, was seeking legal guardianship without parental consent at the time of the interview. I attended a guardianship hearing with her for which she had spent months preparing. She had been caring for her three young great-grandchildren because their parents were abusing them and had no housing. Ms. Harris was living off of her own SSDI and that of a fourth great-granddaughter she had adopted. Having three additional dependents and being unable to work owing to lung cancer was taking its toll. In trying to formalize her relationship with her great-grandchildren, she had confronted several obstacles that had to do with both bureaucratic regulations and the parents' unwillingness to consent.

Ms. Harris's persistence paid off. When we attended her guardianship hearing, she had the paperwork in order. She explained to the judge that her grandson and his girlfriend had left the children in her care, had no place for them, and were struggling to parent them. She was deliberately vague. She didn't mention the abuse, only that "they hadn't returned for the children" and she "didn't know where they were." She kept the focus on needing to get things done for the children, especially regarding medical needs. We looked at her guardianship papers after they had been processed and saw that the children had been "appointed for the following reasons: Both parents are unemployed and unable to provide for children." Her new guardianship status granted Ms. Harris access to the public assistance she so desperately needed.

While family dynamics can be a barrier to receiving public assistance, so too are social welfare policies and program implementation. Three such barriers to TANF receipt were identified: stigma and discrimination, misinformation, and an inability to meet eligibility criteria owing to aging and health-related issues. To minimize the risk of losing their grandchildren and maximize the likelihood of receiving public assistance, study participants acquiesced when confronted with bias or misinformation, satisfied eligibility criteria when possible, bypassed bureaucratic regulations when it was not possible, and did without when all else failed.

Forty-one-year-old Ms. Dewitt decided to care for her newborn granddaughter Neliah because of the conditions in which Neliah lived with her parents. When her seventeen-year-old daughter Portia gave birth to Neliah, she was living with the baby's father and his mother. Ms. Dewitt noticed that her granddaughter was always hungry and that the house was dirty and had rodents. Alarmed, she took Portia to find a job and helped her put Neliah in day care. The job did not last, and Ms. Dewitt found herself in charge of Neliah's day-care transportation and expenses. As Portia started leaving Neliah in Ms. Dewitt's care for extended periods of time, she became concerned for her granddaughter's safety and well-being. She eventually called child protective services and pursued legal guardianship. When Ms. Dewitt asked during the guardianship hearing about available resources, the judge's response not only was stigmatizing but also stopped her from asking for anything more: "When I first got Neliah, I remember trying to get assistance for her was just like the hardest thing. Because they wouldn't give me assistance for her and the judge made me feel like *this* little. She was like, 'Well, if you need assistance for her, if you can't afford to take care of her, why should we give her to you?'"

Ms. Dewitt eschewed the only public assistance available to the grandchild in her care because of the discrimination she experienced. Other study participants also expressed frustration about not receiving benefits, not because they lacked the proper paperwork, but because their doing so as *grandparent* caregivers was questioned (Henderson and Cook 2005). They were also commonly misinformed about the TANF eligibility criteria. In fact, next to parental receipt of public assistance, misinformation about the TANF requirement of legal guardianship was a chief barrier to TANF access for study participants. For example, the fifty-eight-year-old Ms. Toering had cared for seven-year-old Cambria, her youngest son's only daughter, off and on since her birth. Ms. Toering felt that Cambria's mother's care was inadequate and unsafe. Initially, Ms. Toering was not sure whether she should "take" Cambria from her mother. "But this last year I just really—I couldn't take it." After a series of incidents, she contacted DCFS three times—to no avail, because she lacked legal guardianship.

Ineligibility for ongoing public assistance, inaction on the part of the state, and fear that the child's mother would remove her from her care all contributed to Ms. Toering's pursuit of legal guardianship—without the mother's consent and with little assistance from state agents. Ms. Toering told me that, even after obtaining guardianship, "because I went through the guardianship on my own, it's nothing they can do about it as far as helping me out." Although relative caregivers are eligible for TANF child-only grants without being legal guardians of the children in their care, Ms. Toering and others reported that they were told otherwise. Owing to such barriers, fewer than one-fourth of eligible study participants received the $107 monthly stipends.

To pursue the option of applying for TANF family grants for themselves and the child, the grandmothers' incomes had to be included in the benefit calculation. Kinship caregivers in family TANF cases are also subject to time limits and employment and training requirements (Mullen and Einhorn 2000), and so aging and health-related issues often complicated these applications. For instance, when Ms. Charles's drug-addicted daughter went to prison for "fighting with her boyfriend," she stepped in to care for her daughter's two-year-old twins. That was eleven years ago; her daughter's crack cocaine addiction, coupled with an abusive relationship, would make prison entry and reentry a way of life for her. When sixty-four-year-old Ms. Charles applied for a TANF family grant, she was told by her caseworker that she needed to satisfy work and training requirements to receive it. Ms. Charles's age and frail health made participating in the program impossible. "It was hard. I mean I would take them to school, and then I had to go to school. See?... It was hard just for that little $377 I actually got out of it. I pretended like I had gotten hit in the arm because I was tired of going. [laughs] So I just called 'em up one day and told 'em I had a job." When the grant agency learned that she had not completed the program and had not secured a job, they reduced her $377-a-month TANF family grant to a child-only grant of $190 per month. Although she turned sixty-five shortly after throwing in the towel and was able to qualify for SSI, she still fell short of being able to afford private market housing and provide for her two grandchildren while their mother was in prison. So they were living with Ms. Charles's son until she could secure subsidized housing.

Although she desperately needed the medical card that came with public assistance, fifty-nine-year-old Ms. Jena also found it difficult to sustain her participation. Care of her grandchildren was transferred to her when her developmentally disabled daughter "had kids too young, when she was still my dependent." When Ms. Jena sought mental health services for herself and her children because they were the offspring of sexual abuse by her stepfather, the family experienced a downward spiral. When she was awarded workfare, she was allowed to use community service to fulfill the TANF family grant work and training requirement by working at a volunteer assignment at a social service organization for thirty hours a week.[3] Ms. Jena explains why her participation in the program was short-lived: "I guess it became a little bit difficult for me. Again, when I have family problems or whatnot, it's hard on me.

---

3. Workfare programs assign recipients of public assistance to employment without compensation. Workfare is required for persons who do not participate in job search training and work programs but who are not exempt from registration with the job service.

And with the osteoarthritis, the pain that sometimes I get. And dealin' with the issues of my family . . . weighs me down." When Ms. Jena could no longer participate in the program, her resources were cut off, including her access to medical coverage and the $292-per-month cash assistance she received for herself and her fifteen-year-old grandson. While bypassing bureaucratic regulations to maintain subsidized housing enabled Ms. Jena to keep her grandson in her care, her effort to satisfy eligibility criteria did not grant her access to a TANF family grant. Only two grandmothers participating in this study who applied for a TANF family grant qualified for the program.

DISCUSSION

Grandparents find themselves in a marginal position relative to not only judicially favored parents but the state. Inasmuch as family dynamics and state agents hinder grandmothers' efforts to hold on to the resources needed to provide for themselves, their families, *and* their grandchildren, risk negotiation can help them overcome barriers. Risk negotiation enables people to utilize strategies appropriate for their unique circumstances, and using multiple strategies provides tools with which to mitigate the negative impact of structural vulnerabilities on their safety net experiences.

The grandmothers I interviewed struggled not only with family competition over scarce resources but also with the housing authority requiring legal guardianship before they could add children to their leases or apply for subsidized housing—despite an FHA mandate that protects them from such a requirement. Study participants weighed the fluidity and uncertainty that came with grandparent caregiving against a tight subsidized housing market. As such, some would not divulge their household composition for fear of losing their housing subsidies. Others, like Ms. Price and Ms. Bell, assumed guardianship to keep their grandchildren in their care, add them to their leases, or apply for Section 8 status. Still others found themselves locked out of the publicly subsidized senior housing market because of their caregiving responsibilities. Although these grandmothers demonstrated immense agency, their efforts were no match for structural constraints, so several bypassed the regulations to expedite the receipt of public housing or to remain illegally in such housing.

Although thirteen study participants were income-eligible to receive the TANF family grant, only two were able to satisfy the entitlement program's eligibility criteria. Table 1 presents not only the eligibility criteria for safety net programs in Illinois but also the number of respondents who met entitlement program income requirements. Only five grandmothers were able to satisfy the eligibility criteria for subsidized child care. These programs did not align with the lived experiences of grandparent caregivers, many of whom were unable to work owing to poor health or their caregiving responsibilities. Moreover, when grandmothers are the principal child care providers, their role as consumers is largely ignored in the current child care policy, even though most remain in the labor market (U.S. Census Bureau 2010). Although these women had slightly higher wages because of their work longevity, few earned enough to pay directly for child care. Paradoxically, as a result of modifying their labor market participation to care for their grandchildren, some grandmothers lost the income they needed to meet the economic demands of providing such care.

Lacking access to child care challenged custodial grandmothers' efforts to achieve economic self-sufficiency or to escape severe deprivation. Paying for child care made it difficult to pay for health insurance, rent, and utilities. Safe, reliable child care is expensive. Study participants understood why some grandparent caregivers decline to report their full income or devise other strategies to qualify for child care subsidies and other forms of public assistance. Some of those who were unable to pay for child care were compelled to quit their jobs or were unable to secure employment.

The structural lag between GPHHs and safety net programs is compounded by inadequate and punitive welfare policies that engender competition over scarce resources. By acting in the best interests of their grandchildren, grandparent caregivers too often came up short. Without legal protections or publicly recognized authority as parents, they found it difficult to access safety net programs, including TANF child-only grants. While some grandmothers devised strategies to take legal guardianship from the parents, others struck deals with the parents to share resources. Still others simply did without.

**Piecing It All Together:
Resource-Maximizing Strategies**
The grandmothers in the study had to strategize to reduce the severe deprivation their families experienced. While they did what most resource-strapped families do—maximized the resources they could piece together from income, formal support, and informal support—they confronted additional challenges. Among several strategies they used to mitigate material hardship were prioritizing the essentials, pacing consumption, underpaying, and bargain shopping.

Prioritizing the essentials meant using their income to pay the most important bills first. Rent was the most important bill, and for those who were living in subsidized housing and caring for children who had come to the attention of the child welfare system, younger children, or children with special needs, paying utilities was the second priority. Grandmothers unanimously expressed that ensuring that their grandchildren "had a roof over their heads," given that their homes were often those children's last resort, was an additional burden. Even if they had to forgo health care, food, clothing, personal hygiene, or household products, these grandmothers knew that keeping their grandchildren from becoming homeless was their highest priority. Still, housing instability was common.

Study participants paced consumption largely by purchasing needed goods one at a time, paycheck by paycheck. What they could not purchase they often did without; sometimes they waited for donations from family, friends, neighbors, or charitable organizations. Consistent with previous research findings on low-income and female-headed households, civil society, including food pantries, churches, and social service organizations, was an important resource for one-third of the grandmothers in this study (Edin and Lein 1997).

Their family's unique structure and financial needs altered their consumption-pacing behaviors. While the life-course stage of some of the grandmothers was warranting decreased economic resources and less accumulation of material goods, their caregiving roles were placing demands on them typically experienced by parents—the pressure to maintain a dwelling appropriate for children and to incorporate their material needs into the household budget. As such, most of the grandmothers sought opportunities to underpay to maximize their resources by spending less than market value for material items and services; several talked openly about "buying stamps." These opportunities to underpay emerged through personal networks.

When possible, study participants determined *what* their families could do without and *when*. For example, it was not uncommon for them to do without gas in the summer and without electricity in the winter. The vast majority of participants relied on utility assistance programs, and some of them had strategized shortcuts to enable them to qualify for those programs. They increased their odds of receiving public assistance by using their sociodemographic characteristics to fit formal support criteria—for instance, by reporting the disability status of family members.

Kicked by Money Woes: The Implications of Grandparent Caregiving
Grandmothers who care for their grandchildren experience stress that is widely associated with a variety of negative mental and physical health outcomes compared with outcomes for their noncaregiving counterparts, even when controlling for age, race and ethnicity, economic status, education, and marital status. They also have poorer mental and physical health than filial and spousal caretakers, custodial grandparents who provide lesser degrees of care, and members of the general population (Musil et al. 2010).

Elevated depressive symptoms have been found among poor grandmothers. Poor physical health and additional caregiving responsibilities have been identified as sources of stress (Kelley et al. 2000). Moreover, compared with white grandmothers, African American grandmothers may experience higher levels of parenting stress owing to neighborhood characteristics (Park 2005). Like African American custodial grandmothers in other studies, participants in this study were found to experience significant health problems, including diabetes, high cholesterol, obesity, and hypertension (Whitley, Kelley, and Campos 2011). However, the findings also suggest that previous research fails to capture the gravity of the health challenges experienced by low-income black grandmothers raising grandchildren or the exacerbation of health problems caused by financial strain and such barriers as family dynamics, risk negotiation, and lack of access to resources and services. High blood pressure, strokes, heart attacks, diabetes, obesity, and various cancers were widespread among the study participants. Ms. Mizell echoed the sentiment held by most grandmothers participating in this study when I asked about the most challenging aspect of raising their grandchildren. "Money. Money will kick you. There are times I have gone to bed depressed."

CONCLUSION AND IMPLICATIONS

The most significant child welfare legislation in recent years, the Fostering Connections to Success and Increasing Adoptions Act of 2008, authorized competitively awarded discretionary Family Connection Grants to twenty-four awardees to create Kinship Navigator Programs (KNPs).[4] KNPs help caregivers navigate the formal support system by increasing awareness of services and clarifying eligibility procedures. The competitive nature of these demonstration projects means that funding is not available to all states or localities; in 2012 only fourteen states had KNPs. Still, KNPs represent a promising federal policy initiative for assisting grandparent caregivers who provide care outside of the child welfare system. As safety net programs for the poor continue to be politically vulnerable, KNPs might be able to connect vulnerable families to scant available resources, improving their take-up rates and outcomes for children, caregivers, and families in the process.

A population's lived experience amid the rise in GPHHs reveals that a lack of information about available resources and services is only one of a multitude of issues that impede access to formal support systems. KNPs offer a mechanism for systematically assessing family dynamics, which often impedes caregivers' public assistance receipt. By considering intra- and interfamilial dynamics, KNPs can help caregivers pursue available resources by operating as a critical feedback loop between individuals *experiencing* the need for support and those *formulating and implementing* social welfare policies and programs to address it, specifically by reporting structural lags between GPHH needs and those policies.

KNPs also have the capacity to keep pace with rapidly changing, state-driven program availability and eligibility criteria. Recently, Washington, Arizona, Nevada, and Oregon imposed caregiver income requirements when awarding child-only grants, which in most states are based on the child's income. Similarly, most states impose no time limits on child-only grants, but Arizona, Connecticut, North Dakota, and Tennessee do. KNPs can not only monitor such changes but also increase take-up rates by providing correct information about eligibility criteria. State agents routinely—and mistakenly—prevent relative caregivers from receiving available resources by telling them that legal guardianship is required to receive TANF assistance, subsidized housing, or child care.

The first round of national cross-site evaluations indicates that caregivers receiving KNP assistance need less intervention and enjoy better access to public supports (Lin 2014). Based on these results and findings from this study and others, funding is needed for more demonstration projects with strong information and referral, outreach, advocacy, and education and training components, as well as strong family intervention components to help caregivers and parents negotiate.

Additional policy changes that would make safety net programs more accessible to these highly vulnerable families include training

---

4. For details, see the website grandfamilies.org, "Kinship Navigator Programs: Resources," available at: http://grandfamilies.org/KinshipNavigatorPrograms/KinshipNavigatorProgramsResources.aspx (accessed June 1, 2015).

and education "through both HUD and the Fair Housing Initiatives Program, for front line workers who, through no fault of their own, may be misinterpreting policies that affect these families" (Lin 2014, 96). Training and education could also be extended to TANF and the ICCAP. Correct information regarding the legal requirements for GPHHs to receive these public benefits should be disseminated to state agents, owners of privately operated subsidized housing, and relevant support groups to prevent caregivers from being confused about eligibility criteria and their rights.

Interventions that would support employment stability among GPHHs include providing child care subsidies for grandparent caregivers. Providing a period of subsidized child care would enable them to maintain or obtain employment. And finally, part-time work could be accepted to fulfill work eligibility criteria as one step in reducing work requirements to reflect the aging and health issues of grandparents raising their grandchildren.

REFERENCES

Annie E. Casey Foundation. 2012. *Stepping Up for Kids: What Government and Communities Should Do to Support Kinship Families.* Policy Report Kids Count. Baltimore: Annie E. Casey Foundation.

Baker, Lindsey A., Merril Silverstein, and Norella M. Putney. 2008. "Grandparents Raising Grandchildren in the United States: Changing Family Forms, Stagnant Social Policies." *Journal of Societal and Social Policy* 7: 53–69.

Beltran, Ana. 2014a. "Improving Grandfamilies' Access to Temporary Assistance for Needy Families." Policy Brief. Washington, D.C.: Generations United.

———. 2014b. "Policy Update: Federal and State Legislation to Support Grandfamilies." *Grandfamilies: The Contemporary Journal of Research, Practice and Policy* 1(1): 56–73.

Butts, Donna M., Leng Leng Thang, and Alan Hatton Yeo. N.d. "Policies and Programmes Supporting Intergenerational Relations." White Paper. New York: Secretariat of the United Nations.

Copen, Casey. 2006. "Welfare Reform: Challenges for Grandparents Raising Grandchildren." *Journal of Aging and Social Policy* 18(3–4): 193–209.

Cox, Carole B. 2003. "Designing Interventions for Grandparent Caregivers: The Need for an Ecological Perspective for Practice." *Families in Society* 84(1): 127–34.

Edin, Kathryn, and Laura Lein. 1997. *Making Ends Meet: How Single Mothers Survive Welfare and Low-Wage Work.* New York: Russell Sage Foundation.

Falk, Gene. 2014. "Temporary Assistance for Needy Families (TANF): Size and Characteristics of the Cash Assistance Caseload." Congressional Research Service Report R43187. Washington: U.S. Congress.

Fuller-Thomson, Esme, and Meredith Minkler. 2003. "Housing Issues and Realities Facing Grandparent Caregivers Who Are Renters." *The Gerontologist* 43(1): 92–98.

Gleeson, James P. 1999. "Kinship Care as a Child Welfare Service: Emerging Policy Issues and Trends." In *Kinship Foster Care: Policy, Practice, and Research*, edited by Rebecca L. Hegar and Maria Scannapieco. New York: Oxford University Press.

Gustafson, Kaaryn. 2009. "The Criminalization of Poverty." *Journal of Criminal Law and Criminology* 99(3): 643–716.

Henderson, Tammy L., and Jennifer L. Cook. 2005. "Grandma's Hands: Black Grandmothers Speak About Their Experiences Rearing Grandchildren on TANF." *International Journal of Aging and Human Development* 61(1): 1–19.

Johnson, Elizabeth, and Jane Waldfogel. 2002. "Parental Incarceration: Recent Trends and Implications for Child Welfare." *Social Service Review* 76(3): 460–79.

Kelley, Susan J., Deborah Whitley, Theresa A. Sipe, and Beatrice Crofts Yorker. 2000. "Psychological Distress in Grandmother Kinship Care Providers: The Role of Resources, Social Support, and Physical Health." *Child Abuse and Neglect* 24(3): 311–21.

Letiecq, Bethany, Sandra J. Bailey, and Fonda Porterfield. 2008. "We Have No Rights, We Get No Help: The Legal and Policy Dilemmas Facing Grandparent Caregivers." *Journal of Family Issues* 29: 995–1012.

Lin, Ching-Hsuan. 2014. "Evaluating Services for Kinship Care Families: A Systematic Review." *Children and Youth Services Review* 36: 32–41.

Livingston, Gretchen. 2013. "At Grandmother's House We Stay." Social and Demographic Trends Report. Washington, D.C.: Pew Research Center.

Livingston, Gretchen, and Kim Parker. 2010. "Since the Start of the Great Recession, More Children Raised by Grandparents." Social and Demographic Trends Report. Washington, D.C.: Pew Research Center, 2010.

McGowan, Brenda G., and Elaine M. Walsh. 2000. "Policy Challenges for Child Welfare in the New Century." *Child Welfare* 79: 11–27.

Minkler, Meredith, and Esme Fuller-Thomson. 2005. "African American Grandparents Raising Grandchildren: A National Study Using the Census 2000 American Community Survey." *Journals of Gerontology* 60B(2): 82–92.

Mullen, Faith, and Monique Einhorn. 2000. *The Effect of State TANF Choices on Grandparent-Headed Households*. Washington, D.C.: Public Policy Institute/AARP.

Murphy, Yvette, Andrea Hunter, and Deborah Johnson. 2008. "Transforming Caregiving: African American Custodial Grandmothers and the Child Welfare System." *Journal of Sociology and Social Welfare* 35(2): 67–89.

Musil, Carol M., Nahida L. Gordon, Camille B. Warner, Jaclene A. Zauszniewski, Theresa Standing, and May Wykle. 2010. "Grandmothers and Caregiving to Grandchildren: Continuity, Change, and Outcomes over 24 Months." *The Gerontologist* 51(1): 86–100.

Park, Hwa-Ok. 2005. "Grandmothers Raising Grandchildren: Family Well-Being and Economic Assistance." *Focus* 24(1): 19–27.

Perez-Porter, Melinda, and Margaret M. Flint. 2000. "Grandparent Caregiving: Legal Status Issues and State Policy." In *To Grandmother's House We Go and Stay: Perspectives on Custodial Grandparents*, edited by Carole B. Cox. New York: Springer.

Pittman, LaShawnDa. 2014. "Doing What's Right for the Baby: Parental Responses and Institutional Decision-Making of Custodial Grandmothers." *Women, Gender, and Families of Color* 2(1): 32–56.

Roberts, Dorothy. 2003. *Shattered Bonds: The Color of Child Welfare*. New York: Basic Books.

Scommegna, Paola. 2012. "More U.S. Children Raised by Grandparents." Washington, D.C.: Population Reference Bureau (March).

Smith, Carrie Jefferson, and Ana Beltran. 2003. "The Role of Federal Policies in Supporting Grandparents Raising Grandchildren Families: The Case of the U.S." *Journal of Intergenerational Relationships* 1(2): 5–20.

Smith, Carrie Jefferson, and Wynetta Devore. 2004. "African American Children in the Child Welfare and Kinship System: From Exclusion to Over-Inclusion." *Children and Youth Services Review* 26: 427–46.

Swann, Christopher, and Michelle Sylvester. 2006. "The Foster Care Crisis: What Caused Caseloads to Grow?" *Demography* 43(2): 309–35.

Travis, Jeremy, Elizabeth McBride, and Amy Solomon. 2005. "Families Left Behind: The Hidden Costs of Incarceration and Reentry." Washington, D.C.: Urban Institute Justice Policy Center.

U.S. Census Bureau. 2010. *Current Population Survey: America's Families and Living Arrangements*. Washington: U.S. Government Printing Office.

Whitley, Deborah M., Susan J. Kelley, and Peter E. Campos. 2011. "Perceptions of Family Empowerment in African American Custodial Grandmothers Raising Grandchildren: Thoughts for Research and Practice." *Families in Society* 92(4): 110–19.

PART II
Extreme Poverty and Social Suffering

How Institutions Deprive: Ethnography, Social Work, and Interventionist Ethics Among the Hypermarginalized

MEGAN COMFORT, ANDREA M. LOPEZ, CHRISTINA POWERS, ALEX H. KRAL, AND JENNIFER LORVICK

Hypermarginalized populations, such as homeless drug users with acute health problems, are subject to multiple intersecting adversities that result in social exclusion and chronic suffering. Despite this population's high need for health and social services, institutions provide services that are fragmented and often punitive, contributing to further marginality. In this article, we present a hybrid methodological approach that combines clinical social work and ethnography in a study of intensive case management for HIV-positive indigent adults in Oakland, California. We investigate two primary research questions. First, we consider the challenges this population faces in navigating institutions to meet their basic needs, and we demonstrate how organizational irrationality has severe consequences for this population. Second, we grapple with the question of how to ethically engage hypermarginalized participants in research by presenting a clinically informed intervention that is responsive to individual vulnerabilities and also enhances our understanding of institutional failure.

Keywords: ethnography, social work, poverty, incarceration, research methods

"Hypermarginality" refers to a historically contingent social positioning in which inequities coalesce to shape everyday experience. On a concrete level, hypermarginality manifests in individuals as a complex matrix of social exclusion and chronic suffering, including homelessness and housing instability, drug use, serious mental illness, poor health, inadequate access to basic social and medical services, and repeated incarceration. Over time, these phenomena become intensely acute and entangled and must be confronted simul-

All authors are with the Behavioral and Urban Health Program at RTI International. **Megan Comfort** is a senior research sociologist. **Andrea M. Lopez** is a research medical anthropologist. **Christina Powers** is a licensed clinical social worker. **Alex H. Kral** is a senior research epidemiologist. **Jennifer Lorvick** is a senior public health scientist.

This research was supported by funding from the National Institutes of Health (R01MH094090, PI: Kral; R01DA033847, PI: Comfort; and R01MD007679, PI: Lorvick). We thank Jay Borchert, Elizabeth Kita, Reuben Miller, Victor Rios, Megan Tompkins-Stange, Damian T. Williams, and the participants in the Russell Sage Foundation "Severe Deprivation in America" conference for their invigorating and helpful feedback on drafts of the manuscript. We are particularly grateful to special issue editor Matthew Desmond for his detailed comments and insightful suggestions. And we are tremendously appreciative of and indebted to the people who participated in our research, and hope that we have done justice to the experiences they shared with us. Direct correspondence to: Megan Comfort at mcomfort@rti.org, Andrea M. Lopez at alopez@rti.org, Christina Powers at cpowers.contractor@rti.org, Alex H. Kral at akral@rti.org, and Jennifer Lorvick at jlorvick@rti.org; all authors at RTI International, 351 California St., Suite 500, San Francisco, CA 94014.

taneously, both analytically and practically, as they are contemporary syndemics (Singer and Clair 2003). However, for the urban poor in the United States, there exists a particular paradox that has grave consequences: hypermarginalized populations have extremely high and interconnected needs for health and social services, yet the institutions that ostensibly provide those services are not only grossly fragmented but often extremely punitive, and contribute to further marginality by hampering, discouraging, or oppressing individuals seeking help (Lopez 2011, 2014).

In this article, we grapple with two interrelated research questions, one empirical and one methodological. Empirically, we investigate hypermarginalized individuals' processes of institutional navigation, analyzing the challenges that they face as they try to access the basic resources necessary for survival and the ways in which various social institutions introduce or contribute to these challenges. Through a qualitative study of destitute adults diagnosed with human immunodeficiency virus (HIV), we find that when people with complex difficulties encounter medical or social service institutions that cannot address their interwoven needs, they risk becoming categorized as "resistant to treatment" (Buckley and Bigelow 1992) and being further excluded from assistance. A lack of coordination across service institutions significantly exacerbates this risk, as "failure" to perform as required for one service can become grounds for denial of another; for example, serious mental health issues can result in an eviction, which in turn becomes a barrier to obtaining subsidized housing. In addition, hypermarginalized people's contact with the criminal justice system is frequent and heavy, and the various restrictions and mandates placed on them through arrest warrants, criminal records, probation, and parole can pose insurmountable obstacles to meeting requirements for services; an individual with a felony drug conviction, for instance, is ineligible for food stamps. Thus, while hypermarginalized populations interface repeatedly with correctional, medical, and social service institutions, these encounters may merely patch them up from one crisis to the next, or even drive them further into a downward spiral, rather than providing coordinated services to elevate their quality of life.

Methodologically, we pursue the question of how to gather rich, detailed data on the experiences of a highly vulnerable, mobile, and oppressed group. Although information about these individuals can be captured to some extent when they are incarcerated, hospitalized, sheltered, or taken to the coroner's office, there are significant obstacles to enrolling them in research that seeks to follow them across various social institutions, and especially into the interstices between institutions. They often cannot be reached through permanent addresses, directory-listed phone numbers, informational flyers, or other standard procedures for participant recruitment. When they are located through targeted outreach efforts or their contact with a criminal justice, medical, or social service institution, their material circumstances and psychological complexities pose exceptional difficulties for staying in touch. And if a confluence of resourcefulness, rapport, and flat-out luck results in study retention, profound questions arise regarding the ethics of gathering data on the deepest layers of human suffering through non-interventionist, observational research.

Yet without research on people at the margin of the margins, we consistently overlook a small but deeply affected population whose inclusion might alter the results of standard research on urban poverty, and thus we remain ill equipped to determine how to address the literal matters of life and death that afflict society's poorest members. The physician Emily Wang, the sociologist and demographer Christopher Wildeman, and their colleagues have demonstrated that systematically excluding incarcerated individuals from participation in medical research results in lower enrollment and retention rates for African American men in cross-sectional and prospective cohort studies, thereby jeopardizing the validity of conclusions for this population (Wang and Wildeman 2011; Wang et al. 2014). They recommend the careful development of protocols for ethically including prisoners in medical studies, given the long-term benefits of understanding this population's specific health issues. Following this logic, adapting methodological strategies to reach people at the nexus of mental illness, substance use, criminal justice involvement, homelessness, and chronic health conditions will help expand poverty research to cover those at the very bottom of the socioeconomic ladder and thereby illuminate channels for the development of meaningful support services and policy reform to reach the most severely deprived.

In our study of hypermarginalized HIV-positive people's experiences interfacing with an array of social institutions, we developed a methodological model of close collaboration between a clinical social worker and two ethnographers. The social worker provided intensive case management to research participants with the primary objectives of engaging them in regular medical care with an HIV specialist who was part of the research team, increasing adherence to HIV medications, and facilitating the continuity of HIV treatment as participants cycled in and out of correctional facilities. A corollary goal of the improvement in HIV-related health was to help stabilize participants by connecting them to permanent housing, government entitlements (such as Supplemental Security Income, or SSI), and other social services. The social worker therefore worked closely with participants to access and navigate what the medical anthropologist Kim Hopper has termed the "institutional circuits" that populate the lives of the poor: courts, jails, prisons, hospitals, shelters, welfare offices, and the like (Hopper et al. 1997). This process permitted the ethnographers to follow the trajectories of participants step by step as they entered, occupied, and exited a gamut of social institutions; indeed, the collaboration with the social worker provided access to information and situations typically beyond the reach of nonclinician researchers, such as legal documents, medical reports, and hospital examining rooms. We thus were able to undertake our inquiry from an embedded, organizational perspective that shed light on the specific sites of fragmentation within critical services and the implications of this fragmentation for the hypermarginalized.

Intervention research is well established in social work, as is the use of qualitative methods to inform social work practices, and much research on poverty is generated by ethnographers within the discipline of social welfare (Fairbanks 2009; Floersch, Longhofer, and Suskewicz 2014; Gilgun and Sands 2012). We therefore make no pretense that the mere combination of social work and ethnography was particularly innovative. However, our approach introduced an unconventional third party into the traditional researcher-participant dyad—an embedded social worker who through the provision of practical assistance and therapeutic support to participants served as a bridge between them and the ethnographers, while simultaneously becoming a "key informant" through her own participation in navigating the correctional, medical, and social institutions tasked with managing the poor.

We organize this article around the elaboration of three primary strengths afforded by this hybrid social work–ethnography approach. First, we discuss how the social worker's clinical skills and therapeutic background enabled her to form sustainable relationships with participants that could weather periods when they suffered severe mental health deterioration in response to the overwhelming stressors of extreme poverty. Although ethnographic research on people with mental health issues exists (Biehl and Eskerod 2005; Scheper-Hughes 1981), social scientists generally are underequipped to handle psychosis and other serious mental illness or mental health crises among participants, especially when mental health is not the primary focus of a study and the researchers are not clinically trained. In the face of significant mental distress, this lack of preparedness can easily translate into psychological and physical dangers for participants and researchers alike. Having a clinician who was the primary point of study contact permitted us to remain in touch with mentally ill participants through therapeutically supportive means. Ethically, this enabled us to assist and advocate for highly vulnerable participants during times of particularly dire need. Methodologically, our approach permitted us to gather data on participants' encounters with mental health services and, perhaps more importantly, with correctional and social service institutions that were not equipped to meet their mental health needs. These data greatly contributed to our substantive findings about the severe impact of organizational irrationality and disjuncture on people for whom mental health is one among many critical issues.

Second, researchers working with the hypermarginalized must continually confront moments of crisis as participants struggle for survival. As ethnographers such as Philippe Bourgois, Jeffrey Schonberg, and Teresa Gowan have shown, help can be extended during these moments with sensitivity, generosity, and urgency, particularly when time has been invested in developing strong rapport and trust in relationships (Bourgois 1995; Bourgois and Schonberg 2009; Gowan 2010). Incorporating a social worker into the research team provides a formal structure for clinically informed crisis intervention, with the critical advantage of gaining access to medical records, legal files, and other sources of important information that typically are not available to ethnographers but that can be leveraged to assist participants. We elucidate how this advantage played out in our study and reflect on the opportunities offered by these moments to analyze crisis situations from a cross-institutional perspective by giving us an understanding of how information gaps can disrupt continuity of care for suffering people. In addition, our experiences responding to participants' crises raised broader questions regarding the hegemonic "non-intervention" mandate present in much social science research. We grapple with the broader ramifications of a particular form of clinically trained intervention as not only ethically mandated but as central to enhancing the means and lenses through which we understand complex social problems.

Finally, we expound on how the ethnographer–social worker–participant triad reorients the researcher's gaze from perpetual observation of catastrophe and misery to active documentation of attempts to mobilize social service resources, obtain physical and mental health care, and undertake other supportive mediation. Intervening to achieve well-being and assessing better ways to do so are commonplace in clinical social work, which takes human suffering as its starting point and applies itself to relieving this distress (Brandell 2010; Wachholz and Mullay 1997). By contrast, other social science disciplines concentrate on describing, correlating, explaining, or theorizing human suffering as the primary analytic object: the conditions that produce it, the behaviors in which it manifests, and its impact on relationships and institutions such as family life or the economy. We would argue that this tight analytic focus on a "suffering subject" (Lopez 2014; Robbins 2013) and the mandate to not intervene can limit research findings and mask a deeper level of complexity.

The vast majority of the participants in our study were disconnected from the services they desperately needed because, at first glance, they had no mailing address or consistent phone number, they missed appointments, and they struggled to obtain and keep track of documents. However, once the social worker actively intervened to resolve these barriers, massive institutional irrationalities and dysfunctions continued to block participants' access to health care, housing, SSI, and other resources. Helping people through the first steps of connecting to services permitted us to comprehend much more clearly the underlying structural forces at work in their institutional encounters. Thus, applying a social science theoretical lens to the clinical intervention process enriched our analysis of the (mis)management of suffering by social institutions by giving us a unique vantage point from which to, in the words of professor of urban studies Robert Fairbanks (2012, 547), "elucidate translations of policy mandates in local contexts, [and chart] local variations and complex pathways as well as edges, weak spots, contestations, contradictions, and sites of breakdown/failure." As such, the knowledge we gained in our study enabled us to locate the mechanisms through which structural violence operates for hypermarginalized individuals at the specific junctures where organizational irrationality intersects with already entrenched and complex adversity. Our thinking thus advanced from striving to understand how and why people suffer in the abandoned spaces of the city to investigating what happens when they are brought into contact with the front line of the institutions that handle the impoverished.

METHODS

Our data come from the qualitative component of a larger study of HIV testing and treatment among people who use drugs and are involved with the criminal justice system. For the main study (led by authors Alex Kral and Jennifer Lorvick), we conducted a quantitative survey with and provided HIV testing to 2,424 people in Oakland, California, who were age eighteen or over and had used crack cocaine or injected any drug in the previous six months. Participants were recruited through targeted sampling methods, with a highly experienced outreach worker conducting face-to-face recruitment in public settings (Kral et al. 2010; Watters and Biernacki 1989; Watters, Cheng, and Kral 1997). The study had two phases. First, all participants received rapid HIV testing and counseling and completed a computer-assisted personal interview administered by a trained interviewer. Next, those who tested HIV-positive (the majority of whom were already aware of their HIV status) were offered enrollment in an intervention study. HIV-positive participants who were not receiving HIV medical care were offered participation in an intensive case management intervention. Those who were already receiving medical care for HIV were enrolled as a comparison group. Both the intervention and the comparison group participants returned for a survey and blood draw (for future HIV viral load testing) every three months until the study's conclusion in December 2014. In our analyses, we determined that the comparison group was too different from the intervention group to draw any meaningful conclusions; the fact that comparison group participants were already enrolled in HIV care at baseline tended to indicate that they had also managed to connect to basic services, apply for and receive SSI, and take other steps toward stability. Therefore, in this article we discuss only the intervention group.

A total of nineteen participants were enrolled in the intervention between November 2011 and August 2013; all of them received intensive case management through December 2014. Participants included four cis-gender women, two transgender women, and thirteen men. At the time of study enrollment, participants' ages ranged from twenty-six to sixty-five, with five people in their forties and seven people age fifty or older. Sixteen identified themselves as African American, one as Latino, one as Native American and African American, and one as white. No one had stable housing: a dozen people slept in parks, on the sidewalk, in homeless encampments, or in cars, and the rest were temporarily staying in shelters, transitional living facilities, and family members' residences. Three participants were illiterate. Extreme poverty and social dislocation were not new to this group; during a bio-psycho-social intake questionnaire, the social worker (author Christina Powers) documented extensive histories of trauma, addiction, incarceration, mental illness, and victimization for the majority of participants. The overall portrait of our participants that emerged was one of current life conditions being an extension of decades of intense hardship.

The amount of time the social worker spent with each participant varied widely depending on the individual's need in general (for example, people with a higher level of cognitive functioning often required less hands-on help than those with a lower level of ability) and on the given time (for example, less time was spent with participants during their incarceration, but more time was spent with them immediately after their release from custody). During periods of high need, it was not uncommon for her to spend several hours a day three to four days a week with one participant. In contrast to many social workers who are tethered to a specific office, our case management model supported the social worker's full liberty to literally "meet people where they were at"—which included homeless encampments, parks, and street corners—and to accompany them to medical, social service, and other appointments. She also had authorization to visit them when they were incarcerated in the local county jail in order to develop treatment plans for when they would be released. She kept case notes on each interaction with a participant and met weekly with a clinical supervisor who co-signed the case notes and provided supervisory guidance and the opportunity to confer about specific participants or issues. In addition, she held weekly case conferences with an HIV medical provider who was a part of the research team in order to discuss participants' health issues, such as medication adherence, psychiatric developments, and emergency room visits.

Ethnographic data collection (conducted by authors Megan Comfort and Andrea Lopez) began several months after the case management intervention began. We had an initial sense of the serious challenges facing our participants, nearly all of whom were "triple diagnosed" with HIV, serious mental illness, and substance use issues. We also understood from conversations with the social worker how important it was that participants learn to trust her as a clinician, and we hesitated to introduce extra parties into their interactions for fear of confusing participants regarding her role as their primary support person and advocate. We therefore began our qualitative inquiry by gathering data from the social worker herself in the form of weekly, audio-recorded debriefs during which she reviewed her caseload person by person and her calendar day by day with the ethnographers, a procedure we followed for the duration of the case management intervention. In addition to these meetings, several times a week the social worker emailed the ethnographers updates on participants and key events as well as photographs of locales, signs, forms, and other items of interest.

As the social worker's relationships with the participants solidified, she began introducing the ethnographers to those who were mentally and physically well enough to handle the presence of an additional person. All participants had signed consent to be in the research study when they were enrolled in the intervention (and they were regularly reminded of the research component when they completed their quarterly interviews and blood draws), but at this first meeting the ethnographer would conduct an additional informed consent procedure. She would explain what participant observation would entail, clearly establish that she was not a case manager or therapist, and emphasize that the participant could ask her to leave at any time or refuse to participate in any recorded interviews without jeopardizing the receipt of case management services. The ethnographers then made arrangements for one of them to periodically accompany the participant and the social worker on case management–related outings, such as medical appointments.

The degree of direct contact between the ethnographers and the participants varied considerably, guided by the social worker's assessment of a participant's overall mental health stability and of how well the participant could differentiate between the ethnographer's role and the social worker's role; that is, the social worker ensured that the participant did not see the ethnographer as an additional case manager, a view that could have jeopardized feelings of trust and emotional safety if expectations were not met. For those who chronically struggled with serious mental disorders, our protocol was to gather data exclusively through the social worker's report and not risk further disrupting their mental fragility by direct observation or burden these participants with ethnographic interviewing. There were eight participants whom the ethnographers did not meet: four of them were either nearly always incarcerated or in very sporadic contact with the social worker during the study period. In the remaining eleven cases, the ethnography encompassed outreach visits, running errands such as obtaining a money order or picking up a prescription, and attending medical appointments, including mammograms and fittings for dentures and for a prosthetic eye, as well as routine HIV care. Over time, one or more in-depth recorded interviews were conducted with seven participants whom the social worker assessed to be mentally stable (for instance, not veering toward psychosis or paranoia); sometimes these interviews focused on a specific topic of analytical interest, and other times they were used as opportunities to gather more general narratives about a participant's past or present. Importantly, calibrating our ethnographic engagement was an iterative process; as called for by each participant's dynamic psychological state, we alternated between periods of initiating direct contact and periods of stepping back.

WEATHERING SEVERE MENTAL HEALTH DETERIORATION

Multiple participants in our study experienced episodes of psychological deterioration to the point of profound disorientation and psychosis. Often these episodes were characterized by auditory hallucinations (hearing voices, receiving messages from the television or radio) and extreme paranoia. Fluctuations in mental health contribute to the attrition of hypermarginalized individuals in research; the loss of contact with "reality" can easily result in a participant losing contact with researchers, depleting study samples of people who experience severe mental health difficulties. In addition, interacting with someone in such a compromised state without adequate clinical training to address mental health vulnerability raises serious ethical questions and poses risks to both the participant and the researcher.

For instance, Charlie[1] was forty-six years old and had an AIDS diagnosis when he enrolled in the study in June 2012.[2] Upon his release from jail a month earlier, a psychiatrist had diagnosed him with social phobia, paranoid-type schizophrenia, generalized anxiety, depressive disorder, cannabis and cocaine dependence, and alcohol abuse. Charlie was living in a homeless shelter when he joined the study, and two months later he moved into a transitional living facility for former prisoners. He reported having spent the majority of his adult life behind bars and never having had stable housing outside of a correctional facility, in large part because his felony record caused his applications to be rejected. With the social worker's help, he applied and was approved for subsidized housing through Housing Opportunities for Persons with AIDS (HOPWA); he moved into a modest studio apartment in January 2013. Lacking a bed, he slept on a donated comforter that he folded into the size of a cot, remarking that he was used to sleeping on small surfaces from his time in jail. The first time he entered his apartment, he stopped by the building manager's office and told him he was going upstairs, then became flustered when the manager informed him that he could come and go as he pleased. "I thought I had to check in," he mumbled sheepishly to the social worker.

Despite the progress Charlie made in obtaining housing, the social worker observed a progressive decompensation of his mental health in late 2012 and early 2013. Charlie tried to self-medicate his intense anxiety by increasing his drug use, which in turn gave him reason to avoid checking in with his parole officer. He was reincarcerated briefly in early February for the technical parole violation of failing to report his new address and released on March 1 without a supply of his HIV or psychiatric medications.[3] He returned to his studio apartment but was jailed again on May 14 on new charges, which were subsequently dropped. This time, he did not receive HIV or psychiatric medications during the two weeks he was incarcerated or upon release. In late June, Charlie experienced a psychotic break, believing that the police were spying on him via a microchip implanted in his body, a drone that followed him, and an airplane that hovered over his residence. He stopped entering his apartment through the building doorways and instead climbed through a window using a ladder, thinking that the hallway outside of his

---

1. All names are pseudonyms. We thank "Cadillac" for suggesting names for this purpose.

2. Acquired immunodeficiency syndrome (AIDS) is a late stage in HIV disease. Taking HIV medications can maintain the virus in a latent stage for decades, during which HIV-positive people do not experience symptoms of illness. If someone with an AIDS diagnosis does not receive medical treatment, life expectancy falls to one to three years.

3. Under the Eighth Amendment, jails and prisons are required to provide health care, including prescription medications, to incarcerated people. Policies for providing a supply of medication for people upon release from custody vary according to the jurisdiction of the correctional facility. The policy for the county jail in which our study participants were detained was to provide a thirty-day supply of medications for people leaving the jail. Nonetheless, we documented dozens of instances when people were discharged without any of their prescribed medications.

door was under surveillance. Subsequently, he started sleeping in the bushes in order to avoid the apartment altogether because he worried the police would find him there. He was reincarcerated yet again, and the social worker received a call from an attorney who during a legal visit had found Charlie hiding behind a chair with a correctional officer laughing at him. When the social worker visited him in jail shortly thereafter, Charlie had not received any HIV or psychiatric care during the two weeks he had been incarcerated, despite his pleas for medications to help make the drone go away. He was covered in sores from an untreated rash that he scratched until he bled, and he sobbed in distress as they spoke.

Being able to chart this series of events was critical in building our understanding of what constitutes "stable housing" for those whose existence is characterized by severe deprivation not only of economic resources but also of mental and physical wellness. In the absence of psychiatric treatment, and with the omnipresence of criminal justice surveillance, Charlie's mind transformed a safe place to call his own into a treacherous site where he felt exposed and hunted. His struggles clearly indicated his need for a therapeutically and medically supportive living environment as well as a respite from the unrelenting cycle of parole check-ins, police stops, and jail stays. Charlie's ordeal was also instructive for problematizing the concept of correctional settings as "public health opportunities" (Glaser and Greifinger 1993), given his clear need for medical intervention and the lack of response to his anguish when he was behind bars. Yet following a terrified man for the purpose of documenting his trajectory while he was caught in a web of hallucinations would have posed significant and potentially insurmountable ethical issues, and doing so could have compounded the already enormous suffering he was experiencing. Interacting with an ethnographer whom Charlie knew to be someone who was recording his conversations and taking notes on his activities could have aggravated his paranoia, and it would have been logical for him to view the researcher as another part of a malevolent surveillance system. Charlie might even have become violent if he felt the need to protect himself from what he perceived as a tightening circle of intrusion, or if he experienced auditory hallucinations commanding him to strike out. However, avoiding contact with Charlie during a time when he clearly needed intensive help would have left him even more exposed to harm, including eviction, victimization, or self-inflicted injury. In addition, his psychosis was jeopardizing his recently acquired and highly sought-after housing, without which he would be subject to more health and mental health risks.

As a clinician providing intensive case management, the social worker had a clear role that was recognized both by Charlie and by various institutional actors during this tumultuous time; as such, she was able to advocate on behalf of her client while also closely observing his experiences and communicating these observations to the research team. In contrast to ethnographers, who typically seek to limit the impact they have on situations in order to enter as fully as possible into participants' social worlds, a social worker strives to build a "therapeutic relationship" with participants to effect changes in their perspectives and behaviors (McWilliams 2004). Using techniques such as cognitive behavioral therapy, motivational interviewing, and trauma-informed care, a social worker creates a "holding environment" for the relationship in which the individual can feel physically and psychologically safe (Altman 2009; Thompson and Cotlove 2005). For Charlie, this sense of a safe connection to the social worker persisted throughout his mental health decompensation, as evidenced when he asked permission to call her from jail, periodically dropped by her office to request help, and explained to her in detail the various ways in which he believed he was being followed by the police, his strategies for avoiding them, and what the voices he heard were saying to him. From an ethical standpoint, not only did the social worker's presence not incur more risk for Charlie, but she also provided support and worked with him to create a safety plan to mitigate further risks to his well-being.

Importantly, other institutional actors also reached out to the social worker during Charlie's travails: she received calls from or met with the manager of his apartment building, his community-based HIV doctor, the coordinator for HIV care in the county jail, and the attorney who found Charlie hiding behind a chair during the jail visit. Due to Health Insurance Portability and Accountability Act (HIPAA) protections, these interactions were only possible because earlier in their work together the social worker had obtained signed release forms from Charlie giving her permission to communicate with each person in her role as a clinician. Again, these contacts were multifunctional; they served the research purposes of keeping track of Charlie's whereabouts and also provided ways of verifying specific details of his experiences. (For example, the building manager discussed having found the ladder Charlie used to climb into his apartment, and the jail HIV coordinator confirmed that he had not received his medications.) In addition, having access to these institutional actors during a chaotic and troubled time provided the social worker with information and leverage that she could use to help Charlie (for example, asking his community-based HIV doctor to call the jail HIV coordinator regarding his medications, or negotiating with his building manager to avoid eviction). The social worker therefore served as a link between various silo-ed institutions with which Charlie interfaced—a link that simply did not exist in the normal operations of the institutions, despite the overlapping social problems that Charlie was facing. The social worker worked to establish relationships in different institutional arenas in order to facilitate the critical ongoing communication that service providers acknowledged was necessary, but was rarely seen, to stabilize someone with Charlie's complex profile.

INTERVENING IN CRISIS SITUATIONS

Living in a state of perpetual crisis often characterizes deep poverty, and many crises are related to health. From November 2011 through December 2014, five of the nineteen people enrolled in the case management intervention were hospitalized for illness, two were hospitalized for injuries suffered when they were assaulted (one was assaulted and hospitalized multiple times), four were placed on involuntary psychiatric custodial holds, two overdosed on heroin (and survived), and one was shot (and also survived; in total, seven participants had been shot in their lifetime). In addition, fourteen were incarcerated at least once; ten of them returned to jail over ten times.

Studying people who are cycling in and out of correctional, medical, and psychiatric facilities while undergoing life-threatening crises has prompted us to revisit the principles of ethical research and our responsibilities to participants. Institutional review boards (IRBs) typically consider potential "harm" in research as a risk stemming from the research itself—for example, a participant's discomfort with an interview question, a breach of confidentiality, or a side effect from a drug. More than once, however, we found ourselves challenged to intervene on behalf of a participant to protect him or her from harm from a source external to the research. For ethnographers, the imperative to take action under these circumstances can be clouded by questions as to whether it is scientifically appropriate to involve oneself in directing events that are under empirical study. Too much interference may disrupt the patterns and processes being investigated, and ethnographers who do intervene find themselves having to justify their acts (Rios 2011). Further, the likelihood that even ethnographers who are steeped in "applied" approaches to research lack the clinical skills to interact with a population with acute medical and mental health issues makes the question of "intervention" much more ethically complicated with hypermarginalized populations.

Social workers begin from an entirely different point of departure: their presence in a client's life is organized around intervention, and they are equipped with clear guidelines about the ethics of doing so as well as models of practices that have been implemented and analyzed in the discipline (National Association of Social Workers 2008). In our study, the frequency with which crises arose that required clinical intervention affirmed for us that in research with hypermarginalized participants, a protocol for the full "protection of research subjects" ideally would include a highly trained and experienced clinician with competency in crisis management.

A particularly salient example is Hook, who was twenty-six years old and had known he was HIV-positive for three years when he enrolled in the study in May 2012. A sharp dresser with a compact build, Hook had been released from San Quentin State Prison ten days prior to his first meeting with the social worker. He also had an extensive history of mental health issues, with diagnoses of schizoaffective disorder and bipolar disorder and regular auditory hallucinations of voices that he called "the committee." He described himself as "raised by the State of California": he was placed in foster care at age five, entered the juvenile justice system at fourteen, and had not spent more than three consecutive months out of correctional facilities during his adulthood. Ironically, the state was no longer officially responsible for Hook. He had been "realigned" from state parole to county probation as a "non-violent, non-serious, non-sexual offender" under relatively new legislation that aimed to reduce the California prison population.[4] In an interview, Hook expressed bewilderment at being included in this group: "I'm a true violent offender! I've never been arrested for drugs or anything, just violence." Being transferred out of the state system had made Hook ineligible for any of the mental health services or housing resources provided to parolees.

Four days after enrolling in our study, Hook was shot in the arm while standing outside of the homeless shelter where he had been staying. His assailant was a man confined to a wheelchair owing to his own gunshot injury years prior. The attack was captured by video surveillance, but despite camera footage and a name, no arrest was ever made. Hook was required to move out of the shelter after he was released from the hospital because staff feared that the perpetrator, who had been seen hanging out in the neighborhood and had specifically targeted Hook, might return to look for him. Two weeks later, during a meeting with the social worker, Hook requested that she take him to the county psychiatric hospital because he feared he was having a mental breakdown. After several hours there, Hook reported that he felt better, and because he did not meet the technical criteria for a "5150" involuntary hold, he was released from the hospital.[5] The social worker took him directly to a transitional housing program for former prisoners and negotiated to have him admitted. If she had not been there, it is unclear where he would have slept that night, since the hospital did not have mechanisms in place to ensure that a person has somewhere to stay when released.

Over the next four months, Hook was in and out of touch with the social worker as he resumed using crack cocaine, was expelled from the transitional housing program, lost thirty pounds from his muscular frame, and stopped taking his HIV and psychiatric medications. During a visit with Hook at his mother's residence in mid-August, the social worker noted signs of an impending psychotic break, but he was unwilling to accompany her to see his doctor. In late September, Hook called the social worker from the county hospital where he was being treated for an as-yet unidentified illness, and she visited him there. The hospital staff reported that he had been threatening them and they had called security multiple times; that night Hook left the hospital against medical advice. The next day a physician called the social worker to tell her that Hook had been diagnosed with methicillin-resistant staphylococcus aureus (MRSA) in his bloodstream and that it would probably be swiftly fatal if left untreated. The social worker received this phone call only because Hook had signed the release of information form, which allowed communication between her and his doctors.

4. California Assembly Bill 109 is referred to by the California Department of Corrections and Rehabilitation as the "cornerstone of California's solution to reduce overcrowding, costs, and recidivism." Implementation of "realignment," as it is colloquially known, began in October 2011.

5. Under section 5150 of the California Welfare and Institutions Code, a clinician or a criminal justice authority can confine people against their will for seventy-two hours if they are considered to be a danger to themselves or others owing to a mental health disorder. The term "5150" is commonly used colloquially to refer to being placed on such a hold (for example, "She can't come today, she was fifty-one-fifty-ed") and as a synonym for "crazy" (for example, "When he told me I couldn't have what I wanted, I went fifty-one-fifty").

Even knowing that the infection would likely be fatal, without the social worker, the hospital had no formal institutional procedures to locate Hook to inform him of his grave situation.

In the social worker's clinical evaluation, Hook's mental health had decompensated to a point that he was unable to understand the gravity of his medical situation and therefore had not made an informed decision to refuse treatment when he left the hospital. After consultation with the full research team, she and an outreach worker who had known Hook for years through the homeless shelter went to look for him. They found him at a house known to be frequented by drug users, and the social worker explained the MRSA infection to him and his risk of sudden death. Drawing on established therapeutic models of intervention, she framed returning to the hospital for treatment with her support as a proactive choice that Hook could make to save his life. He decided that he would return, and upon arrival the social worker helped ensure that he was readmitted immediately rather than forced to wait in the extremely busy and chaotic emergency room. Soon thereafter, he nonetheless began exhibiting psychotic symptoms and acting menacing toward the medical personnel, at which point he was deemed a threat to others and forcibly restrained under the 5150 code by three deputies (two of whom he recognized from the county jail).[6] The social worker was allowed to be by Hook's bedside once he had been administered antipsychotic medications, and she remained there into the evening, advocating for his needs and supporting him emotionally. When she went to visit him the next day, he was calm and no longer restrained, although he had been moved to a respiratory isolation unit and the social worker had to don a hospital gown, gloves, and facial mask before entering. An infectious disease specialist spoke with her and said that the MRSA had spread to Hook's lungs and would require between four and eight weeks of treatment with intravenous antibiotics.

As with Charlie, Hook's trajectory from prison through the homeless shelter to the streets with several loops through the emergency room provides rich data for analyzing correctional, social, and medical systems from the vantage point of the extremely poor. From being ejected from the shelter for being a gunshot victim to being allowed to walk away from life-saving medical treatment while submerged in psychosis, Hook's repeated encounters with "care" institutions deepened his deprivation and placed him at high risk of death. In retrospect, it is hard for us to fathom what our experience with Hook would have been like without the social worker guiding us. From the early days of his study involvement, Hook repeatedly cycled through medical and psychiatric settings that would have been off limits to someone who was not a clinician and did not have formal clearance under HIPAA to be privy to confidential information. When the physician notified the social worker of Hook's MRSA diagnosis and the danger it posed, he was only able to do so because of this clearance. The social worker's clinical understanding of Hook's mental health issues alerted her to the need to intervene quickly, and she possessed the therapeutic skills necessary to do so, along with on-the-ground knowledge of where he might be located. Chillingly, the most likely scenario for Hook's study participation had the social worker not been a part of the team would have been a rapid loss of contact as his psychosis set in, followed by news of his death from an untreated MRSA infection.

TURNING THE LENS ON POVERTY-PROCESSING INSTITUTIONS

Upon entering the study, twelve participants had been in correctional facilities within the last year, but their contact with other institutions was minimal. Only one person possessed an official California state identity (ID) card, three had makeshift correctional ID cards that identified them as parolees, and fifteen had no form of ID. Apart from one person who was able to work (tellingly, the same person who had an official ID), all participants were eligible for some form of government support, yet three were receiving nothing at all, and nine

---

6. For a discussion of the overlap of criminal justice authorities in correctional facilities and public hospitals, see the sociologist Armando Lara-Millán's (2014) study of emergency room waiting areas.

were receiving substantially less than they were due (for example, only food stamps when they were eligible for monthly income through SSI).

Impoverished people, especially those with the compounded issues of mental illness and drug use, are often held responsible for their inability to connect with social services, and indeed, it can be difficult to determine whether individual issues, such as illiteracy or a tendency to miss appointments, prevent them from accessing resources. In our study, the early steps of case management typically centered on securing basic survival needs, such as making doctor appointments, obtaining a state ID card, seeking a shelter bed, applying for SSI, and connecting to resources such as food pantries, free meal programs, and subsidized bus passes. The social worker's repeated undertaking of these activities—often multiple times with the same individual, as even brief incarcerations or hospitalizations resulted in lost ID cards and derailed application processes—provided the opportunity to observe how even a skilled social welfare professional working carefully to follow bureaucratic procedures, submit required paperwork, and attend mandatory appointments continually encountered major setbacks and institutional barriers.

Returning to Charlie's story provides an apt example. Upon release from his jail stay for the parole violation of not reporting the address of his new subsidized apartment, Charlie and the social worker attended a check-in meeting with his parole officer. At this meeting, they were informed that Charlie would not be allowed to use his apartment as his address of record for parole because it was in the county adjacent to the one in which he was required by parole to live. The social worker explained that Charlie would be homeless if he could not stay in the HOPWA housing and asked if special accommodations could be made, such as applying for a transfer of Charlie's county of parole. The parole officer refused and reiterated that Charlie would be considered to have violated his parole if he occupied his apartment.

The social worker's account of this conversation was invaluable for instructing us about the significant housing challenges faced by parolees (not to mention challenges faced by drug-using, mentally ill, HIV-positive parolees). The parole officer's unwillingness to help problem-solve the conundrum that a man could be condemned to homelessness when housing had been made available to him because of a medical condition, even when asked for such help by a case manager working with the parolee, brought into sharp relief the Kafka-esque ways in which highly bureaucratic systems create additional hardships for the people under their control (Lipsky 1980). The total disconnect between the parole administration and the low-income housing system, even when the social worker attempted to mediate between them, rendered what should have been a milestone in improving Charlie's quality of life into a further barrier to his well-being. Not incidentally, this conflict fueled Charlie's perceptions that the police were hunting him and greatly complicated the social worker's efforts to help him manage his mental health: whereas the microchip, drone, and airplane were hallucinations, it was utterly (sur)real that he was prohibited to reside in an apartment leased to him and for which he was paying rent, especially considering that he had been chronically homeless and adequate, affordable housing in the San Francisco Bay Area is extremely hard to come by.

Ideally, partnerships between parole officers and social workers could advance common goals of helping marginalized people obtain housing, access health care, find employment, and reconnect to family life. This possibility could occasionally be glimpsed when an "old-school" parole officer facilitated the social worker's request to refer a participant to drug treatment, as would have been more likely to happen in the past, when community supervision professionals commonly had a background in social work (Lynch 2000; Simon 1993). More often than not in our study, however, we documented not only a disintegration of the potential alliance of social and parole services but outright contention, typically when parole officers disallowed housing options or threatened reincarceration for drug use relapse and the social worker could no longer be confident that information she possessed would not be used against the parolee. These communication breakdowns generated additional work for the social worker, who had to help participants develop strategies for managing the problems stemming from parole restrictions, which also often affected others in the participant's network.[7]

Cadillac's case is illustrative. Cadillac was fifty-one years old when he enrolled in the study in September 2012. He had been diagnosed with HIV while in jail in 1994, the same year he was viciously assaulted with a baseball bat and suffered a traumatic brain injury that left him with significant cognitive impairment. Like Charlie, Cadillac had a viable residence that was outside of his county of parole—the house of his oldest sister, Sherry. Sherry cared deeply about Cadillac and struck up a regular, mutually supportive communication with the social worker by text and phone as soon as Cadillac signed consent for them to be in touch. In the autumn of 2013, when her brother was released after one of his many jail stays, she offered to let him live in a comfortable "in-law" unit connected to her house while he attended an outpatient drug treatment program during the day. The parole officer denied authorization for this arrangement because Sherry lived in a county that was adjacent to Cadillac's county of parole, not in it. Cadillac then turned to his sister Linda, whose residence was in his assigned county and therefore would be acceptable to the parole officer. Linda was less financially secure than Sherry and had struggled recently with her own drug addiction; nevertheless, she hesitantly agreed to let her brother sleep in the living room, all the while expressing misgivings about the destabilizing impact he might have on her sobriety. Soon thereafter, the parole officer came to the residence for a routine check, but he forgot to bring Linda's apartment number. When Linda returned home from work, she was mortified to learn that the parole officer had knocked on nearly every one of her neighbors' doors looking for her brother. Furious, she called the parole officer and said that Cadillac could no longer live with her. The parole officer retorted that being homeless was a violation of Cadillac's parole, and if he no longer had a residential address, a warrant would be issued for his arrest. In the wake of this conversation, the social worker and Sherry were caught in a flurry of attempts to find an available shelter bed in Cadillac's county of parole while trying also to persuade Linda not to put her brother out until he had a place to go, especially given that her embarrassment and anger were a result of the parole officer's actions, not Cadillac's. At her limit and worried about her own health, Linda refused. The shelters were full. The social worker strategized with Cadillac how to safely store and remember to take his HIV medications when living outside. And Sherry painstakingly assembled a backpack for her brother with clean socks, disinfectant wipes, lip balm, a blanket, and other survival items for life on the streets.

In analyzing the penal regulation of poverty in neoliberal societies, the sociologist Loïc Wacquant points to how the social ills afflicting the destitute are cast as problems to be managed by the disciplinary, regulatory "Right Hand" institutions of Pierre Bourdieu's "bureaucratic field," and he notes that police, courts, and corrections figure prominently among these state actors (Bourdieu 1992, 1993; Wacquant 2010, 2014). Charlie's and Cadillac's housing struggles are apt examples of Right Hand management: despite vigorous efforts by the social worker and their family members to connect them to supportive "Left Hand" institutions, the final authority rested with the parole officers. Yet, even when participants were handled by hospitals and social service programs, the chronic draining of funding from Left Hand institutions under neoliberal governance left them exposed to neglectful, irrational, and punishing treatment.

Take the case of Crystal, who was thirty-five years old in March 2012 when she joined the study. At that time, Crystal was on probation and parole, although she spent the vast ma-

---

7. Though we have discussed the issue of confidentiality at various points in this article, we want to reemphasize here that any communication or collaboration conducted between the social worker and the parole officer was done by the request of the clients and with a signed release form. In accordance with clause 1.07(c) of the National Association of Social Workers (NASW) Code of Ethics, the social worker disclosed the "least amount of information necessary to achieve the desired purpose" per the client's request and with a signed release.

jority of her time in the study in jail; over the ensuing months, we documented her being released and reincarcerated in as few as four days. A survivor of a childhood and adolescence saturated with physical, sexual, and emotional abuse, Crystal had been living on and working the streets since age eleven and had been using crack and heroin since fourteen. Her social network had remained relatively insular and continued to include a man several decades older than her with whom she had been sexually involved since arriving on the streets and who regularly assaulted her. After one attack, Crystal was found bloody, disoriented, and wearing only her underwear by a passing motorist, who stopped to help and phoned the social worker at Crystal's request. The social worker called an ambulance and met Crystal at the hospital, where they spent the afternoon and evening waiting for examinations and X-ray results. Around 10:00 PM, Crystal's wounds were determined not to need further treatment and she was discharged. The hospital had provided her with a standard-issue gown, but no other clothes. Because Crystal had not wanted to press charges against her attacker (which she fatalistically told the social worker would do nothing more than put her at risk for retaliation), she was not provided with a placement in a domestic violence shelter. She thus was sent out into the dead of night barefoot, in a hospital gown and underwear, with no money, no ID, and no place to go.

The social worker managed to track down a women's shelter that agreed to admit Crystal that night despite her lack of an ID card as required (the social worker provided this from a photocopy the next day, along with clothes and shoes for Crystal) and her decision not to press charges (which became grounds for Crystal being asked to leave the shelter several days later). Had Crystal been on her own, she would have had to figure out a way to traverse the five miles between the hospital and the general area where she usually stayed, and when she arrived there—bruised, exhausted, barely dressed, and barefoot—she would probably have been dependent on her assailant for help, since he was her primary social connection and she had no other resources. When spelled out in detail, such institutional abandonment plainly reads as egregious and stunningly counterproductive. In Crystal's case, however, employees at an overcrowded public hospital were contending with limited resources in a chaotic environment, and they did not violate formal protocol regarding the minimal requirements for intervention (Ansell 2011). This situation nonetheless contributed to the multiple compounded physical and psychological assaults Crystal endured.

Yeheskel Hasenfeld, a professor of social welfare, distinguishes between "people processing" and "people changing" institutions: the former have relatively short-term contact with clients and deploy their activities on the boundaries of the organization, while the latter sustain long-term contact with their wards (students, patients, prisoners) and locate their activities within the center of the organization (Hasenfeld 1972). Over the two and a half years of our study, we observed innumerable instances of what could be called institutional "poverty-processing," whereby standard procedures, bureaucratic adherence to regulations, and other forms of "business as usual" worked against, jeopardized, or failed to protect someone in need of care to the point of effacing his or her personhood. There was the time when Crystal, who had been creating a plan with the social worker to enter a residential drug treatment program immediately upon her release from jail so that she would not resume her substance use, was suddenly set free without advance warning late on the Wednesday afternoon before Thanksgiving. Unsurprisingly, Crystal had relapsed when the social worker returned to work after the four-day weekend. Being released early from jail before a major holiday may on its surface seem compassionate, but it is much more complicated for people facing compounded adversities who do not have family to welcome them home. If there had been established coordination between service providers inside and outside of the jail, it would probably have been determined that early release on a long weekend and the risks posed in terms of drug use and personal safety would actually be *antithetical* to the established treatment plan.

Or consider the saga of PeeWee, who decided to turn himself in for an outstanding warrant as a means of getting sober. He binged on his final stash of drugs, poured his heart out to the social worker during a "last supper" at a fast-food restaurant, and then was paradoxically turned away at the jail because the fingerprint scanning machine was broken and they could not verify his identity. Doggedly returning the next day, he was again refused, this time because the clerk erroneously claimed that there was no warrant issued for him. Two weeks later, on the heels of a drug run that left him gaunt and with open sores on his lips from smoking crack, he asked the social worker to take him to the jail for a third time; there he was finally admitted on the original warrant. This scenario points to the perplexing way in which institutional engagement is unpredictable for this population and policies (or lack thereof) create further instability.

And then there was Moan, who after months of homelessness was notified that he had qualified for subsidized housing and was encouraged to come immediately to look at his new apartment. Hours after viewing the studio, as he gathered his scarce belongings in preparation for moving in the next day, the social worker received a call from an administrator who told her that Moan could not live in the building after all because he had failed the eviction check. Eviction records are commonplace among the extremely poor, whose prior evictions are often due to irregular and unreliable sources of income that must be juggled across multiple competing demands; this blemish then perpetuates their housing instability (Desmond 2012). Indeed, in some more progressive areas (such as certain subsidized housing buildings in San Francisco), eviction history is not weighed in housing eligibility because it is assumed to be one of the major bureaucratic barriers keeping people from securing housing. Despite the social worker's vehement protests, Moan was barred from the apartment building and continued to live on the street. Six months later, he was admitted to a respite bed in a homeless shelter owing to his diminishing health and multiple hospitalizations.

The list of instances of failed institutional coordination and de facto punitive institutional practices we compiled is a long one. There is the common practice of releasing people from county jail in the middle of the night, with no option other than to wait huddled at the bus stop until dawn when public transportation starts running. There is the federal Shelter Plus Care program's requirement that an individual be in a homeless shelter or live on the streets in order to be eligible for a subsidized housing unit; thus, while waiting to ascend the eighteen-month waiting list, applicants are technically not allowed to live with family members or to scrape together a temporary housing option. There is the program's further demand that, after being on its waiting list for a year or longer, homeless people must be reachable by phone and then able to produce scads of documents (including photo ID and proof of income) within one week in order to advance to the next step, even though they are not formally connected to a social worker through the housing program to help them prepare for this hurdle.

Having an embedded social worker allowed us to distinguish the features of poverty-processing institutions from the litany of personal difficulties that are levied against the extremely poor as explanations for their own misery. Before we undertook this research, we and many others were well aware that illiteracy, drug use, mental health crises, and sickness make it hard for impoverished people to follow through on the myriad applications and processes they are obliged to complete in order to receive the basic elements for leading safe, healthy lives, and that those living outside the reach of health and social welfare institutions are tremendously vulnerable (Bourgois 2009; Braveman and Egerter 2008; Phelan et al. 2004; Sidel 1998; Wildeman and Muller 2012). In principle, introducing the case management component should have mitigated or resolved many related obstacles: the social worker's phone was never cut off, she was cognitively equipped to fill out countless forms, she stored original paperwork in her filing cabinet and electronic records in her computer, and her bulging calendar reminded her of every appointment and deadline. These skills and resources did help, to be sure: eight participants were approved for SSI, and two received presumptive SSI benefits for a period of time; nine obtained housing; nearly all saw a doctor, and many began taking HIV medications; several of them managed to spend dramatically longer periods of time outside of correctional facilities before being reincarcerated; and (not to be taken for granted) everyone stayed alive. And yet, for each accomplishment there were multiple setbacks as the social worker and participants navigated the maze of underfunded, rigidly bureaucratized institutions that served more as gatekeepers withholding the protections of social integration than as conduits to those protections. These setbacks would have been challenging for anyone, but in the context of the chronic suffering, mental health crises, and acute health emergencies of our participants, their emotional and physical tolls were even more dire.

CONCLUSION

Through our hybrid approach to studying the experiences of HIV-positive, indigent adults navigating various institutional contexts with the assistance of a clinical social worker, we were able to deeply probe questions of how and why very poor and very sick people continue to be severely deprived of the resources they need. This research yielded substantive findings with concrete policy implications and generated methodological reflections on the ethics of conducting research with hypermarginalized populations. Ethnographically documenting the provision of intensive case management by an experienced clinician permitted us to enrich our analysis with a perspective from the "inside" and to gain information about the precise sticking points, glitches, and breakdowns of institutions rather than having to settle for superficial explanations such as "the patient did not show up for the appointment" or "the client's phone has been disconnected." Directly intervening in participants' lives highlighted that the social worker–participant dyads encountered major obstacles when a single institution could not address the participant's needs beyond a relatively narrow purview and that cross-institutional collaboration was required. Highly salient in these scenarios was organizational irrationality, not only in the inability of single institutions to take a broader perspective on the complex problems that afflicted their patients or clients, but also in the massive disconnect between institutions—to the point that they undermined each other by operating at cross-purposes.

The social worker's efforts were paramount in building our understanding of the irrationality at play. The fact that a skilled professional working full-time to obtain services for her clients by bridging agencies, fostering connections, and trying to reconcile the requirements of multiple entities met with considerable opposition and formidable stumbling blocks forcefully revealed that correctional, medical, and social service institutions have not been designed to be comprehensible and accessible, least of all to hypermarginalized individuals. This tops our list of policy implications stemming from this research: just as university systems are expected to be intelligible to their students and retirement programs provide clear counsel and support to their investors, institutions delivering services to extremely poor people should be obliged to make their procedures understandable to and usable by those who show up on their doorstep. Having social workers be a part of this effort would be ideal, particularly for people who are new to the institution or in crisis, but the widespread need for them could be alleviated if procedures were more transparent, coherent, and explained in clear language. Flexibility with regard to the specific issues of poverty (for example, lacking access to a phone or being unable to make photocopies or fill out complicated forms) is also critical.

Our findings also support the necessity of increasing institutional capacity in public hospitals, social services, and community supervision settings (for example, probation and parole) to more fully serve a hypermarginalized clientele with complex and overlapping needs. Narrow service mandates necessarily lead to "poverty-processing," as there is no way to meaningfully improve the well-being of a severely deprived patient or client by focusing on one problem in isolation. Under these circumstances, overwhelmed service providers may become fatalistic and reduce their assistance to the bare minimum, knowing that their efforts will soon be undone by forces outside of their control. Care and treatment of an individual become reduced to managing the immediate issue at hand as swiftly and economically as possible, without violating rules but also without consideration of other conditions that contribute to his or her suffering. The impoverished are continually processed through the "institutional circuits" (Hopper et al. 1997) that may provide temporary relief but lack the breadth and resources to effect actual change. The resulting frustration often destabilizes the client's health and mental health even further. We can imagine the difference it might have made, for example, had a psychiatrist been included in Hook's treatment team as soon as he was admitted to the hospital with what turned out to be a MRSA infection. With appropriate support and advocacy, he might never have left the hospital against medical advice, and his extended stay for intravenous antibiotics could have provided an opportunity for therapeutic services such as substance use treatment, mental health counseling, and stabilization on antipsychotic medications.

When a "one-stop shop" for comprehensive services is not feasible, it is critical to establish coordination and dialogue across institutions at the local and state levels. In the course of the three years of our study, the social worker was able to establish strong professional ties with several people in key positions at the county jail, Oakland's main homeless shelter, a legal clinic for indigent clients, and a nurse at an HIV clinic. These partnerships provided a glimpse of how efficiently integrated services could operate when there were willing parties on both sides and clients had signed HIPAA releases. For instance, the HIV services coordinator at the county jail, rather than requiring the participant to place a collect call from a public phone monitored by correctional officers, would call the social worker while the participant was in her office to coordinate care, and the three would talk on speakerphone. The homeless shelter coordinator would contact the social worker when a respite bed opened to ask whether a participant was in need. The social worker would alert attorneys at the legal clinic when a participant was incarcerated so that they could schedule a meeting at the jail and applications for housing or government benefits did not get derailed by missed appointments. And the nurse would send a brief update to the social worker after conducting a home visit to let her know if a participant seemed destabilized. Importantly, all of this cooperation occurred informally: the individual actors reached out to each other, obtained the necessary releases, and communicated among themselves without direction from the organizational level to do so. Although highly beneficial to the participants—not to mention a time-saving collegial resource for the professionals—there was neither institutional support for this kind of service integration nor any official mechanisms for creating or sustaining it. When an individual left a job, the collaborative tie was broken, and it was not always possible to reestablish it. Institutional integration therefore must be created with attention to developing formal cross-agency policies, providing training to employees on collaborative protocols, and dedicating adequate financial resources to these processes.

Our hybrid approach not only generated data from an embedded perspective that enriched the policy relevance of our findings but also provided very direct assistance to some people living in deep poverty. Such a methodology is familiar to social work and public health researchers but is less accepted as "scientific" by social scientists, who consider it ethically problematic. There is a school of thought in the social sciences that intervention invalidates findings because the researcher becomes implicated in the processes under study, altering them in ways that might not have "naturally" occurred. We engage this argument on several levels. First, as discussed at length in this article, intervention can move research into new realms of complexity by permitting us to probe beneath the obvious: merely documenting that an illiterate person with mental health issues and a criminal justice record has a hard time filling out the required paperwork for his SSI and housing applications is not particularly innovative or helpful. But realizing that SSI and housing remain elusive to him even with the support of a clinical social worker sheds light on institutional operations, structural violence, and the types of reforms necessary to address hypermarginality. In sum, with an appropriate research design, intervention does not impede our learning but rather helps us learn more.

Second, we must consider the ethics of non-interventionist research with hypermarginalized populations. Is it ethical for us, as individuals with careers, research funds, and informed ideas about how to improve people's lives, to be bystanders documenting other human beings' suffering when we have the option to do otherwise? We take the stance that in the current era of poverty research, scholars should challenge themselves and each other to develop methodologically rigorous and ethically grounded studies that confer concrete benefits on participants, such as linkage to services, direct assistance, and other forms of help. To be sure, the mode of intervention in each study must be tailored to the researchers conducting it and the resources available and designed with extreme caution and sensitivity. Underestimating the level of skill and expertise required to meet the needs of hypermarginalized people risks exacerbating their already entrenched and overwhelming issues. Our experienced clinical social worker was equipped with over a decade of training in the unique needs of this population, trauma-informed care, and crisis intervention. Clearly, graduate students conducting solo fieldwork who have no clinical training should not attempt to provide "case management" simply because they "want to help." Direct services should only be provided with appropriate clinical training and not simply with the intention of "doing good" for research participants.

Scholars at every level of seniority, however, in concert with IRBs, could think about the obligations we may have to participants beyond protecting them from potential harms of the research. Many ethnographers and others conducting field-based studies regularly face this question when participants need a ride, a meal, help finding a service agency's phone number, or some other low-grade favor. Although appropriate responses are usually not codified in the research protocol, it is commonplace for researchers in the field to provide these resources out of feelings of ethical compulsion and social norms of reciprocity, even if they often downplay or do not mention such responses in publications, owing to concerns about scientific acceptability. We encourage more dialogue and openness around these issues, in the vein of the sociologist Victor Rios's (2011) argument that practical support should be inherent to the study of disadvantaged groups. Acknowledging that it is ordinary to lend a hand when participants are in need would legitimate such interactions, animate discussions with colleagues and IRB members about best practices for engaging in them, and lay the groundwork for the broader inclusion of intervention in social science research.

Validating and adopting "compassionate practices" that can be used by individual researchers is only a first step. As Rios (2011) has noted, simple acts of help are unlikely to produce actual change in participants' lives, even if they are meaningful interpersonally and ethically. The solid foundation of knowledge developed by previous poverty research and the desperate circumstances of contemporary hypermarginalized populations call us to move forward and embrace intervention research that can improve participants' well-being and identify concrete policy recommendations for real structural change. Such research requires adequate funding to hire qualified practitioners and support them to do difficult work. In our study, we did not encounter any drawbacks to providing the intervention, perhaps in large part because our social worker had extensive training and experience and we were diligent about providing her with clinical supervision, a mileage allowance so she could be mobile, paid vacation and sick leave, and other optimal work conditions so that she could do her job well and avoid burnout. Conducting a cost-benefit analysis was beyond the scope of our study, but future research could compare the cost of resources dedicated to high-quality staff support and the expenses avoided or curtailed through reduced recidivism, decreased need for emergency room care, and other cost savings that accompany improvements in a population's social stability and mental and physical health.

We note that our efforts to stabilize our participants—to move them off the street and into housing, to provide them with a steady income by signing them up for SSI, to improve their health by connecting them with medical care—

were an uphill battle and at best produced incremental improvements rather than radical transformation. We take this to be a substantive finding, but not a methodological justification. Had our intervention vastly ameliorated people's circumstances and thereby significantly changed empirical outcomes, our study design would have been equipped to understand the processes by which that happened. Again, this possibility highlights the utility of making intervention itself the focus of study in order to excavate and explicate the institutional conditions, structures, and relationships that promote or inhibit change, rather than fixating on suffering subjects with no intention of altering their plight. With the collaboration of skilled practitioners, appropriate ethical guidelines, and a rigorous study design, there is no reason for researchers to hold back from working to effect social change.

REFERENCES

Altman, Neil. 2009. *The Analyst in the Inner City: Race, Class, and Culture Through a Psychoanalytic Lens.* New York: Routledge.

Ansell, David A. 2011. *County: Life, Death, and Politics at Chicago's Public Hospital.* Chicago: Chicago Review Press.

Biehl, João, and Torben Eskerod. 2005. *Vita: Life in a Zone of Social Abandonment.* Berkeley: University of California Press.

Bourdieu, Pierre. 1992. "La Main gauche et la main droite de l'État." *Lignes* 15(March): 36–44.

———. 1993. *The Field of Cultural Production.* New York: Columbia University Press.

Bourgois, Philippe. 1995. *In Search of Respect: Selling Crack in El Barrio.* Cambridge: Cambridge University Press.

———. 2009. "Recognizing Invisible Violence: A Thirty-Year Ethnographic Retrospective." In *Global Health in Times of Violence*, edited by Barbara Rylko-Bauer, Linda Whiteford, and Paul Farmer. Santa Fe: School of Advanced Research Press.

Bourgois, Philippe, and Jeff Schonberg. 2009. *Righteous Dopefiend.* Berkeley: University of California Press.

Brandell, Jerrold R., ed. 2010. *Theory and Practice of Clinical Social Work.* New York: Columbia University Press.

Braveman, Paula, and Susan Egerter. 2008. "Overcoming Obstacles to Health: Report from the Robert Wood Johnson Foundation to the Commission to Build a Healthier America." Princeton, N.J.: Robert Wood Johnson Foundation.

Buckley, Ralph, and Douglas A. Bigelow. 1992. "The Multi-Service Network: Reaching the Unserved Multi-Problem Individual." *Community Mental Health Journal* 28(1): 43–50.

Desmond, Matthew. 2012. "Eviction and the Reproduction of Urban Poverty." *American Journal of Sociology* 118(1): 88–133.

Fairbanks, Robert P., II. 2009. *How It Works: Recovering Citizens in Post-Welfare Philadelphia.* Chicago: University of Chicago Press.

———. 2012. "On Theory and Method: Critical Ethnographic Approaches to Urban Regulatory Restructuring." *Urban Geography* 33(4): 545–65.

Floersch, Jerry, Jeffrey Longhofer, and Jacob Suskewicz. 2014. "The Use of Ethnography in Social Work Research." *Qualitative Social Work* 13(1): 3–7.

Gilgun, Jane F., and Roberta G. Sands. 2012. "The Contribution of Qualitative Approaches to Developmental Intervention Research." *Qualitative Social Work* 11(4): 349–61.

Glaser, Jordan B., and Robert B. Greifinger. 1993. "Correctional Health Care: A Public Health Opportunity." *Annals of Internal Medicine* 118(2): 139–45.

Gowan, Teresa. 2010. *Hobos, Hustlers, and Backsliders: Homeless in San Francisco.* Minneapolis: University of Minnesota Press.

Hasenfeld, Yeheskel. 1972. "People Processing Organizations: An Exchange Approach." *American Sociological Review* 37(June): 256–63.

Hopper, Kim, John Jost, Terri Hay, Susan Welber, and Gary Haugland. 1997. "Homelessness, Severe Mental Illness, and the Institutional Circuit." *Psychiatric Services* 48(5): 659–65.

Kral, Alex H., Mohsen Malekinejad, Jason Vaudrey, Alexis N. Martinez, Jennifer Lorvick, William McFarland, and Henry F. Raymond. 2010. "Comparing Respondent-Driven Sampling and Targeted Sampling Methods of Recruiting Injection Drug Users in San Francisco." *Journal of Urban Health* 87: 839–50.

Lara-Millán, Armando. 2014. "Public Emergency Room Overcrowding in the Era of Mass Imprisonment." *American Sociological Review* 79(5): 866–87.

Lipsky, Michael. 1980. *Street-Level Bureaucracy: Dilemmas of the Individual in Public Services.* New York: Russell Sage Foundation.

Lopez, Andrea M. 2011. "Ethnography at the Intersection of Policy, Place, and Moral Sentiments: Locating Structural Factors and Discursive Fields in the Everyday Lives of Women Who Use Drugs." Paper presented to conference at Prevention Research Center. Berkeley, Calif. (September 27).

——— 2014. "The Paradoxes of Poverty: Hypermarginality and Ideologies of Intervention in the 'Compassionate' City of San Francisco." PhD diss., University of New Mexico.

Lynch, Mona. 2000. "Rehabilitation as Rhetoric: The Ideal of Reformation in Contemporary Parole Discourse and Practices." *Punishment and Society* 2(1): 40–65.

McWilliams, Nancy. 2004. *Psychoanalytic Psychotherapy: A Practitioner's Guide*. New York: Guilford.

National Association of Social Workers (NASW). 2008. "Code of Ethics." Available at: http://www.socialworkers.org/pubs/code/code.asp (accessed May 14, 2015).

Phelan, Jo C., Bruce Link, Ana Diez-Roux, Ichiro Kawachi, and Bruce Levin. 2004. "'Fundamental Causes' of Social Inequalities in Mortality: A Test of the Theory." *Journal of Health and Social Behavior* 45(3): 265–85.

Rios, Victor M. 2011. *Punished: Policing the Lives of Black and Latino Boys*. New York: New York University Press.

Robbins, Joel. 2013. "Beyond the Suffering Subject: Toward an Anthropology of the Good." *Journal of the Royal Anthropological Institute* 19(3): 447–62.

Scheper-Hughes, Nancy. 1981. *Saints, Scholars, and Schizophrenics: Mental Illness in Rural Ireland*. Berkeley: University of California Press.

Sidel, Ruth. 1998. *Keeping Women and Children Last: America's War on the Poor*. New York: Penguin.

Simon, Jonathon. 1993. *Poor Discipline: Parole and the Social Control of the Underclass, 1890–1990*. Chicago: University of Chicago Press.

Singer, Merill, and Scott Clair. 2003. "Syndemics and Public Health: Reconceptualizing Disease in Bio-Social Context." *Medical Anthropology Quarterly* 17(4): 423–41.

Thompson, Mark J., and Candace Cotlove 2005. *The Therapeutic Process: A Clinical Introduction to Psychodynamic Psychotherapy*. Lanham, Md.: Jason Aronson.

Wachholz, Sandy, and Bob Mullaly. 1997. "Human Caring: Toward a Research Model for Structural Social Work." *Canadian Social Work Review* 14(1): 23–42.

Wacquant, Loïc. 2010. "Crafting the Neoliberal State: Workfare, Prisonfare, and Social Insecurity." *Sociological Forum* 25(2): 197–220.

——— 2014. "Marginality, Ethnicity, and Penality in the Neoliberal City: An Analytic Cartography." *Ethnic and Racial Studies* 37(10): 1687–1711.

Wang, Emily A., Jenerius A. Aminawung, Christopher Wildeman, Joseph S. Ross, and Harlan M. Krumholz. 2014. "High Incarceration Rates Among Black Men Enrolled in Clinical Studies May Compromise Ability to Identify Disparities." *Health Affairs* 33(5): 848–55.

Wang, Emily A., and Christopher Wildeman. 2011. "Studying Health Disparities by Including Incarcerated and Formerly Incarcerated Individuals." *Journal of the American Medical Association* 305(16): 1708–09.

Watters, John K., and Patrick Biernacki. 1989. "Targeted Sampling: Options for the Study of Hidden Populations." *Social Problems* 36(4).

Watters, John, Y. Cheng, and Alex Kral. 1997. "Toward Comprehensive Studies of HIV in Injection-Drug Users: Issues in Treatment-Based and Street-Based Samples." *Substance Use and Misuse* 32: 1709–14.

Wildeman, Christopher, and Christopher Muller. 2012. "Mass Imprisonment and Inequality in Health and Family Life." *Annual Review of Law and Social Science* 8: 11–30.

Understanding the Dynamics of $2-a-Day Poverty in the United States

H. LUKE SHAEFER, KATHRYN EDIN, AND ELIZABETH TALBERT

Shaefer and Edin (2013) have found a large rise in "extreme poverty"—defined as cash income of no more than $2 per person per day, for a month or calendar quarter—among U.S. households with children between 1996 and 2011. This article explores some underlying dynamics of this phenomenon, referred to here as "$2-a-day poverty," presenting evidence from both qualitative fieldwork and quantitative analysis of the Survey of Income and Program Participation (SIPP). The rise in $2-a-day poverty has been concentrated among children experiencing it chronically—that is, for seven or more months during a calendar year. Both qualitative and quantitative evidence find that a large majority of children experiencing $2-a-day poverty live in households where an adult worked during the year, while only a small proportion live in households accessing TANF. Finally, households experiencing $2-a-day poverty appear to be more likely to face material hardships than other low-income households.

Keywords: poverty, welfare, social policy, low-wage work, material hardship

The 1990s was a period of major change to federal means-tested income transfer programs targeting low-income families with children in the United States. The 1996 welfare reform replaced a federal entitlement program, Aid to Families with Dependent Children (AFDC), with a more restrictive program, Temporary Assistance for Needy Families (TANF), which offers time-limited cash assistance and imposes work requirements on able-bodied recipients. Following this change, the cash assistance caseloads fell from 4.7 million families per month in 1994 to 1.7 million in 2013. Never during the Great Recession era did the TANF caseload rise

H. Luke Shaefer is associate professor at the University of Michigan School of Social Work and Gerald R. Ford School of Public Policy. Kathryn Edin is Bloomberg Distinguished Professor at the Zanvyl Krieger School and Bloomberg School of Public Health at Johns Hopkins University. Elizabeth Talbert is a doctoral student in sociology at Johns Hopkins University.

Luke Shaefer's time on this research was supported in part by the National Science Foundation under grant no. SES 1131500. The authors thank participants in the 2013 University of Chicago EINet Symposium, "Employment Instability and the Safety Net"; members and staff of the Council of Economic Advisers; session participants at the annual conference of the American Sociological Association; participants at the Russell Sage Foundation conference "Severe Deprivation in America;" and Indi Dutta-Gupta for helpful comments on earlier versions of this work. The opinions and conclusions presented here are solely those of the authors and should not be construed as representing the opinions or policies of the National Science Foundation or any other entity. Direct correspondence to: H. Luke Shaefer at lshaefer@umich.edu, School of Social Work, University of Michigan, 1080 S. University Ave., Ann Arbor, MI 48109; Kathryn Edin at Kathy_edin@jhu.edu, Zanvyl Krieger School, Johns Hopkins University, Department of Sociology, 533 Mergenthaler Hall, 3400 N. Charles St., Baltimore, MD 21218; and Elizabeth Talbert at etalber2@jhu.edu, Zanvyl Krieger School, Johns Hopkins University, Department of Sociology, 533 Mergenthaler Hall, 3400 N. Charles St., Baltimore, MD 21218.

above 2 million families. Even in the worst economic times, TANF serves only a small fraction of the families that AFDC once did.

While cash assistance through AFDC and TANF has declined in significance, other means-tested income transfer programs have grown since the 1990s. Supplemental Nutrition Assistance Program (SNAP) caseloads fell during the late 1990s along with TANF caseloads, but SNAP rebounded in the 2000s as a result of the relaxation of some eligibility requirements and the weak economy of the Great Recession. In addition, the value of refundable tax credits like the Earned Income Tax Credit (EITC) increased a number of times, with expansions in the early 1990s and changes made as part of the 2009 American Recovery and Reinvestment Act. These benefits are conditional, however, on earnings from work: they increase in value as earnings rise to a point.

Taken in total, the changes to federal means-tested income transfer programs during the 1990s led to a net increase in means-tested income transfer aid flowing to poor families with children in the United States as low-income families benefited from growing access to refundable tax credits and relaxed SNAP eligibility rules. However, most of the increase in aid has been concentrated among families with earnings (Ben-Shalom, Moffit, and Scholz 2012), and thus there may have been a concurrent rise in the number of households surviving on very low levels of cash income (Shaefer and Edin 2013). In addition, much of what remains available to the nonworking poor comes in the form of in-kind aid rather than cash transfers.

Several studies have documented an increase in the number of the "disconnected": single mothers with neither earnings nor welfare (Blank 2007; Loprest 2011; Turner, Danziger, and Seefeldt 2006). These studies find that as many as one-quarter of single mothers were disconnected for at least a four-month period in 2009, a large increase since the mid-1990s. Luke Shaefer and Kathryn Edin (2013) built on these findings by broadening the study population to all poor households with children and accounting more fully for sources of unearned and in-kind cash income. They developed a metric of extreme poverty, adapted from the World Bank's metric of global poverty: subsistence below a level of $2 per person per day. Across three alternative definitions of income, they find that there was a marked rise in extreme poverty beginning in the late 1990s and continuing into the 2000s, well before the Great Recession began.

Their estimates of the increase in the proportion of non-elderly households with children experiencing extreme poverty between 1996 and 2011 vary depending on what is counted as income. When the cash value of SNAP, refundable tax credits, and housing assistance is accounted for, there is a 45.5 percent increase; when only cash income (including TANF) is considered, there is a 152.9 percent increase. As of mid-2011, roughly 1.65 million households with over 3.55 million children were reporting cash incomes of no more than $2 per person per day. Shaefer and Edin (2013) also find that the rise in extreme poverty is concentrated among the households most likely to have been affected by welfare reform and that, descriptively, the decline in cash aid from AFDC and TANF is a major factor in understanding this trend.

Building on Shaefer and Edin (2013), Laurence Chandy and Cory Smith (2014) estimate the rate of $2-a-day poverty for all U.S. households rather than only for households with children. They also account for a wider variety of in-kind programs (such as the National School Lunch Program, imputing a cash value for food eaten by kids at school). Despite these differences in their analyses, their baseline results "are roughly of the same magnitude as those of Shaefer and Edin and serve to reaffirm their core findings" (Chandy and Smith 2014, 4).

Chandy and Smith also compare income estimates to estimates on household consumption from the Consumer Expenditure (CE) survey and find what they consider to be a weak relationship between very low levels of reported income and very low levels of reported consumption. Based on this evidence, they argue that the American poor consume more than their incomes would suggest. This analysis depends, however, entirely on the quality of the CE data. There is evidence that the survey may be unrepresentative of households at the very bottom (see the appendix), and the CE survey has very low-quality measures of income. These shortcomings of the CE may explain why Chandy and Smith find a weak relationship between income and consumption.

While the Shaefer and Edin (2013) results offer important evidence of trends in income levels at the very bottom of American society, their analysis raises many new questions. Do children typically experience only short spells of what we refer to here as $2-a-day poverty (equivalent to "extreme" poverty in the earlier paper),[1] or is the typical experience more one of longer periods of such deprivation? Under what circumstances does a family fall into a spell of $2-a-day poverty? Finally, is the experience of $2-a-day poverty associated with a greater degree of material hardship than other forms of poverty?

To more fully develop our understanding of the dynamics of $2-a-day poverty in the United States, we present findings from both qualitative data collected by the authors and new analyses conducted on the SIPP. First we offer a case study from our qualitative fieldwork. We then present new results from analyses of the SIPP that offer a fuller understanding of the duration of spells, the circumstances that lead a family to enter a spell of $2-a-day poverty, and the degree to which $2-a-day poverty is associated with an elevated risk of material hardship.

DATA AND METHODS

Since 2012, we have engaged in what we call "iterative" mixed methods research on $2-a-day poverty in the United States, conducting both qualitative and quantitative research simultaneously, with each line of inquiry informing the direction of the other. For example, a key finding from our qualitative research has been that job loss is a common precursor to a spell of $2-a-day poverty. This has led us, in turn, to examine more fully the relationship between work and the risk of entrance into a spell of $2-a-day poverty using the SIPP. When we identified, through our quantitative research, a concentration of $2-a-day poverty in the southeast region of the United States, we opened additional qualitative field sites to better understand $2-a-day poverty in this key region. We have also noted in our ethnographic work that a spell of $2-a-day poverty often precipitates housing instability, and so we have focused on the incidence of housing instability as one measure of well-being in our quantitative work.

Qualitative Methods

Our ongoing ethnographic research has been conducted in four field sites with eighteen families who, when we first met them, had recently lived under the $2-a-day threshold for at least three months' time, and usually for much longer. Our field sites are located in Chicago, Illinois; Cleveland, Ohio; Johnson City, Tennessee; and a number of small towns in the Mississippi Delta.

In each field site, we partner with local non-profits referred to us by community members. We leave materials in the lobbies of these agencies, volunteer, and approach families who come seeking services. Because many among the $2-a-day poor are isolated from such sources of aid, we also enlist the help of trusted community members in neighborhoods where we know many families are struggling.

We have met with all of the families in our sample over a period of at least six months and in many cases for more than a year, interviewing each family multiple times, observing their daily activities, and following the events of their lives. We examine the events surrounding each family's spells of $2-a-day poverty and, in collaboration with our study team, identify common themes that emerge across cases. This investigation was approved first by the institutional review board (IRB) at Harvard University and currently by the IRB at Johns Hopkins University.

Quantitative Methods

Data for this line of research come from the SIPP collected by the U.S. Census Bureau. The SIPP is a nationally representative, longitudinal, multistage, stratified sample of the U.S. non-institutionalized population, collected in panels ranging from two to five years. The estimates presented here are for three calendar

---

1. We changed our terminology because the frequent use of "extreme poverty" interchangeably with the official Census Bureau designation of "deep poverty" confused readers.

years: 1996 (before states were required to implement the 1996 welfare reform),[2] 2005 (after the economy had recovered from the mild 2001 recession), and 2012 (the last year for which the 2008 SIPP panel can produce calendar-year estimates). The U.S. unemployment rate was roughly comparable in 1996 (5.4 percent) and 2005 (5.1 percent), and both followed years with comparable unemployment rates. The unemployment rate in 2012 was higher, at 8.1 percent.

Because of the unstable nature of households, we use the child as the unit of analysis that is followed over time. Calendar-year weights in the SIPP allow us to follow a nationally representative sample of children eighteen years old and younger who remained in the SIPP sample for the full calendar year under study. We select a sample of children ages zero to eighteen assigned calendar-year weights by the SIPP (so that we can follow them for a full year) for the years 1996, 2005, and 2012. We restrict our sample to children in households with annual incomes no more than 150 percent of the official poverty threshold during the calendar year under analysis.[3] We also restrict our sample to children in households with low assets, defined as a net worth of less than 300 percent of the poverty line.[4] Standard errors are adjusted using Stata's svy routine to account for the SIPP's complex survey design.

Some researchers might prefer a consumption-based measure of a household's resources for an analysis such as this one, given the extent to which poor Americans may access noncash aid. We continue to use an income-based rather than consumption-based measure in part because of concerns regarding the quality of the available survey data that capture household consumption (see the appendix). But more importantly, *our central argument is that cash resources have a particular salience in the United States.* The various forms of noncash aid available to the American poor are important—even vital. Yet reductions in the accessibility of *cash* among the poorest of the poor in America signal a decline in a critical component of "capability" well-being, to borrow from Amartya Sen (1999). To be without cash income in the United States is to be without a flexible resource that is vital to having a chance of bettering one's circumstances. As two experts on global poverty put it, living without cash in the United States might be thought of as a kind of "purgatory," and the rise of $2-a-day poverty here may "imply a severe form of poverty in both a practical and intangible sense" (Chandy and Smith 2014, 15).

Our household income measure includes the resources of all individuals living in a housing unit: labor market earnings, retirement benefits, cash income from public programs like TANF, reported income from friends and family members outside the household (such as child support), and income from informal sources.[5] All income values are adjusted to January 2011 dollars using the Consumer Price Index for All Urban Consumers (CPI-U). Misreporting of income and public-program participation is a problem in major household

---

2. By 1995, many states had begun to implement new welfare programs through waivers granted by the U.S. Department of Health and Human Services (DHHS) and caseloads had begun to decline. However, these waivers were far from universal. We use 1996 as our starting time point because the Census Bureau undertook a major overhaul of the SIPP starting with the 1996 panel. This overhaul included changes to some variables, changes in the way the survey was administered, and changes in the length and size of panels, causing concern that trends relative to point estimates from prior panels might be the result of design effects.

3. We also examine results using alternative annual income cutoffs of 125, 185, and 200 percent of the poverty level. Results are substantively similar, fluctuating slightly in line with the respective restrictions.

4. We also examine results using an alternative restriction based on having liquid assets with a value that would keep a family out of poverty for three months or less. Again, results are substantively similar. We use the definition based on net worth to weed out households with high housing equity but low levels of liquid assets.

5. We recode negative income values to cash income rates above our $2-a-day poverty threshold because negative income values in the SIPP are often related to investments and tend to be from households with high incomes in other months.

surveys, but the SIPP does comparatively well relative to its peers in terms of reporting rates (Meyer, Mok, and Sullivan 2009). The SIPP has higher reporting rates for public-program participation than comparable surveys, and it asks many detailed questions about sources of income, both from formal employment and informal sources. Because administrative earnings records are insufficient for capturing informal income among the poor, the SIPP is the best choice for this study (see the appendix for more details).

We present estimates using two definitions of household income. The first is reported cash income from all sources (akin to the income measure used to calculate a family's official poverty status). The second definition adds SNAP benefits for an adjusted income measure, making the assumption that $1 in SNAP benefits equals $1 in cash. SNAP is the largest federal means-tested near-cash income transfer program in the United States and appears to have the largest impact on spells of $2-a-day poverty of any public means-tested income transfer program, if counted as cash (Shaefer and Edin 2013).

In this analysis, we require that a child report at least *three* months during a calendar year with a household income below the threshold of less than $2 per person per day (approximated as $60 per person per month) to be counted as experiencing a spell of $2-a-day poverty. Beyond this, in order to examine whether changes in $2-a-day poverty in the child's household have been marked by an increase of relatively short or long spells, we distinguish between "episodic" and "chronic" spells of $2-a-day poverty. We consider a child to have experienced episodic $2-a-day poverty if the household reports a monthly household income below the $2-a-day poverty threshold for at least three months but no more than six months over the course of a calendar year. We consider a child to be in chronic $2-a-day poverty if the child's household reports a monthly household income below the $2-a-day poverty threshold in at least seven months over the course of a calendar year.

Measuring Material Hardship

The SIPP is the primary source of nationally representative data on material hardship in the United States (Ouellette et al. 2004). We present bivariate estimates of the association between the experience of $2-a-day poverty and the experience of some forms of material hardship, reported at a single point in time during the calendar year being analyzed. These are drawn from the SIPP's adult well-being topical module in the 2008 panel.[6] It should be noted that the timing of this topical module does not necessarily coincide with a spell of $2-a-day poverty, and thus some reports from families below this threshold over the course of the year may be from a time period when they had a higher income. This may bias downward the association between $2-a-day poverty and material hardship.

We present estimates of rates of residential instability (captured in the core SIPP data by the number of residential address changes reported during the calendar year), a measure of housing quality, a measure of food insecurity, a measure of medical hardship, and an aggregate hardship measure (whether or not the household experienced any of these hardships). The SIPP household food security measure does not correspond exactly to the official U.S. Department of Agriculture (USDA) food security measures included as an annual supplement to the Current Population Survey (CPS); however, it is used in several studies and is closely related to the official food security measure (Nord 2006; Ratcliffe, McKernan, and Zhang 2011).

RESULTS

Case Study: Monique

Monique, an African American mother of two, wears a secondhand pair of jeans and a well-worn sweatshirt. Hair pulled back in a tight ponytail, she keeps a bright expression on her aged thirty-three-year-old face and is prone to express gratitude for the fact that though she's experienced so many trials, she has come through them. During those times over the past year when she's had a place of her own, its living room has been furnished sparingly,

---

6. These modules were administered at a point-in-time during waves 6 and 9. We report results from wave 6, which are reflective of 2010. Findings are substantively similar when wave 9 is used.

with only a plastic milk crate and one vinyl hassock to sit on. During various spells among the $2-a-day poor, she and her two boys have found themselves in homeless shelters in Birmingham, Chattanooga, and Johnson City, Tennessee. She's also had spells living with kin—or having kin live with her—in order to save on rent.

Despite her hardship, Monique is rarely without a job, usually maintaining some type of employment by registering at temp agencies when permanent work isn't available. She gets SNAP benefits but hasn't received cash assistance since shortly after her youngest son was born. Though she believes she may be eligible for disability insurance—a pinched nerve in her leg causes her quite a bit of pain—she refuses to apply. "People say, 'Oh, girl, you get your disability,' and I can think to myself and say, 'Oh, you know it would be nice, but after a while, I'd get bored with just sitting in the house.'" Utility shutoffs are common in Monique's home, she and the boys wear used clothing gleaned from the Goodwill in town, and she walks to work—sometimes for several miles—because she lacks money for public transportation.

Monique has dipped in and out of $2-a-day poverty multiple times over the course of her life. She is a Birmingham, Alabama, native and survived a childhood riddled with abuse at the hands of her drug-addicted mother. After her mother's boyfriend kicked her out of the house at age twelve, Monique bounced between foster care and her grandfather's home. Monique's grandfather was intent on instilling traditional values in his granddaughter, which she says kept her on the straight and narrow. Monique remained a virgin until age eighteen and completed high school. She went on to become a certified nurse's assistant. When she was twenty-one, Monique gave birth to her first son; her second son, fathered by the same man, was born three years later. Shortly thereafter, the boys' father was incarcerated.

One day in Birmingham when her sons were playing outside, "the bullets started flying." Monique ran outside and grabbed the children, and while she hurried them inside, a stray bullet just missed her face and singed her hair. "I could smell my hair [burning]." She moved out of that neighborhood, where violence was intensifying, and into her uncle's home several neighborhoods away, but still didn't feel safe. Not only did she not really trust her uncle—his substance abuse issues were well known in the family—but she couldn't forget her brush with that bullet. "I felt like I had been at war and I was shell-shocked and I was paranoid." Monique decided she and her sons needed to move somewhere safer—Chattanooga, Tennessee. A phone call revealed that there was a spot in a family homeless shelter there. The woman on the other end of the phone told Monique, "Yeah, yeah, we have somewhere for you to stay."

Upon their arrival in Chattanooga on a Greyhound bus, however, the homeless shelter had no open beds. Still, the staff assured them that a spot would open up in just a few days' time. Monique had saved a little of her tax refund for the security deposit on an apartment and had hoped to save more by staying in the homeless shelter while searching for a job. Now she felt that she had no choice but to check her family into a cheap motel—one that mainly served transients and prostitutes—while she waited, at $70 a night. As each day ticked by, Monique's cash reserves dropped. Finally, she was informed that a spot at the shelter would open up in just three days' time, on Monday. If she used every penny of her remaining cash, she would still be $83.90 short of what she needed to get through the weekend. The motel required payment in advance. She wrote a check for the remaining amount, knowing there was nothing in her bank account. Maybe they would be in the shelter by the time the check bounced and she could pay it back when she finally found a job.

The next day Monique received a call from the motel office asking her to come to the lobby. She told her young boys to keep watching cartoons; she would be back soon. Upon entering the lobby, two police officers arrested Monique—the check she had written had already bounced and the motel was pressing charges. Though her children were upstairs, Monique decided not to mention them to the police; she figured she would be back before they even missed her. Monique knew firsthand what happened to children who became enmeshed in the child welfare system, even temporarily, and wagered that the probability of the children being found alone in a motel room was low.

While Monique was down at the station, one of the boys started to cry, and the noise was reported to the manager, who again called the police. Monique was charged with child neglect, and the boys were removed from her custody. "Things went down from there," Monique says. "They prosecuted me, I went to jail, and I lost my kids for sixteen months. All for $80." After being released from jail, Monique went to work to regain custody. On earnings from temporary employment, she managed to secure a place to live—a requirement for regaining custody—while also dealing with court appearances, psychologist and counselor visits, and the worst depression of her life. She says she didn't know "how I was going to make it without [my sons]." Eventually, she would get them back, one of the greatest moments of her life.

In the meantime, and unbeknownst to her, she was accumulating a huge child support arrearage owed to the state of Tennessee for the sixteen months her kids were in the foster care system—she reports that it was compounded at an interest rate of 15 percent. As soon as Monique found a stable job—a part-time shift at McDonald's in Johnson City where she was forever begging for enough hours—the state began to garnish her check. "After all my working, I would make three or four hundred dollars in my check and have $94 [to take home], because of the child support they took out of it. There were times we lived on $150 a month—thank goodness for food stamps."

Monique has not been able to apply for public housing assistance since the family's move to Johnson City. In fact, because of a $400 unpaid bill to the Chattanooga Housing Authority, where she had found housing after regaining custody of the boys, Monique believes she is "banned" from receiving any form of housing assistance. She's been living in a tiny, ramshackle house on the rural outskirts of Johnson City where the landlord sometimes allows her to perform repairs in lieu of much of the rent—which is supposed to be $400. She's also taken in her uncle as a boarder—he's supposed to pay the utilities—$50 for water and $270 for the electricity that provides lighting and heat. But as it turns out, he's been spending all of his disability check on drugs. Her church helped her keep up with the water bill, but the electricity was shut off. Then, in a January cold snap, the pipes in the home burst, forcing the family to vacate the property. Monique begged a friend to take them in temporarily.

At one point during their time in Johnson City, Monique acquired work at a paper factory a few towns over. "I didn't have enough for a taxi. . . . The taxi was going to charge me $18 and I'm like, I couldn't [afford it]." Without a car and because the bus system didn't run anywhere near the factory, Monique walked two hours each way during the first week of the job: "I walked to work and got up at four in the morning since I didn't know how long it was going to take me." Finally, she found a coworker who could give her a ride. Her income qualifies her for free bus passes on the Johnson City transit system, but the sprawl of the city makes this form of transportation only intermittently useful. "It's hard for me to find a job that I can get to on the bus. Everywhere that is hiring you gotta have a car, so that's like a holdback for me. I can't afford a car—I can barely afford to have a roof over my kids' heads."

Monique strives to create a better life for her children. Though her limited cash resources make it difficult to provide basic needs, she finds ways to cover those needs and occasionally to treat her sons to something fun. She gets $497 in food stamps and uses "every last one of them." Monique does what she can to make sure her sons get special experiences during their childhood, even if she has to get creative. "They'd say, 'Mommy, we want a Happy Meal.' [So] I would walk to the Dollar Store and buy them a toy and take a paper and staple the ends of it and take some French fries, make 'em a hamburger and put it on a tray when they were little, and that was their Happy Meal . . . they were happy! . . . I wanted to be frugal, so we still sometimes have to push it to make it."

As her children have gotten older, she has tried to explain to them why they can't always have treats: "I explain to them, 'Look, we can't go out because we have to pay this light bill.'" Monique buys her children's clothing at Goodwill or goes to clothes closets and yard sales; she provides for their needs before her own.

She buys only one pair of used shoes a year. Monique has a state-provided cell phone and does not have cable or Internet. She and her sons are covered by the TennCare health insurance. Her sons attend free after-school programming and play on the school's basketball team, yet are unable to afford new basketball shoes or uniforms.

Despite the challenges Monique faces, she remains optimistic about her future. She strives to always have a backup plan: "If you don't got no backup plan, you ain't got no plan." At last contact, Monique had decided that she wanted to move on, to leave Johnson City and try to get stable work at a soda pop factory in North Carolina, where she has heard they are hiring. Her desires are modest but hinge on stability for herself and her sons: "I'm going to say ten to twelve dollars an hour with at least thirty to forty hours a week. . . . I want a car, but is that hindering me? Heck no, it's not hindering me. Just stability. My main goal is having something that looks stable, that's mine . . . and it ain't goin' nowhere—it's comfortable, solid. . . . My determination is over the edge, I'm telling you. I'm going to be one of those people that's going to make it."

Synthesis of Qualitative Findings

Monique's story highlights a number of themes present in many of the stories of the eighteen respondent families included in our ethnographic research. First, many of the respondents facing $2-a-day poverty found themselves in a cascade of hardship, experiencing not just a month or two of such circumstances but longer or recurring spells. Those in the worst circumstances found themselves experiencing the condition chronically. Second, job loss was a common precursor to a spell of $2-a-day poverty. Low pay, unpredictable schedules, and a lack of sufficient hours permeate the low-wage sectors of the economy where many of our respondents found work. Finally, material hardship is a common experience among the $2-a-day poor, but its forms may look different than for other Americans. For instance, Monique and her sons experienced a significant degree of housing instability. In some months, however, she might not respond affirmatively to a standard material hardship question about whether she had fallen behind on her rent, a standard indicator used to measure housing security.

NATIONAL ESTIMATES FROM THE SIPP

How many households with minor children are there in the United States like Monique's? Has the rise of $2-a-day poverty been concentrated among those experiencing long or recurring spells?

Figure 1 presents estimates from the SIPP of the number of unique children in the United States who experienced a spell (multiple spells by the same child not counted) of episodic $2-a-day poverty (between three and six months in length) during the calendar years 1996, 2005, and 2012. The full vertical bars, including both the upper and lower segments, represent the number of unique children experiencing episodic $2-a-day poverty based on household cash income in each of these years. The lower portions of these bars represent the number of children experiencing episodic $2-a-day poverty based on adjusted household income, which includes both cash and SNAP benefits as described earlier.

Based on the cash income–only definition, we find that the number of children experiencing *episodic* $2-a-day poverty rose from 1.27 million in 1996 (1.7 percent of all children) to 1.58 million in 2005 (2.0 percent of children), and then to 1.89 million in 2012 (2.4 percent of children). In 2012 this rise represents a statistically significant increase in the probability that a child will experience an episodic period below the threshold of $2 per person per day, relative to 1996 (after accounting for population growth).[7] For reasons explained later, the overall growth in the number of children experiencing $2-a-day poverty for three to six months during a calendar year is lower than what was found by Shaefer and Edin (2013) for overall $2-a-day poverty.

---

7. This is determined by a bivariate regression predicting the risk of $2-a-day poverty based on a year dummy, with a sample restricted to observations from 1996 and 2005, and then 1996 and 2010.

Figure 1. Unique Children in Episodic $2-a-Day Poverty over the Course of a Calendar Year, 1996, 2005, and 2012

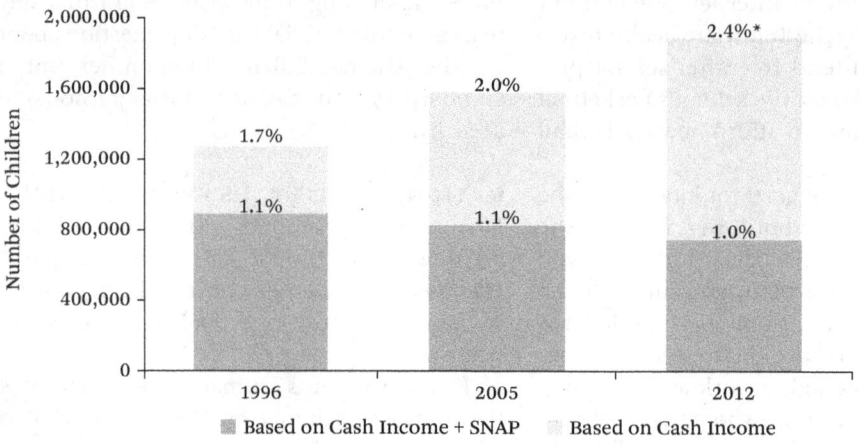

Source: Authors' calculations from SIPP, 1996, 2004, and 2008.
Notes: Calendar-year weights are used. Horizontal axis measures number of unique children; percentages of children and statistical significance appear at the top of the bars. Income dollars are adjusted to January 2011 dollars. A child must be eighteen or younger, must have an annual household income of 150 percent or less of the poverty line, and must have low assets to be counted in any $2-a-day poverty group. Episodic extreme poverty is defined as three to six months below a household income of $2 per person, per day.
*$p < 0.5$

Further, as shown by the lower portion of the bars—where SNAP is counted as cash—we find no increase in the number of children experiencing an episodic spell among the $2-a-day poor. This means that all of the increase in the prevalence of episodic $2-a-day poverty between 1996 and 2012 is driven by children in households that have cash incomes below the $2-a-day threshold but are accessing SNAP. The number of children in this category grew 97.4 percent between 1996 and 2005, and 200 percent between 1996 and 2012.

Figure 2 presents estimates from the SIPP of the number of unique children experiencing a spell of *chronic* $2-a-day poverty—seven months or more below this threshold, the condition most common in our ethnographic work among households like Monique's—during the calendar years 1996, 2005, and 2012. The changes over time in this group are more dramatic than for episodic spells. As of 1996, the SIPP found fewer than 400,000 children experiencing a spell of chronic $2-a-day poverty based on household cash income (0.5 percent of children). By 2005, this number had reached 894,000 (1.2 percent of children), and by 2012 the SIPP registered 1.33 million children (1.7 percent of children) in households experiencing seven months or more among the $2-a-day poor—a 241 percent increase between 1996 and 2012.

Further, there is also a statistically significant increase in chronic $2-a-day poverty based on adjusted household income. In 1996 there were 196,000 children who had reported incomes that classified them as experiencing chronic $2-a-day poverty when SNAP was taken into consideration. By 2005 this estimate had risen to 342,000 children, and by 2012 there were 478,000 such children, based on SIPP estimates—144 percent higher than in 1996. The estimates in 2005 and 2012 both represent statistically significant increases in the risk of chronic $2-a-day poverty relative to 1996. As with the episodic results, however, the greatest increase in $2-a-day poverty occurred among

Figure 2. Unique Children in Chronic $2-a-Day Poverty over the Course of a Calendar Year, 1996, 2005, and 2012

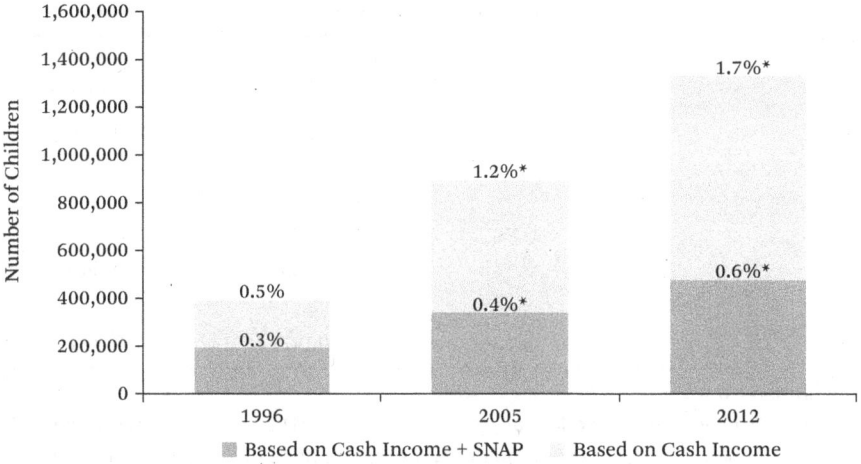

Source: Authors' calculations from SIPP, 1996, 2004, and 2008.
Notes: Calendar-year weights are used. Vertical axis measures the number of unique children; percentages of children and statistical significance appear at the top of the bars. Income dollars are adjusted to January 2011 dollars. A child must be eighteen or younger, must have an annual household income 150 percent or less of the poverty line, and must have low assets to be counted in any $2-a-day poverty group. Chronic extreme poverty is defined as seven or more months below a household income of $2 per person, per day.
*$p < 0.5$

children in households receiving SNAP but with cash incomes below the $2-a-day poverty threshold. The size of this group increased 339 percent between 1996 and 2012.

Thus, when using the definition based on cash income only, figures 1 and 2 show increases in both episodic and chronic $2-a-day poverty relative to 1996. The increases in chronic $2-a-day poverty relative to 1996 are proportionally larger than for episodic $2-a-day poverty, no matter which definition is used. These figures further reveal a statistically significant and substantively large increase in chronic $2-a-day poverty even after accounting for SNAP. Thus, it appears that the changes in $2-a-day poverty found in Shaefer and Edin (2013) were driven by increases in the prevalence of chronic more than episodic $2-a-day poverty. It also appears that, for both figures, the largest growth in $2-a-day poverty has been among children on SNAP but with household cash incomes below $2 per person per day.

Characteristics of Children in $2-a-Day Poverty

Table 1 presents selected characteristics of children in 2012 by poverty status, comparing higher-income children (those living in households with annual cash incomes above 150 percent of poverty) in column 1 to "other low-income" children (those living in households with annual cash incomes of no more than 150 percent of the poverty level but not experiencing $2-a-day poverty) in column 2, and children experiencing either episodic or chronic $2-a-day poverty in column 3. Owing to sample size limitations, we examine the characteristics of children in $2-a-day poverty based on the cash-only definition and include those experiencing both episodic and chronic $2-a-day poverty together in one category.

In 2012 low-income children were far less likely to be non-Hispanic white than higher-income children, but children who experienced $2-a-day poverty were no less likely to be non-

Table 1. Characteristics of Children by Poverty Status, 2012 (Proportions)

	Higher-Income	Other Low-Income	$2-a-Day Poverty
Race			
White, non-Hispanic	0.622	0.318	0.327
Black	0.102	0.213	0.246
Hispanic	0.170	0.380	0.340
Household type			
Married	0.793	0.505	0.379
Female-headed	0.145	0.420	0.540
Region			
Southeast	0.236	0.262	0.321

Source: Authors' calculations from SIPP, 2008.

Notes: Calendar-year weights used. Income dollars adjusted to January 2011 dollars. A child must have annual household income of 150 percent or less of the poverty line and have low assets to be counted in any $2-a-day poverty group.

Hispanic white than other low-income children. Among both categories of low-income children, about one-third were non-Hispanic white, compared to 62.2 percent of higher-income children.

Table 1 estimates show that 37.9 percent of children in $2-a-day poverty were in married households, as opposed to 50.5 percent of other low-income children and 79.3 percent of higher-income children. Children experiencing $2-a-day poverty were the most likely of any of the three categories to be in a household headed by a single female: 54.0 percent of these children lived in a single female-headed household, as opposed to 42.0 percent of other low-income children and just 14.5 percent of higher-income children.

Table 1 further reports on a source of regional concentration of the $2-a-day poor. The Southeast region includes the states often referred to as the "Deep South" and Appalachia, where we find Monique and her boys.[8] In 2012 the SIPP found that 32.1 percent of children experiencing a spell of $2-a-day poverty lived in the Southeast, compared to 26.2 percent of other low-income children and 23.6 percent of higher-income children.

Figure 3 reports on two key characteristics of the households of children by poverty status. The first characteristic is the proportion of children living in a household that reported TANF receipt in the SIPP over the course of the 2012 calendar year. The second is the proportion of children living in a house where an adult member worked in a formal job for at least one full month over the course of 2012. Only 1.8 percent of higher-income children lived in households that reported TANF receipt in at least one month of 2012. Still low but somewhat higher, 11.4 percent of children in low-income (but not $2-a-day poverty) households reported TANF receipt during the year, as did 10.8 percent of households with children who experienced $2-a-day poverty during 2012. Thus, children experiencing $2-a-day poverty were not noticeably more likely to access TANF than other low-income children. For both groups, the rate of TANF receipt was low. Presumably, virtually all of the children living in $2-a-day poverty ought to have been eligible for TANF.

The bars on the right track the proportion of children living in a household where an adult member worked for at least a full month during

---

[8]. The Southeast includes Alabama, Arkansas, Florida, Georgia, Kentucky, Louisiana, Mississippi, North Carolina, South Carolina, Tennessee, Virginia, and West Virginia.

Figure 3. TANF Receipt and Household Work Effort Among Children by Poverty Status, Calendar Year 2012

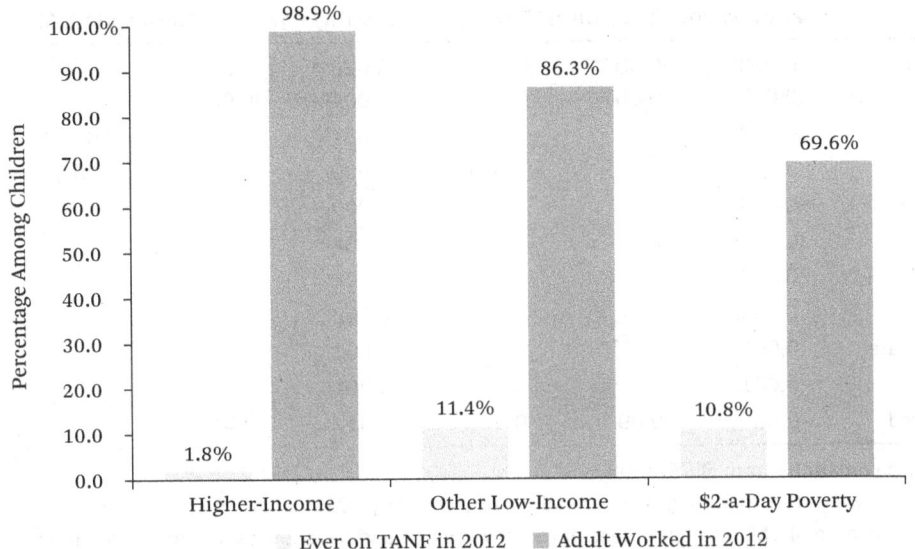

Source: Authors' calculations from SIPP, 1996, 2004, and 2008.
Notes: Calendar-year weights are used. Income dollars are adjusted to January 2011 dollars. A child must be eighteen or younger, must have an annual household income of 150 percent or less of the poverty line, and must have low assets to be counted in any $2-a-day poverty group.

the course of the calendar year. Among higher-income children, such work effort was nearly universal—98.9 percent of children with annual household incomes above 150 percent of the poverty line lived in a household with this level of labor force attachment. The large majority of children in low-income families not experiencing $2-a-day poverty also met this threshold of labor force attachment, with 86.3 percent living in a household where an adult worked for at least one full month during the year. While a lower percentage of children experiencing $2-a-day poverty lived in a household with this same labor force attachment compared to children from the other two income thresholds, a large majority, 69.6 percent, did so: that is, in 2012 seven in ten children among the $2-a-day poor lived in a household where an adult worked for at least a month during the year. This finding is consistent with the finding from our ethnographic work that respondents were actively engaged in the labor market for at least part of the year. As we saw with Monique, disruptions in formal-sector market work seem to precipitate a spell among the $2-a-day poor.

Fixed-Effects Analysis Predicting Changes in $2-a-Day Poverty Status

Table 2 presents a fixed-effects linear probability regression model predicting child-specific changes in $2-a-day poverty status. Fixed-effects ordinary least squares (OLS) models subtract all variables by their mean, causing all static characteristics such as race and sex to fall out of the regression model.[9]

The goal of this analysis is to see if child-specific changes in $2-a-day poverty status are associated with child-specific changes in other household characteristics. Monthly SIPP data for the calendar year 2012 are clustered by child. The independent variables included in this

---

9. Results from a fixed-effects logistic regression model were substantively similar.

Table 2. Fixed-Effects Linear Probability Regression Results: Predicting $2-a-Day Poverty Among U.S. Children, 2012

	$2-a-Day Poverty by Cash Only			$2-a-Day Poverty by Cash and SNAP		
Working adult in household	-0.098**	-0.098**		-0.028**	-0.028**	
	(0.007)	(0.007)		(0.004)	(0.004)	
TANF receipt	-0.079**		-0.073**	-0.031**		-0.029**
	(0.013)		(0.013)	(0.009)		(0.009)
Number of children	-0.006			0.000		
	(0.008)			(0.004)		
Number of adults	-0.007*			-0.004		
	(0.003)			(0.002)		
Unemployment rate	0.001			-0.001		
	(0.001)			(0.001)		
Overall R-squared	0.08	0.09	0	0.01	0.01	0

Source: Authors' calculations from SIPP, 2008.
Notes: Analysis is unweighted. Income dollars are adjusted to January 2011 dollars. A child must have annual household income of 150 percent or less of the poverty line and have low assets to be counted in any $2-a-day poverty group.
*$p < .05$; **$p < .01$

model are monthly measures indicating the presence of a working adult, reported TANF receipt during the month, the number of children in the household during the month, and the number of adults in the household. The last two are included to capture the extent to which changes in household composition are related to changes in $2-a-day poverty status. Also included is the child-month-year state seasonally adjusted unemployment rate.

We find that a change in the presence of a working adult in a child's household is an important predictor of a change in $2-a-day poverty status. Also predictive are changes in TANF receipt and changes in the number of adults in the household. Columns 2, 3, 5, and 6 report on model variations that include a single predictor: first, whether there was a working adult in the household (columns 2 and 5) and then whether the household reported TANF receipt (columns 3 and 6). In both cases the point estimates remain consistent with the results from the model in columns 1 and 4.

However, the R-squared values suggest that the variable capturing the presence of a worker in the household contributes more to explaining variation in the outcome than does TANF receipt. Indeed, change in the work effort of adults in the households in which children reside seems to be an important predictor of changes in $2-a-day poverty status.

Material Hardships Among the $2-a-Day Poor

Table 3 reports on estimates of the rates of select material hardships experienced by children in $2-a-day poverty during 2010 relative to other low-income children and higher-income children. We use 2010 data because this was the first year in the 2010 panel in which material hardship outcomes were collected. The first hardship represents the proportion of children who moved over the course of the 2010 calendar year.[10] We examined this hardship in lieu of the material hardship outcomes associated with standard housing costs because of the high

---

10. Of course, some moves are indicative of positive outcomes for children, such as a move to a better neighborhood or a move for a parent's new job. But housing affordability is a key issue among poor families in the United States, and housing instability is associated with numerous poor outcomes.

Table 3. Material Hardships Among Children by Poverty Status, 2010 (Proportions)

	Higher-Income	Other Low-Income	$2-a-Day Poverty
Residential instability	9.0%	13.2%	22.9%*
Housing problem	10.8%	20.4%	19.0%
Food-insecurity	9.2%	24.4%	28.1%+
Medical hardship	6.7%	14.0%	19.7%*
Any of these hardships	27.9%	48.6%	59.0%*

Source: Authors' calculations from SIPP, 2008.
Notes: Calendar-year weights are used. Income dollars are adjusted to January 2011 dollars. Material hardship outcomes are merged from wave 6 of the 2008 SIPP panel. A child must have annual household income of 150 percent or less of the poverty line and have low assets to be counted in the $2-a-day poverty group. Because of small sample size, adjustment using the svy routine could not be executed. Statistical significance is based on an unadjusted regression with indicators differentiating higher income, low income, and $2-a-day poverty. Findings significant at the 0.05 level are robust to alternative specifications, and marginally significant findings are sensitive to specification. All point estimates remain substantively similar for 2011. All $2-a-day poverty estimates are statistically significantly different from estimates for higher-income children at the 0.05 level or greater.
+$p < .10$; *$p < 0.5$

rates of residential instability among our qualitative sample. Among higher-income children, 9.0 percent had one or more residential moves during the year. The same was true of 13.2 percent of other low-income children. Among children experiencing $2-a-day poverty, 22.9 percent moved at least once over the course of the year—a rate nearly ten percentage points higher than the rate of residential instability experienced by other low-income children.

We find roughly the same levels of physical housing problems between the two groups of low-income children. However, estimates also suggest that children in $2-a-day poverty are more likely to experience food insecurity: 28.1 percent reported household food insecurity, compared to 24.4 percent of other low-income children and 9.2 percent of higher-income children. The rate of food insecurity among the $2-a-day poor is significantly different from the rate for other low-income children only at the 0.10 level.[11] Children among the $2-a-day poor also appear to be more likely to live in households reporting that a household member did not see a medical professional when they needed to because of cost. Nearly 20 percent of children in $2-a-day poverty lived in households reporting medical hardship, compared to 14.0 percent of other low-income children and 6.7 percent of higher-income children.

Taken together, these hardship results offer suggestive evidence that children experiencing $2-a-day poverty are more likely to experience material hardships than other low-income children, not to mention higher-income children. In fact, in terms of the risk, $2-a-day poor children were far more likely to have experienced at least one of these hardships in 2010 compared to other children, with nearly 60 percent reporting one or more of them. This is 10.4 percentage points above the rate for other low-income children, and 31.1 percentage points above the rate for higher-income children.

Sensitivity Analyses

Although the results from Shaefer and Edin (2013) and from this article appear robust in finding an increase in the number and propor-

---

11. See table notes for limitations to the testing of statistical significance.

tion of children reporting very low levels of income in the United States over the past fifteen years, all of these results remain subject to bias. It is possible that, insofar as SIPP respondents misreport their income, our estimates are biased upward. It is also possible that, insofar as SIPP respondents facing $2-a-day poverty drop out of the sample (owing to residential instability), our estimates are biased downward.

In spite of the potential for misreporting on income and public-program participation, the SIPP remains the best source of nationally representative data currently available for this investigation. It would not be appropriate to use administrative earnings records, since these undercount income earned "off the books," which is particularly common among the poor. The SIPP, in fact, records more income among the poor than any other major household survey. As for public-program reporting rates, the SIPP does well relative to other major surveys, and SIPP reporting rates for most public programs did not fall over our study period in a way that would explain a dramatic and steady increase in $2-a-day poverty.

Further, our original estimates were initially motivated by Kathryn Edin's qualitative fieldwork, through which she found herself interacting with more and more families who were surviving on no cash income. Our current fieldwork has taken us to four field sites, where we have interacted with eighteen families who would fit the $2-a-day poverty profile if they were SIPP respondents.

Still, it would be beneficial to have the SIPP results externally validated by some other source of data. Given that the greatest increase in the $2-a-day poverty population is among those reporting SNAP benefits, we turn to the SNAP administrative records. Households receiving SNAP benefits must verify their incomes for eligibility purposes usually every three to twelve months, depending on their state and status. Families can face stiff legal penalties if they knowingly misrepresent their income to increase their SNAP benefit levels.

Annual reports produced from SNAP administrative data have provided the total number of households with children in the United States receiving SNAP benefits who report no other source of income. Based on these reports, figure 4 presents these annual totals with a dashed trend line, starting in 1996 and ending in 2012. In 1996 there were 316,000 SNAP households with children who reported no other source of income. This number began to rise in 2002 and by 2005 had increased to 599,000. By 2012 there were 1.2 million such households. This represents a substantial increase in the share of all households with children in these circumstances, and an increase in the share of all SNAP households. Thus, this increase cannot be explained simply by rising rates of SNAP receipt in the population.

The closest comparison point for this trend line available in our SIPP estimates is the total number of $2-a-day poverty households with children who report SNAP receipt. In the boxes plotted in figure 4, we present these SIPP-based population estimates in the form of unduplicated households in this state for the years 1996, 2005, and 2012. These population estimates prove to be remarkably close to the corresponding household counts from the SNAP administrative records in 1996 and 2005. Our SIPP estimates fall behind SNAP administrative data estimates as of 2012, suggesting that our SIPP estimates are on the low side.

Thus, the key findings of this investigation have been substantiated, to the extent possible thus far, through both quantitative and qualitative means, with each line of inquiry informing the other. As a final note, it is worth mentioning that misreporting of income itself suggests adverse outcomes, such as engagement in the underground economy. For example, in Kathryn Edin and Laura Lein's study *Making Ends Meet* (1997), which they conducted in four cities just prior to welfare reform, many welfare recipients were forced to work "off the books" to survive. Eight percent reported work that was illegal in and of itself (not just because it went unreported to welfare caseworkers and the IRS); the most common such work involved selling sex.

DISCUSSION

The results presented here support and shed further light on what is reported by Shaefer and Edin (2013). When we examine children longitudinally, we find that the changes in the inci-

Figure 4. SNAP Households with Children Reporting No Other Source of Income (Administrative Records)

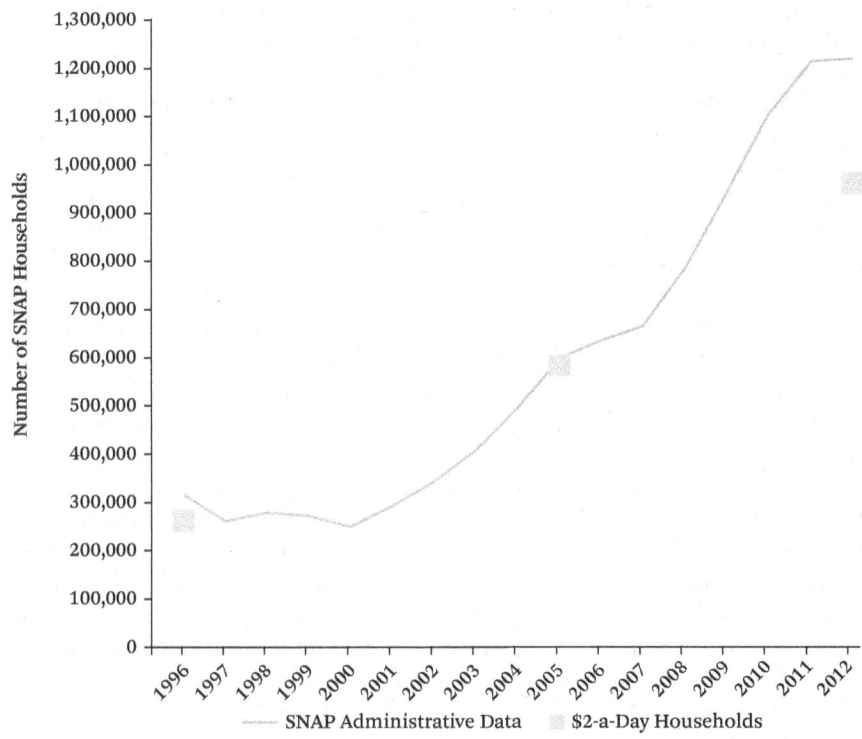

Source: Authors' calculations from U.S. Department of Agriculture, Food and Nutrition Service, "Characteristics of Supplemental Nutrition Assistance Program Households," fiscal years 1996–2013. Yearly reports available at: http://www.fns.usda.gov/ops/supplemental-nutrition-assistance-program-snap-research (accessed October 1, 2015).
Notes: These households report no other countable income. Boxes represent comparable estimates from SIPP $2-a-day poverty households.

dence of $2-a-day poverty are concentrated among children experiencing such a state chronically—that is, for seven or more months during a calendar year. Growth in chronic $2-a-day poverty is seen using both the cash-only definition and after accounting for SNAP, the nation's largest means-tested transfer program. We find that 69.6 percent of children who experienced $2-a-day poverty in 2012 lived in a household where an adult worked for at least one full month over the course of the year, while only 10.8 percent lived in households that reported receipt of TANF during the year. Not surprisingly, we find that change in the employment of household adults is a key predictor of change in $2-a-day poverty status. Finally, we find evidence suggesting that households experiencing $2-a-day poverty are more likely to face certain material hardships than other low-income households and higher-income households.

These results suggest that SNAP plays a vital role at the very bottom of the income distribution, but they also raise the question of the proper cash value of $1 in SNAP benefits for households that are highly resource-constrained. For households with other resources, economic theory suggests that SNAP and cash are roughly equivalent, increasing a family's budget constraint except in the region marked by very low food expenditures. However, it is unclear for families with no or very few resources how a dollar of SNAP should be valued relative to a dollar in cash.

The descriptive analyses presented here also do not clarify the exact causal mechanisms leading to such a large rise in $2-a-day poverty in the United States. We hypothesize that the virtual disappearance of a cash safety net for nonworkers has played an important role, as well as the extended period of high unemployment that has accompanied the Great Recession. A number of sensitivity analyses described here and in Shaefer and Edin (2013) offer suggestive evidence that this is correct. Yet future research must seek to more fully assess the causal relationship between the welfare reforms of the 1990s and the rise of $2-a-day poverty.

Whatever the exact causal relationship, the results presented here lend more evidence to the assertion that there has been a fundamental shift in the circumstances of households with children at the very bottom of the bottom in the United States. What's more, the rising rates of spells of very low income found by Shaefer and Edin (2013) are concentrated among children experiencing such spells chronically rather than episodically. Such findings raise important questions about the adequacy of the U.S. means-tested income safety net.

APPENDIX
Measuring Extreme Deprivation in the United States: Is Consumption the Right Measure?

Consumption measures of poverty attempt to take the resources that families expend on current consumption and assign them a cash value, with the goal of estimating a total dollar value for what that family consumes over some period of time. Some researchers argue that a consumption-based measure of poverty may more directly reveal the resources available to families and be a more direct measure of material well-being than an income-based measure of poverty (Bavier 2014; Meyer and Sullivan 2003). Chandy and Smith (2014), for example, report that the World Bank prefers a consumption-based measure of poverty when estimating rates of global poverty (although some countries do use income-based measures), in part because people in developing countries often survive solely on resources that never take the form of cash, such as raising and tending to livestock or subsistence farming.

Some research offers evidence that consumption estimates from national representative surveys have a stronger association with key material hardship outcomes among some population subgroups, such as single mother households (Meyer and Sullivan 2003). However, to our knowledge there is no paper that shows that consumption is better than income in measuring hardship across the board, and the two measures generally paint qualitatively similar pictures of well-being among poor families with children. On the other hand, for some sub-groups, such as the mature population, there is preliminary evidence that income is much more clearly associated with material hardship than consumption (Charles et al. 2006). A great deal more research is needed to determine which is the more uniformly superior "instrumental" measure of well-being for the U.S. population.

Yet in efforts to evaluate changes in consumption among the poor over the past two decades, we are confronted with significant shortcomings of available data. The primary source of data for such analyses is the Consumer Expenditure Survey (CE). Recent evidence suggests that for the purposes of measuring low levels of income and consumption over the period of 1996 to 2010, the CE data may be deeply flawed (Bavier 2014).

A broader literature has for some time noted a divergence in trends between consumption poverty estimates produced by the CE and income poverty estimates from the Current Population Survey (CPS) since roughly the year 2001 (Meyer and Sullivan 2009). Until recently, these studies have called into question the value of income-based poverty measures. However, Bavier (2014) argues that the divergence of income poverty estimates yielded by CPS (and by extension the SIPP) and CE consumption poverty estimates after 2001 is not explained by fundamental differences in what is captured by a consumption-based poverty measure as opposed to an income-based measure. Rather this divergence may be the result of differences between the CE sample and the (much larger) samples of other major household surveys.

Bavier finds that trends in poverty rates based on adjusted income (accounting for taxes and public program benefits) in the CPS and consumption data from the CE matched quite closely during the period between 1984 and 2000. However, after that point in the CE, *both* the consumption poverty estimates *and* the income poverty estimates began a rapid decline that followed a starkly different path from income poverty rates recorded in the CPS and other major household surveys over this period. Thus, if one were to look only at the income poverty estimates from the CE, one would see the same divergence from the income data of the other major household surveys that one sees in the CE's consumption data.

Some researchers have raised questions about this analysis in terms of whether Bavier's calculation of income in the CE was conducted correctly. However, Bavier ushers in another test of the CE's representativeness using consumption data from the Panel Study of Income Dynamics. PSID did not include a full battery of household expenditure questions until the mid-2000s, and even today the reference period for these questions is not consistent across expenditure questions. Yet when PSID expenditure questions that remained consistent starting in 1999 are compared to the results from a similar set of questions in the CE, the resulting divergence leads to the same conclusion as the previous test—that of the CE breaking away from peer surveys after 2000. The PSID consumption data remain in line with the CPS and its peers, while the CE takes a different path. Thus, at the very least, there is considerable disagreement across the primary nationally representative data sources that can be used to construct trends in expenditure and consumption poverty estimates.

Furthermore, the CE is currently undergoing a major redesign as a result of widespread concerns about data quality.[12] Thus, we are of the opinion that the CE data should not be used in an analysis that examines trends in the prevalence of households with very low resources over time.

Misreporting of Income and Public Program Participation in Household Surveys

Misreporting of income is a problem in major household surveys, but the SIPP does comparatively well relative to its peers in terms of reporting rates (Meyer et al. 2009). Analyses find that the SIPP records the highest level of aggregate income among families in the lowest income quintile, far more than the CPS or American Community Survey (Czajka and Denmead 2008). SIPP asks many detailed questions about sources of income, both from formal employment and from informal sources.

Reporting rates for public program participation are typically reflected by the difference between counts of participants yielded by surveys and counts of participants from administrative records (reported as the proportion of survey counts to administrative counts). In all household surveys, public program participation is nearly always lower than is reflected in administrative totals, but the SIPP has much higher reporting rates, on average, than its peer surveys. Most importantly, available evidence finds that SIPP reporting rates for most public programs have not fallen steadily over the study period in a way that could explain the increase in rates of $2-a-day poverty.

Further, evidence from available studies is suggestive (although far from definitive) that misreporting of program participation is greatest among low-income families with existing sources of income—those who may cycle onto and off public programs in relatively short periods (Meyer and Goerge 2011). Thus, when examining families at the very bottom with few other sources of income in a given month, it is not clear the extent to which misreporting of public program participation will occur.

REFERENCES

Bavier, Richard. 2014. "Recent Trends in U.S. Income and Expenditure Poverty." *Journal of Policy Analysis and Management* 33(3): 700–18.

---

12. http://www.bls.gov/cex/ce_gemini_redesign.pdf (accessed October 1, 2015).

Ben-Shalom, Yonaton, Robert Moffitt, and John Scholz. 2012. "An Assessment of the Effectiveness of Anti-poverty Programs in the United States." In *Oxford Handbook of the Economics of Poverty*, edited by Philip N. Jefferson. Oxford: Oxford University Press.

Blank, Rebecca M. 2007. "Improving the Safety Net for Single Mothers Who Face Serious Barriers to Work." *Future of Children* 17(2): 183–97.

Chandy, Laurence, and Cory Smith. 2014. "How Poor Are America's Poorest? U.S. $2 a Day Poverty in a Global Context." Policy Paper 2014-03. Washington, D.C.: Brookings Institution.

Czajka, John, and Gabrielle Denmead. 2008. "Income Data for Policy Analysis: A Comparative Assessment of Eight Surveys: Final Report." Washington, D.C.: Mathematica Policy Research, Inc. Available at: http://www.mathematica-mpr.com/publications/PDFs/incomedata.pdf (accessed October 1, 2015).

Edin, Kathryn, and Laura Lein. 1997. *Making Ends Meet*. New York: Russell Sage Foundation.

Loprest, Pamela. 2011. "Disconnected Families and TANF." Research Brief 2. Washington, D.C.: Urban Institute, Office of Planning, Research, and Evaluation (OPRE).

Meyer, Bruce, and Robert Goerge. 2011. "Errors in Survey Reporting and Imputation and Their Effects on Estimates of Food Stamp Program Participation." Working Paper 11-14. Washington: U.S. Census Bureau Center for Economic Studies.

Meyer, Bruce, Wallace Mok, and James Sullivan. 2009. "The Under-reporting of Transfers in Household Surveys: Its Nature and Consequences." Working Paper 15181. Cambridge, Mass.: National Bureau of Economic Research.

Meyer, Bruce, and James Sullivan. 2003. "Measuring the Well-Being of the Poor Using Income and Consumption." *Journal of Human Resources* 38(S): 1180–1220.

——. 2009. "Five Decades of Consumption and Income Poverty." Working Paper 14827. Cambridge, Mass.: National Bureau of Economic Research.

Nord, Mark. 2006. "Survey of Income and Program Participation 2001 Wave 8 Food Security Data File Technical Documentation and User Notes." Washington: U.S. Department of Agriculture (USDA), Economic Research Service. Available at: http://www.nber.org/sipp/food_security/2001.pdf (accessed October 1, 2015).

Ouellette, Tammy, Nancy Burstein, David Long, and Erik Beecroft. 2004. "Measures of Material Hardship: Final Report." Washington: U.S. Department of Health and Human Services (DHHS) (April). Available at: http://www.aspe.hhs.gov/sites/default/files/pdf/73366/report.pdf (accessed October 1, 2015).

Ratcliffe, Caroline, Signe-Mary McKernan, and Sisi Zhang. 2011. "How Much Does the Supplemental Nutrition Assistance Program Reduce Food Insecurity?" *American Journal of Agricultural Economics* 93: 1082–98.

Sen, Amartya. 1999. *Development as Freedom*. New York: Alfred Knopf.

Shaefer, H. Luke, and Kathryn Edin. 2013. "Extreme Poverty in the United States and the Response of Federal Means-Tested Transfer Programs." *Social Service Review* 87(2): 250–68.

Turner, Lesley, Sheldon Danziger, and Kristin Seefeldt. 2006. "Failing the Transition from Welfare to Work: Women Chronically Disconnected from Employment and Cash Welfare." *Social Science Quarterly* 87(2): 227–49.

When There Is No Welfare: The Income Packaging Strategies of Mothers Without Earnings or Cash Assistance Following an Economic Downturn

KRISTIN S. SEEFELDT AND HEATHER SANDSTROM

The 1996 welfare reform law sought to reformulate single mothers' income package, replacing cash welfare checks with paychecks. However, many single mothers have not been able to do that and have neither earnings nor cash assistance. Among a sample of single mothers in Los Angeles and southeast Michigan, we find that when single mothers lose jobs and do not receive cash assistance, they package income from a variety of sources (such as other public assistance programs and informal child support), find others in their social networks to pay their bills, or move in with others. However, their income packaging strategies are fraught with challenges. Benefits from certain public programs are difficult to secure; financial assistance from friends and family members can quickly vanish, particularly if a partner is deported or jailed; and doubling up with others often leads to living in crowded and unsafe conditions.

Keywords: single mothers, welfare reform, economic survival, income packaging

"Welfare [does] not pay enough to cover a family's monthly bills." This statement by Kathryn Edin and Laura Lein (1996, 254) challenged a popular conception in the 1990s that welfare recipients were able to live adequately on public benefits, so much so that they became "dependent" on them. In their large-scale study, Edin and Lein (1997) documented the various strategies that low-income single mothers used in the early 1990s to obtain enough income to pay the bills. In addition to welfare checks and food stamps, poor women might work informal jobs, obtain help from friends and family, seek out the assistance of boyfriends, and visit community agencies. Packaging together all of these forms of assistance, women were able to make ends meet (Edin and Lein 1997).

Yet the 1996 welfare reform law, the Personal Responsibility and Work Opportunity Reconciliation Act (PRWORA), sought to re-

Kristin S. Seefeldt is assistant professor of social work at the University of Michigan. **Heather Sandstrom** is senior research associate at the Urban Institute.

This project was funded by the Office of Planning, Research, and Evaluation in the Administration for Children and Families, U.S. Department of Health and Human Services, under contract #HHS P23-337-0207. The authors' thank Emily Schmitt and Matthew Borus, federal project officers, for their support of this work, Sandra Huerta and Max Sokoloff for excellent research assistance, and Pamela Loprest for her guidance on the project. Direct correspondence to: Kristin Seefeldt at kseef@umich.edu, School of Social Work, University of Michigan, 1080 S. University Ave., Ann Arbor, MI 48109; and Heather Sandstrom at hsandstrom@urban.org, Urban Institute, 2100 M St. NW, Washington, D.C. 20037.

formulate single mothers' income package. Instead of receiving welfare checks, poor mothers were expected to work in the formal economy for paychecks. Other policies, such as the Earned Income Tax Credit (EITC) and access to child care assistance, were expanded to make low-wage work more appealing. Many mothers did leave the welfare rolls for work (or started reporting wages from jobs they already held). Yet, for a small but growing number of families, a paycheck was not replacing a welfare check. The low-income single mothers in these families were not employed, nor were they receiving cash assistance from the Temporary Assistance for Needy Families (TANF) program, which replaced the welfare program that Edin and Lein's single mothers had used in the early 1990s. Researchers and policymakers began referring to these women as "disconnected" in that they were attached to neither the labor market nor the welfare system (the one that had historically provided cash, as opposed to in-kind benefits).

Studies have established that the number of disconnected families has grown over time, from about 12 percent of all low-income single mothers in 2004 to about 20 percent in 2008 (Loprest and Nichols 2011). Other estimates have broadened the definition of disconnected mothers to include all low-income mothers not working and not receiving TANF, regardless of past TANF receipt, including those who are ineligible because of either their immigration status or TANF time limits (Loprest 2011). Compared to other single mothers who are not disconnected, they face more employment barriers (Loprest and Zedlewski 2006) and are more likely to face severe deprivation, at least in terms of income: using Survey of Income and Program Participation (SIPP) data, Pamela Loprest and Austin Nichols (2011) find that the median annual income, excluding other household members, of disconnected mothers is only $535. Although many studies have attempted to count and characterize the number of disconnected families, one largely unanswered question remains: How do these women survive economically? What does their income package look like when they are not working and are also not using cash assistance? The United States is a cash-based economy, and not having earnings from work or cash welfare benefits may make financial coping extremely difficult (Edin and Shaefer 2015).

In this article, we use qualitative interview data from a sample of low-income women with children living in two distinct locations—southeast Michigan and Los Angeles, California—to begin to examine the economic survival strategies of mothers who have found themselves without earnings and without welfare benefits in the aftermath of the Great Recession. We address the following three questions:

1. What are the circumstances under which low-income women lose jobs and welfare benefits or do not take up welfare?

2. What do they do to manage financially during periods when they have no earnings and no cash welfare?

3. Are their financial coping strategies adequate and sustainable? For whom and under what circumstances?

LITERATURE REVIEW
Who Are the Disconnected?

Both during the welfare reform debates in the 1990s and after implementation of PRWORA, many researchers, policymakers, and advocates wondered whether poor single mothers would be able to meet the demands of the law. Among other provisions, PRWORA mandated that in order to receive cash benefits through the TANF program, adult recipients would need to find jobs. After receiving benefits for five years—or less at state discretion—most adult recipients would no longer be eligible for cash assistance, having hit the so-called welfare time limit. Although TANF caseloads declined dramatically in the years following welfare reform's passage, not all former recipients left TANF for work, and even those who did often worked in unstable and low-paying jobs (Danziger 2010). Analysts began referring to poor families that had no TANF cash benefits and no job earnings as "disconnected." That is, they were disconnected from the labor market and from one of the few sources of public cash aid available to this population.

To count the number of disconnected families, a clear definition needed to be developed;

over time researchers and policymakers focused on narrowing the types of economic supports that a disconnected family could receive so that the resulting group represented potentially the most economically disadvantaged of all poor, single-parent families. One of the first analyses on this topic (Loprest 2003) defined the disconnected as former welfare recipients who were not currently receiving TANF benefits, not working, not living with a working spouse, and not receiving disability benefits. Other studies built on this definition (for example, Blank and Kovak 2009; Ovwhigo, Kolupanowich, and Born 2009; Turner, Danziger, and Seefeldt 2006), including or excluding various other types of benefits and income brought in by other adults in the household.

Estimates of the prevalence of disconnected families vary depending on the definition used, although most studies find fairly similar proportions. Loprest (2003) found that just under 10 percent of former recipients nationally were disconnected (that is, not working, not receiving welfare, not living with a working spouse, and not receiving disability) at a point in time in 1999, although that figure rose to 13.8 percent in 2002. Lesley Turner, Sheldon Danziger, and Kristin Seefeldt (2006) found that about one-tenth of low-income women who had formerly received TANF in one county in Michigan were chronically disconnected; that is, they had not worked or received TANF for at least one-quarter of the months over a six-and-a-half year period (in other words, for at least twenty out of seventy-nine months). The most recent estimates (Loprest and Nichols 2011) show that the percentage of disconnected single mothers (regardless of prior TANF participation) has increased substantially over the last decade: about one in eight low-income single mothers were disconnected in 1996 and 1997, but about one in five experienced disconnection in 2008.

In addition to estimating the prevalence of disconnectedness, these studies also examined the characteristics of the disconnected and found, in general, that the disconnected are more disadvantaged than other single mothers in the domains of health, substance abuse problems, education levels, and learning disabilities (Loprest 2003; Turner, Danziger, and Seefeldt 2006). Although they report housing problems at levels similar to those of other former recipients, the disconnected appear to have more food-related hardships, such as skipping meals and running out of food (Loprest 2003).

More limited is any information on how women become disconnected and the challenges they face in connecting to the public assistance system when they are in between jobs. Rebecca Blank and Brian Kovak (2009) documented a variety of reasons that women become disconnected, the most common being loss of earnings (58 percent of all spells). Turner and her colleagues (2006) similarly found that most women in their sample became disconnected because they lost a job, not because they lost welfare benefits.

Not surprisingly, disconnected mothers are quite poor (Loprest and Nichols 2011). In 2008 median annual income for these mothers was just $535. When including income from other household members, that figure rises to just over $18,000. About 30 percent of disconnected mothers are the only adult in the household, while the remainder live with at least one other adult. Unknown from survey data is whether income is shared across the household.

Income estimates often do not include benefits from public programs. Although the term "disconnected" might imply to some that these families have no interactions with the public benefit system, about half of disconnected mothers receive food assistance through the Supplemental Nutrition Assistance Program (SNAP), formerly known as food stamps. About one-fifth receive housing assistance, and 14 percent report that the household receives some other kind of public transfer. Additionally, survey data may not capture the extent to which women receive other types of financial assistance that are more difficult to quantify, such as having a family member who purchases groceries or pays certain bills. For poor women, earnings and public benefits alone are known to be inadequate and must be supplemented if families are to get by. Single mothers without welfare and their own earnings might be connected to a variety of these types of support, so perhaps it is more accurate to characterize them as lacking earnings and cash welfare rather than as "disconnected."

The Income Packaging Strategies of Poor Single Mothers

Poor families, not just those who are termed "disconnected," have long had to piece together income from various sources, because money from any one source (such as welfare benefits or earnings) is never enough. Carol Stack's classic *All Our Kin* documented the complex networks of familial and "fictive kin" that existed in a poor African American community in the 1960s. Communal child-rearing, sharing and swapping of household items, and the trading "back and forth [of] food stamps, kids, clothes, money, and everything else" were common strategies of economic survival (Stack 1974, 35). This "cooperative lifestyle," as Stack termed it, helped poor families survive the uncertainty of the labor market and the idiosyncrasies of the welfare office by providing a stable network of individuals who could always be relied upon for help.

In perhaps the most detailed accounting of poor women's economic coping strategies, Edin and Lein (1997) found that public assistance benefits rarely covered families' most basic needs, which included rent, food, and transportation, although they were able to cover about three-fifths of their expenses from these two sources. To "make ends meet," women relied on contributions from family members and friends, including formal and informal child support from noncustodial fathers and contributions from current boyfriends (both live-in and not), as well as unreported or off-the-books work. Although life on welfare was not at all lucrative, more mothers chose to stay on the rolls than to work because child care and transportation costs, along with the potential loss of Medicaid benefits, made taking a low-wage job a costly prospect.

Piecing together these sources of support posed new challenges each month, Edin and Lein (1997) note, in part because of instability in the various supports and in part because of poverty in the networks in which women were embedded. Further, more recent research has brought into question just how much kin support poor families receive, particularly African Americans. Whereas white families are more likely to provide financial support to their kin members, in black families support is usually in-kind, such as transportation and child care (Sarkisian and Gerstel 2004). Additionally, receiving help from a friend or family member often comes with the expectation that the favor will be returned sometime in the future. In some relationships, this reciprocity can be time-consuming and demanding, further straining already limited resources (Domínguez and Watkins 2003; Hogan, Eggebeen, and Clogg 1993).

While cohabiting partners may contribute toward bills, rent, and other expenses, this additional source of income may not be stable for low-income mothers, for several reasons. First, about two-thirds of cohabiting relationships among economically disadvantaged couples will dissolve rather than end in marriage (Lichter, Qian, and Mellott 2006). When these relationships do end, women's economic situation declines, averaging about a 33 percent decline in household income among a population already more likely to be poor, whereas men experience little change in income (Avellar and Smock 2005). Second, resident male partners may have obligations outside of the household. Rates of multiple partner fertility (having children with more than one partner) have increased over recent decades (Carlson and Furstenberg 2006). For families with low income, this can mean that already thin resources must be spread across two or more households.

These patterns of family instability may not hold for all racial and ethnic groups, such as Mexican Americans, whose cultural background allows cohabitation to be seen as a type of "surrogate marriage," particularly for individuals of lower socio-economic backgrounds (Castro Martin 2002, 35). *Una unión libre* (a consensual union) is an informal type of marriage with a long history in Mexico (Ojeda 2011). A qualitative study comparing the attitudes of young women on either side of the U.S.-Mexican border found that while Latinas in the United States viewed cohabitation as a potential "testing" period for a couple, young women living in Mexico equated cohabitation with a consensual union, an alternative family form in which to live with a partner and have children (Ojeda 2011).

Third, men who partner with low-income women are likely to be similarly economically disadvantaged (Sinkewicz and Garfinkel 2009). Men with lower levels of education have fared poorly in the last several decades as technological advances have favored the more educated in the labor market. Real wages for young men in the twentieth percentile of the earnings distribution dropped between 1979 and 2007, as did the wages of high school graduates. The employment rates of high school–educated young men also declined across this time period, with African American men faring the worst: more than one-quarter of young African American men did not formally work for pay at any point during 2007 (Danziger and Ratner 2010). Instability in their relationships and their partners' low earnings can make cohabiting low-income women unable to depend on a partner's income during a spell of disconnection.

Formal child support may also not be consistently paid. A study of low-income single mothers in Wisconsin found that while 89 percent had received a child support payment at some point during the previous year, only 56 percent had received payment in ten of the twelve months, and 40 percent had received a regular amount for at least ten months (Ha, Cancian, and Meyer 2011). Informal payments, while perhaps a more flexible option for parents with unstable income or changing needs, cannot be enforced legally and are not subjected to automatic payment mechanisms such as wage withholding. Thus, informal payments may be an even less stable source of support. Fathers may also be less likely to provide informal support when mothers go on to have additional children with other men. They often target support directly at their biological children (for example, by purchasing clothes for them) rather than provide support that can be shared across the household (Cancian and Meyer 2011).

In Edin and Lein's (1997) study, cash welfare payments, although not generous, provided a consistent financial base for many single mothers. Under current regulations, to the extent that cash welfare is at all stable, assistance is available for a limited period of time. For those who are unable to make or sustain the transition from welfare to work, how might financial coping strategies differ when welfare is no longer in the equation? A qualitative phone study of ninety-five disconnected families conducted in 2002 provides some information on this group's income packaging strategies (Zedlewski et al. 2003). More than half of families used food stamps, and 37 percent received some form of government housing assistance. Another 37 percent received help with housing costs from family members, so that the vast majority were able to receive some financial contribution to what very likely was their largest expense. Help from noncustodial parents came in the form of regular, formal child support payments for about two-fifths of the sample. Nearly two-thirds received help from friends and family, but most of that assistance was reported to be relatively small. Just under one-third received regular help from private agencies and charities, and just over one-third reported income from informal employment.

These data were collected, however, prior to the Great Recession; although there had been a recession in 2001, it was relatively mild by comparison. We might expect that a prolonged economic downturn would affect the ability of other family members to help out or of noncustodial parents to provide child support, if these individuals lost jobs. Moreover, the Great Recession along with its aftermath has been the first real test of the nation's reformed safety net during a period of economic difficulty. Trend data show that TANF caseloads remained relatively flat during the worst of the Great Recession, suggesting that perhaps even more families were without cash assistance during extended periods of unemployment. Finally, we know little about the consequences for these mothers of engaging in particular economic survival strategies. This article attempts to provide some insight into these issues.

METHODS
Sample
We drew participants from Los Angeles, California, and southeast Michigan, two areas with relatively high concentrations of low-income families, in order to maximize our ability to recruit mothers who were not working or receiving public assistance. The two sites were chosen for a couple of other reasons as well. First, we were already involved in survey projects in these areas and were able to leverage

the survey data to identify potentially eligible families.[1] Second, the demographics of these communities allowed us to focus on two groups: noncitizen immigrants, who are overrepresented among the disconnected, and African Americans, who are slightly underrepresented (Loprest and Nichols 2011). These two sites also have different labor markets and costs of living, allowing for an exploration of differences in economic survival strategies.

To qualify for participation in the study, respondents had to be:

1. Low-income, unmarried women with at least one resident child under the age of eighteen
2. Not currently working for pay and not currently receiving TANF or Supplemental Security Income (SSI) for themselves; or, if currently employed, having experienced at least six cumulative months of unemployment in the past two years, during which time they did not receive cash benefits from TANF or SSI for themselves and were caring for a resident child

Potentially eligible survey respondents were notified about the study and then screened, if they were interested, for eligibility. In Los Angeles, fifty-six women were fully screened, and thirty-five were determined eligible. Of the thirty-five who were eligible, twenty-nine completed an interview. In Michigan, thirty-five women were screened, with twenty-three meeting the study eligibility criteria. Twenty-two Michigan respondents were interviewed, for a total of fifty-one women across the two sites.

Procedures

Data were collected in the summer and fall of 2013. Interviews were semistructured and lasted approximately ninety minutes on average. All interviews were conducted in English in Michigan, whereas the majority of respondents (twenty-two out of twenty-nine) in Los Angeles were interviewed in Spanish and the rest in English. The interviews were audio-recorded to later produce full transcriptions. Only one woman in Los Angeles declined being recorded; in that case, a research assistant took detailed handwritten notes and subsequently wrote a memo containing a full account of the interview that was used in the analysis.

The interview guide explored many topics related to participants' experiences, including their reasons for not working, their participation in public assistance programs, and their experiences of material hardship. Because of the project's interest in learning how low-income families manage without earnings and cash assistance, we focused much of our inquiry on the various financial sources of support the women received, including support from other household and family members, boyfriends, the fathers of their children, and other individuals. In addition to asking directly about financial help they might have received from others, we requested an accounting of all the money and benefits they had received in the previous month and asked them to specify the sources of the money they received to pay bills and buy groceries and items for their children. We also asked the women to complete a social network diagram in which they identified the people in their lives who supported them in different ways—financially, emotionally, with child care, and so on—and described the closeness of those relationships. Women also identified people who were sources of stress in their lives.

We imported the transcripts into NVivo software for text analysis. The research team developed a coding scheme from the research questions and coded and analyzed a priori and emergent themes across interviews. Specifically, researchers coded the segments of interview text in which respondents discussed a particular topic, such as their experiences of hardship. Analysis of the coded text revealed common themes across respondents as well as similarities and differences across the two sites.

---

1. Study participants were recruited based on their participation in either the Best Start Los Angeles Pilot Community Evaluation, led by the Urban Institute and the Center for Healthier Children, Families, and Communities at the University of California–Los Angeles, or the Michigan Recession and Recovery Study, conducted by the National Poverty Center at the University of Michigan.

RESULTS

Sample Characteristics

The twenty-two participants in Michigan were on average thirty-six years old, ranging in age from twenty-seven to fifty-one. Nearly all were African American, while two identified as white and one as biracial. On average they had 3.5 children, including adult children, and 2.7 minor-age children. Half of the women had a resident child under age five. Their education and employment experiences were quite heterogeneous. Seven of the twenty-two women had not finished high school (although three of these women had GEDs), while another six had completed only high school, eight had completed some college, one held an associate's degree, and two had finished their bachelor's degree.

The twenty-nine participants in Los Angeles were slightly younger than those in Michigan—thirty-one years old on average, their ages ranging from eighteen to forty-six. They all self-identified as Latino or Hispanic, except for one African American. Twenty-five of the twenty-nine Los Angeles participants were immigrants, including eighteen from Mexico, four from El Salvador, and three from Guatemala. One woman had immigrated within the past five years, eleven others had immigrated between six and ten years ago, and the remaining women had come to the United States as children or adolescents. All participants in the Los Angeles site had a three-year-old child at the time of the interview (because the sample drew from an existing survey sample of mothers who had given birth in Los Angeles between December 2009 and September 2011, three years prior to data collection for this study); most had at least one other child. Most Los Angeles participants had no more than a high school education; some immigrant mothers had completed the equivalent of a sixth-grade education in their country of origin. Seven women had some postsecondary education, but none had a college degree.

Why Were the Study Participants Not Working or Receiving Cash Assistance?

Analyses of interview data uncovered the reasons why the women in our sample were not working or receiving cash assistance. Table 1 summarizes those results. In Los Angeles, most (twenty) of the women voluntarily left the labor force when they had children. Most of these women cited a belief that it is better for children to have their mother home with them, at least until they start school. Others reported that motherhood left them with no choice but to stay at home because of limited child care options, limited job opportunities (especially jobs with a schedule that fit working mothers' needs), or pressure from a partner who would not allow them to work outside the home.

Table 1. Paths of Study Participants to No Earnings and No Cash Assistance

	Los Angeles	Southeast Michigan
Laid off; did not apply for TANF	3	3
Laid off; subsequently hit TANF time limit	0	3
Quit job; did not apply for TANF	20	4
Quit job; subsequently hit TANF time limit	0	4
Fired from job; did not apply for TANF	1	3
Fired from job; subsequently hit TANF time limit	0	1
Fired from job; lost TANF for other reasons	0	1
Left job for health reasons (disabled); did not apply for TANF	1	2
Left job for health reasons (disabled); lost TANF for other reasons	0	1
Never worked	4	0

Source: Authors' calculations.

Four women had never worked since arriving in the United States.

The majority of the women in Los Angeles had never used TANF, and when they exited the labor market they did not apply. Depending on their immigration status, these mothers may not have been eligible themselves for TANF. Documented immigrants may not receive TANF until they have been in the country five years, and undocumented immigrants are never eligible. Although mothers of citizen children might have been able to receive cash assistance on their children's behalf, beliefs held by the immigrant community kept many mothers from applying. Six women told us that if they used TANF, their children would later be forced to repay the cash assistance, either directly or through military service.[2] Another five women reported that taking TANF could negatively affect their chance of obtaining citizenship. Indeed, immigration law allows individuals who are deemed likely to become "public charges"—that is, who rely on public cash assistance such as TANF—to be denied entry into the country or lawful permanent residence. According to the U.S. Department of Homeland Security (2009), however, the "public charge" clause does not apply during the naturalization process.

In Michigan, almost half of the women first lost a job, either through layoffs, quitting, or being fired, and then later lost TANF benefits. The other half did not apply for TANF when they lost or left a job. Of those who lost TANF, one-third reached the time limit. The state initially did not have a formal time limit; instead, Michigan used state funds to pay benefits for families that had reached the sixty-month federal limit. Starting in 2006, the state instituted a forty-eight-month limit, counting only months in which benefits were received from the date of implementation going forward. A new administration sought to revise the policy, counting all months of TANF receipt since 1996. Between 11,000 and 15,000 families suddenly lost benefits in 2012 when an injunction was lifted that had previously barred the state from "starting the clock" in 1996. These families were allowed to reapply when a lawsuit was filed challenging the constitutionality of this provision, but many did not (French 2012). Other families had already lost benefits under a 2007 policy that implemented a forty-eight-month time limit (counting months of TANF receipt since 2007). The policy at the time interviews were conducted limited TANF receipt to cases that had not exceeded forty-eight months of assistance since 2007 or sixty months since 1996.

For example, both Gina and Claudette had last received TANF in February 2013 after hitting the sixty-month limit.[3] Gina had lost TANF earlier in 2011 but then, because of the lawsuit, was allowed to reapply. Until she lost her job, Claudette had not received TANF since the late 1990s. When she reapplied in 2012, she found out that she could collect only a few months of benefits. Although Monica, a young mother with a severely autistic child, was not exactly sure when she had reached the time limit, she was one of those who lost benefits because of the state's initial time limit policy, losing benefits in 2007 or 2008. Other than Claudette, most of the women reported being unaware that they were close to reaching the time limit and having found out only a month in advance that their benefits would be stopped.

Other women had been dropped from TANF owing to other rules, such as the state's work requirement. Fifteen years earlier, Ginger had applied for disability benefits through the SSI program. When she was denied, she reapplied and reapplied after each subsequent denial. While her applications were pending, she had been able to receive TANF benefits without having to attend a job search program. In 2007 Michigan changed its policy, giving caseworkers discretion to send SSI applicants to the job search program. Despite being disabled enough to receive state payments for a home health aide to help with household chores, her caseworker deemed Ginger capable of attending. After several sessions, Ginger stopped going, saying that the pain from her various med-

---

2. In 2011 at least one media outlet reported that the state of California was seeking to recoup overpayments (benefit payments made in error) from the adult children whose parents had been overpaid. A lawsuit was subsequently filed, and the state settled the case by agreeing to halt the practice (Miranda 2011).

3. All names have been changed.

ical conditions made it too difficult to sit all day in a classroom. She was promptly dropped from the rolls. Lisa had been attending the job search program and found it helpful, but then she moved and her new place was not on a bus route. Without transportation, she could not attend the program. Lisa alerted her caseworker to the predicament, but she still lost her benefits. Finally, a few women received Unemployment Insurance (UI) benefits when they lost their jobs, but those benefits also ran out. One woman applied for TANF but then lost these benefits when she reached the time limit, another transitioned into a disability program, and still another found a new job.

The study participants in Michigan who did not apply for TANF upon loss of employment believed that they did not need it because they had other sources of support or because they thought the program's requirements were too burdensome. At an earlier time, Michelle was on TANF. She told a story of wanting to leave the TANF job search program to pick up her son when his school let out in the afternoon. However, she was told she would be penalized for doing so. She said, "If I tell you, 'Okay, my son is in school, you want me to come to [the job search program] nine till four, and I'm telling you my son get out at two-thirty. Who's going to pick him up at two-thirty if I don't have anybody to pick him up?'. . . They say, 'Okay, if you go, you're out the door, and then you can't come back in.'" When Michelle lost her job in 2011, she decided she would not apply for TANF.

Some of the women—four in Michigan and seven in Los Angeles—were working by the time we interviewed them. Three women in Michigan restarted work with the same employer after a temporary layoff. The fourth had just recently found a new job. The jobs held by the Los Angeles mothers were mostly off the books, paid very low wages, and offered irregular work. Some of these women went back to work when their partner left or lost a job. Most of the women who wanted to work reported being unable, however, to find jobs. The poor economy in Michigan and issues related to immigration status and child care needs in Los Angeles kept most of the women in the study unemployed.

Six women in Michigan reported being laid off, primarily because their employers were facing economic difficulty. The restaurant in which Susan worked slowed down more than usual one winter, and she was laid off. Kiana lost her job when the public school system privatized part of its workforce in an effort to save money. Other women were either fired or left jobs when a problem arose. All of them had expected to be able to find another job, but as the economy worsened they found themselves struggling to do so. Michelle, a Detroit resident, quit her job as a nurse's aide when the cost of gas rose and the commute to her suburban employer became, as she judged it, too expensive. She hoped to find a similar job within the city limits, but given the few available jobs in Detroit, her odds of doing so seemed slim. Altercations with supervisors led Linda to quit her job and Gina to be fired. Linda enrolled in a training program to be a medical bill coder, a job purportedly in great demand as health care providers moved to electronic recorders, but no one actually was hiring. Gina was initially not bothered when she lost her cashier job; with a couple of exceptions, she had never held any job for more than a couple of months, and she had always been able to find another. But in 2008 the Great Recession was in full force, and that next job never materialized for her.

The more time passed since their last job, the more difficult these women perceived it to be to find a new one. Gina noted, "It's just been the space [on my résumé]. The first thing [employers] say, 'Well, what you've been doing for these last five years or six years?'" And the women were correct in thinking this was a factor: recent research has found that the chances of receiving an interview for a job decline by 45 percent for those who have been unemployed eight months or more compared to those who have been unemployed only one month (Kroft et al. 2014).

Although most of the women in Los Angeles were not actively looking for a job and instead were staying home with their children, they noted that even if they wanted to work, they would face significant challenges. Quite a few mothers were concerned about finding child care that was safe and affordable. Others believed that their limited proficiency with English would severely limit their job options. Immigration status was another issue. Rosa, a

Guatemalan immigrant, had found work in a factory after she first arrived in the country. But she quit when she heard a rumor that some authority was going to be checking Social Security numbers. Mayra, who also lacked documentation, reported running out of her workplace one day when her father called to tell her that immigration authorities were in the neighborhood. The few who were actively seeking employment cited lack of education and experience as reasons why employers were not responding to their applications.

In total, the women in Michigan had been without work and cash welfare anywhere from six months to five years, and most of those spells were ongoing. The Los Angeles respondents had been without work and cash welfare between six months and eight years; on average they had longer spells than the Michigan respondents. But despite not working and not receiving cash assistance, women were getting money and paying for some, if not all, of their expenses.

Income Packages of Mothers Who Were Neither Working nor Receiving Cash Assistance

Although the experiences of the women in Los Angeles and Michigan were relatively distinct in terms of TANF use and employment history, their income packaging strategies were quite similar. First, the majority of the women in Los Angeles and all but one woman in Michigan were receiving food assistance through SNAP. All eligible families (which included all twenty-nine participants in Los Angeles) received additional food assistance through the Special Supplemental Nutrition Program for Women, Infants, and Children (WIC). Half of the Michigan sample also received housing assistance, either through Section 8 vouchers or by living in public housing, and one woman received assistance through a transitional housing program after leaving a homeless shelter several years earlier. With no earnings, their rent was effectively zero, eliminating a potentially large expense.

Beyond these strategies, five approaches to financial survival during disconnection emerged: (1) relying on children or other household members' SSI payments; (2) cohabiting with a working partner; (3) having former partners pay for major expenses; (4) having family members pay for major expenses; and (5) doubling up with another household. A final strategy, which we label "last-resort," was used by just a couple of women. Women also supplemented these primary sources of income with cash from informal work. These strategies were not necessarily mutually exclusive—a woman might live with a working partner and have a child who received SSI. For the most part, however, one strategy was more dominant than others.

Relying on SSI

Receipt of SSI for one's self was an exclusion criterion from this study, but several families received SSI benefits on behalf of their children—two in Los Angeles and five in Michigan (although one Michigan family had just begun receiving the payment). Yesenia, a recent immigrant mother, relied heavily on the disability payment she received for her seven-year-old with severe special needs. She was unable to balance work outside the home with the demands of caregiving and also could not find regular employment without working papers, so the payments she received provided financial support for her family. Two of Monica's four children received SSI, and her cohabiting boyfriend had his own payment.

In Michigan, an SSI payment of more than $600 a month is generally more than a family might receive under TANF ($492 for a single parent with three children). For California families, it is unclear whether an SSI check would be more than what a family could receive from TANF without knowing the immigration status of the family.[4]

---

4. The average monthly TANF benefit in California for a single-parent family with three children and no other income is $638 (Floyd and Schott 2013). However, families that have been in the country as legal residents for less than five years or are in the country without documentation are not eligible. Citizen children may be eligible for TANF; the average monthly benefit for a family with one citizen child is approximately $380 (Mauldon et al. 2012). Depending on the family size and legal status of family members, TANF benefits could be less than, similar to, or greater than what a family would receive if one child was on the SSI rolls.

Living with a Working Partner
Living with an employed partner was the most common strategy for women in Los Angeles but was very rare in Michigan (twenty-four versus only two). In all but one case, the mother and her cohabiting partner had at least one child together. Compared to the six women in Los Angeles who were living without other adults, those who were cohabiting were generally less disadvantaged economically. Living with a working partner also gave these women the opportunity to exit the labor market and stay home with their children. Although these relationships brought these women more economic security than they were likely to have had otherwise, their situations were not always stable. Partners generally worked low-wage jobs, and some were immigrants who lacked working papers and took whatever irregular work they could find. A few had experienced bouts of unemployment themselves. Some of the women were not at all aware of what their partners did, what their schedules were, and how much they earned. Those who knew what their partner earned generally reported low incomes of about $12,000 a year or less.

Receiving Assistance from Nonresident Fathers
Fathers did not have to be living with their families to provide generous assistance, particularly when mothers became disconnected. In half the cases in Michigan, the children's fathers, at a minimum, were paying for any costs associated with their children, including school clothes, after-school activities, and any extras the child might need. This assistance was over and above what these men might have been paying, or would have been ordered to pay, in formal child support. In five of these eleven cases, the fathers were doing even more, essentially supporting the family entirely during the period of disconnection.

Kiana was laid off and then ran out of unemployment benefits (which she received only for a couple of months). When asked what she did once this happened, she laughed and play-acted picking up a phone, saying, "Hello, baby daddy. I'm not working. I need some help." She continued, saying, "He stepped up to the plate. He's been taking care of us for the last couple of years." Describing what the children's father would do for them financially in a typical month, she said: "Well, the rent is $700. You figure light and gas bill between $200 and $250, [the children's] cell-phone bills, $200 for cell-phone bills, and just miscellaneous stuff that they might need, maybe he'll give about maybe $300 or $400." In other words, the children's father was contributing about $1,400 every month. Kiana purchased food for the family using her SNAP benefits, but that was her only expense. She stated very clearly, however, that previously their situations had been reversed and she had been supporting him. Given the literature on the instability of formal and informal child support payments, the extent to which women were supported by ex-partners was rather surprising, although many of these women had children with only the one partner, perhaps indicating a tighter bond between the family and the noncustodial father.

Receiving Monetary and Other Help from Family
Parents and other family members were also able to provide income support during periods of disconnection by giving cash, paying bills directly, or a combination of the two. This was the primary form of economic support for one woman in Michigan; other women in both sites used familial help in combination with earnings from partners and SSI payments. Claudette, a longtime public employee, lost her job, exhausted her unemployment benefits, and went on TANF, but then reached the time limit. Although she characterized herself as "facing hardship" financially, her mother was able to provide her with cash. When asked if her mother ever helped her out, Claudette said: "Oh yes, 100 percent. Yes, I'm very blessed to be the only child. No other body's begging in the pockets." Claudette's mother provided cash only for absolute necessities, however, not for anything she considered frivolous. "She's very firm. You got to be strict with like, phone, something necessary. No getting no hair done, no shopping, no nothing like that."

Kim, on the other hand, routinely received cash from her parents without any strings attached. She lived rent-free in a house owned by her parents, received SSI for one of her children, and, once she reached the TANF time limit, was routinely provided by her parents with $200 to $300 a month in cash. Diana, a mother of three who emigrated from Mexico when she was eleven, did not have her parents nearby to turn to, but she did rely on the support of her college-age son. He helped pay the rent with his financial aid money, the survivor benefits he collected from his deceased father, and the money he earned working at a clothing retailer during school breaks. Her son had recently been admitted to a psychiatric hospital after having a stress-induced anxiety attack, however, so Diana was receiving support from her brother, multiple close friends and neighbors, and her pastor, who helped pay her bills and provided free child care for her two young daughters.

Julie, who was caring for her mother after surgery, described her family as one where everyone always shared. Her brother gave her a car when hers broke down, and her parents gave her money to help pay bills. She said that this type of giving back and forth was typical in her family and did not occur just because she had been temporarily laid off from work. She said, "Whatever you need, if you don't have it, the other one will help, yeah. They [family] are like that, always have been."

Doubling Up
Receiving money directly from family members was less common in the Los Angeles sample, but family members often provided assistance through sharing housing. In twenty-one of the twenty-nine cases in Los Angeles, participants lived—or had recently lived—with parents, in-laws, siblings, or cousins. In a few cases, these arrangements were temporary, emergency solutions when families had been evicted from their homes or faced possible eviction. In the majority of cases, however, relatives lived together to reduce housing costs, given the very high cost of living in the city. Some women discussed how household members would pool their resources from earnings and public benefits to pay the bills and purchase food and necessary household items. Others split housing costs but otherwise kept expenses separate. But when someone in the household lost a job, others were available to help keep a roof over everyone's head.

In Michigan, four women reported doubling up as a result of a drop in income, from either losing a job or losing benefits. With no cash income to pay rent, women moved in with family members or friends or moved between various households.

Last-Resort Strategies
A few Michigan respondents resorted to other measures when money ran tight. Gina sold her plasma; she was such a regular at the donation center that she was given a debit card loaded with cash after each trip. Arlene frequented bingo halls, claiming that the money she won could "carry me a long way" financially. Ginger, one of the poorest women in the Michigan sample, received only $368 in SNAP benefits each month. Although she lived in public housing and did not have to pay rent or utilities, she had no way to purchase other necessities, such as toilet paper, school supplies for her daughter, or even shoes for herself. (At the time of the interview, she was wearing an old pair of slippers in lieu of shoes.) When asked how she managed with no cash income, she said she asked people she knew for money. Often these were men who wanted something from her in return. She said, "I'm telling you, but being of the male species they might want things, and stuff like this here. I just be fed up. I get so overwhelmed, you know. I get angry and I get a bitterness inside with just the man species period."

Supplementing with Income from Informal Work
Many women were able to supplement these strategies by working in the informal economy, such as caring for children, cleaning homes, cutting and styling hair, providing transportation to neighbors, and making and selling food. For immigrants who lacked working papers, the line between what they considered a regular job and informal work was often blurred because of their limited employment options. Some Los Angeles participants described any paid work (such as babysitting or

selling goods out of their home) as a job, whereas others performing the same kind of work said that they were doing it on the side to make a little money.

Another set of women had what might be considered small businesses. Kiana, unemployed since 2009, cleaned out rental properties and readied them for new tenants. She got referrals from friends and enlisted her three teenage children to help. Taurean did landscaping in the summer and shoveled snow in the winter. She reported finding work by going door to door in various neighborhoods. Andrea and her partner sold street food from a cart.

Are These Income Packaging Strategies Adequate and Sustainable?
Between public benefits, family support, and informal employment, mothers were usually able to piece together enough to obtain housing and food and to pay at least some of their bills. But how secure and sustainable were these strategies? We examine each in turn.

The Stability of Public Benefits
Although many of the women in Michigan were dropped from the TANF rolls and the women in Los Angeles avoided the program, other public assistance programs seemed to provide a fairly reliable source of support. As noted earlier, the vast majority of the women were receiving SNAP benefits, and because so many were neither working nor receiving TANF, the amount of SNAP benefits they received was quite substantial, sometimes in excess of $500 a month. Compared to TANF, women described SNAP as easier to use, in part because it was perceived as less intrusive. Janice, a mother in Michigan, said that SNAP caseworkers were "not in your business." Furthermore, she said, "it's no problem [getting SNAP] because maybe once a year or once every six months you have a phone interview. I don't even have to go to their office. I couldn't tell you what my worker looked like."

While TANF caseloads rose only slightly during the Great Recession, the number of SNAP recipients increased dramatically (Rosenbaum 2013). However, recipients risk losing the benefit if they commit fraud. Gina made a little bit of money from driving people in her car and had, until recently, been getting many of her bills paid by an ex-partner. Her only real source of income that was hers was her SNAP benefit card. Gina had recently moved, but since she had no cash to pay her rent, she gave her card to her landlord and allowed him to shop first when the card was replenished each month. Gina worried that he would not return the card in a timely fashion or would leave her without enough on the card to feed her children. If Gina's arrangement had been uncovered, however, she could have lost her benefits entirely.

WIC was also a stable source of nutrition assistance for mothers who were pregnant or had young children. Women in Los Angeles in particular expressed their appreciation of the program, saying that it was much easier to obtain and maintain than other public benefits and carried less stigma since it was a program for children. Still, some women reported recent food insecurity in their households. Most said that they had not run out of food completely but rather got very low on provisions. As Jessica described it: "There's always some food, maybe that day we won't eat the meat we wanted, but there are other things to make, like soup, vegetables."

Once secured, housing assistance was not easily lost. However, as is well known, obtaining publicly funded housing can be extremely difficult. Claudette had been receiving Section 8 since 2007, although she said she first applied in the mid-1990s, when her oldest child was born. Taurean waited ten years to receive a Section 8 voucher. For these women, living in public housing also might mean remaining in a place they did not like. Ginger, Arlene, and Julie all lived in the same public housing complex in a Detroit suburb. They described it as crime- and drug-infested, particularly the units farther away from the main road. (They all cautioned the first author not to "go to the back.") But the fact that their rent was zero when they had no other income kept them in place.

Cash from the SSI program provided the sort of stable income floor that welfare benefits might have done before 1996. But SSI is hardly a perfect substitute. An individual must have a health or mental health problem that meets the Social Security Administration's definition of disability. Although women who received SSI for their children did not report any problems obtaining the benefit, a couple of women in Michigan had been attempting for more than ten years to get on the rolls themselves.

The Consequences of Relying on Support from Partners and Family

Most of the women living with a working partner had more cash coming into the household compared to those using other survival strategies. This is not surprising, and in fact some studies of disconnected families exclude such women from their count, since the household is not disconnected from the labor market. But this strategy is viable over the long run only to the extent that the partner remains employed and remains in the household. In Los Angeles, some male partners were reported to have fairly stable jobs, but others worked intermittently, in construction as day laborers or in factories where hours went up and down based on production schedules. How much money the male partner brought in varied from month to month.

Cohabitation did not always protect women financially during periods of unemployment. Shonda had been with her boyfriend for more than twenty years, during which time they had four children together. Their economic situation was always precarious, but she characterized their relationship as one where they "had each other's back": "If I'm working and he's not, I take care of all the bills and stuff and everything. It's like vice versa. I'm the working mom and he's the home mom. Then it might switch. He's the working person and I'm the home person. Sometimes we both work." However, when they both lost their jobs at the same time, Shonda had already reached Michigan's TANF time limit, and soon they could no longer afford their rent. Each moved in with their respective parents. Shonda's partner was trying to find a job so that they could afford a home of their own again, and she reported that his frustration at being unemployed for so long was starting to cause stress and affect their relationship.

Several of the women lived with a working partner purely for economic reasons. Cohabiting appeared to be Yesenia's only option for financial survival. A thirty-one-year-old mother in Los Angeles, Yesenia had come to the United States from El Salvador eight years earlier and had arranged to live with a man twenty years her senior who was from her hometown and had been established longer in the United States. He cared for her, and they eventually began a relationship, having two children together. Yesenia received SSI for her older son, but she could not find employment since she did not know any English, had only a sixth-grade education, and was undocumented. It became apparent during her interview that Yesenia rarely left her home, had no family or friends, and was very isolated and depressed. When asked if she had plans to marry someday, she replied, "No, I don't know, but my heart is not in it to get married." Without the support of her children's father and the disability payments she received for her son, she would have had great difficulty making ends meet, but she also reported suffering emotionally.

Financial assistance, whether from a live-in partner or someone else, could also quickly vanish. The threat of deportation hung over the heads of many mothers in the Los Angeles sample. If not deported themselves, their partners might be, and a crucial source of income would be quickly eliminated. The father of Diana's youngest two children had helped her buy clothes, diapers, and food for their children, but after he was deported her life spiraled downward—she lost her job (because she could not find reliable and affordable child care), and she was forced to move when the house she rented went through foreclosure. She relied on the generosity of family and her church to get by. In talking about her partner's deportation, she said, "It's been hard. That's when everything became ... harder, because that's when I really knew I was on my own now." Several years earlier, the father of her older two children had died; thus, none of her children had a father available to provide support.

Women with citizen-partners were also in danger of quickly losing this important source of economic support—for example, through death or incarceration. Gina had been receiving substantial financial help from the father of one of her children. She referred to him as "my main source of income," and he paid all her bills. Just weeks before the interview, he died unexpectedly. The anxiety in Gina's voice was noticeable as she talked about facing a utility shutoff, since she lacked the money to pay the bill. His parents had told her that they would help her financially, but thus far they had not. Gina was very reluctant to ask them directly for money, since they had just lost their son, but she also knew that she needed to find a way to pay her utility bill. Her relationship with another child's father was extremely acrimonious; he had successfully petitioned for the removal of their child from Gina's care, citing her unstable living arrangements as evidence of unsuitability to parent. Between 2011 and 2013, Gina estimated, she had stayed in at least eight different places, usually the houses of friends or cousins, leaving when she and her five children wore out their welcome.

Even in situations where financial assistance was generous and reportedly given gladly, being dependent on others could take an emotional toll. Janice quit her job when she was unable to get enough hours and child care was becoming difficult to secure. Her own father and her children's father stepped in to take care of her financially. Between the two of them, all the bills were paid. She said, "My dad helps out extremely a lot. The kids' dad helps out extremely a lot. I'm covered between the two of them. They're not going to let us be without." She continued, talking about why she believed they were so willing to help: "I guess the biggest thing for my dad and the kids' dad is they understand that I will go to work. It's not like I just choose to sit here and just be unemployed." Even though Janice had not worked in more than three years and admitted that her job search efforts were not always as diligent as they might be, it was important to her to construct a self-image as someone who was not taking advantage of the generosity of others and was prepared to take a job. She also noted that by taking their help, she was losing some of her autonomy: "Sometimes it's stressful because I like my own money. I like to be my own boss. Sometimes, when you're asking someone for something or someone doing something, they feel like they have some type of control over you. Sometimes it bothers me."

While Kiana and Janice were grateful for the help they were receiving and in fact elected not to apply for TANF benefits because of this help, their comments reflected some mild unease about being the recipient of this generous support. Throughout the interview, Janice made reference to not wanting to burden those who helped her and needing to make sure her father and ex-partner knew how much she appreciated their help. Both Janice and Kiana also talked about being used to having control over financial decisions when they were working and earning their own money. Having to rely upon their ex-partners made them cautious about spending. For example, Janice reported that she would not turn on the heat in her house until it became "extremely cold" and would tell her children to put on more layers if they were cold. She said that she did this to keep the heating bill down, since she was not the one making the payments. Kiana, whose ex-partner paid all of the bills, believed that other family members were gossiping about her and saying things such as, "'Oh, she's not working. She's living off her baby daddy.' Just stuff like that."

Women who were doubling up, whether by choice to save money or because they had no other option, were living in very crowded conditions. When she lost her job and lost her apartment, Shonda moved back in with her mother in the house she grew up in. However, other family members were facing similar challenges, and they also landed with Shonda's mother. In total, five adults and one child (Shonda's son) lived in a small house that was overcrowded and cluttered. The front door opened up into a small living room that contained a cot where Shonda's grandfather slept along with some chairs and a television. Plastic bins stacked floor to ceiling contained the belongings of those who had moved in. During the interview, several different people came in and out of the house, sitting on the chairs in the living room and talking, even though the grandfather was sleeping. Shonda's small niece was there at the time and attempted to show off her crawling skills, but she had to navigate around the very small spaces between the chair legs. Shonda and her eight-year-old son shared one of the bedrooms, which also held belongings from her house that she had taken with her.

Overcrowding also posed safety concerns. Few infants and toddlers had safe sleeping arrangements; most slept with a parent, other children, or both. Like the women in Michigan living in public housing, the economic need to remain doubled up kept many Los Angeles women in locations they deemed unsafe or undesirable.

Similar to relying on the earnings of others, doubling up as a strategy works only when housing is stable. Pauline moved in with her mother when she lost her job after her car broke down; her job required substantial amounts of driving, and she had no money for repairs. Pauline's teenage daughters had rooms on the main floor of the house, but Pauline and her son had to stay in the basement, which was dark, dank, and lacking in privacy. The arrangement, however, was rent-free. Unfortunately, Pauline's mother had just started to have some financial difficulties herself, and Pauline worried that soon her mother might not be able to pay the mortgage and the house would go into foreclosure.

The Instability of Informal Jobs and the Problems with "Last-Resort" Strategies

For most of the women who engaged in informal work, being able to make money depended on others needing and paying for the services they provided and, for some jobs, being able to physically do the job. Gina had a working minivan and gave friends rides for money, but how much she received was completely dependent on how much her riders were willing to pay. Andrea, who had the street-corner food business, referred to this work as "not so stable," since some days they had more customers than others. Arlene frequently babysat to make extra money, although she reported that her most recent client owed her $700; Arlene had watched this woman's child for months but never received any payment. Claudette tried to make extra money by planning parties and weddings, making floral arrangements, and tending to other details, but "people really don't want to pay what it takes for you to put into that work," she said. "Because they doing, you know, the brides want certain things, but when you start telling them [how much it will cost], they be like, 'Well, wait a minute, no, I'm fixing to save money here. Why, I could do that myself, you know.'" Taurean had been making money doing yard work in the warm months and shoveling snow in the winter, but once her pregnancy was further along, she had to give up that work.

Finally, some of the last-resort strategies were not without danger. Ginger, whose multiple health problems prevented her from working and who had no cash coming into the household, sometimes relied on male friends to pay bills or buy her groceries. However, she recognized the challenges inherent in accepting help from men who, she said, "might want things." Discussing a man who recently went to the store for her, she elaborated:

> He wants to stay the night, and thinking he's gonna get over. No, you're not gonna get over on me. Just because you bought me eight rolls of tissue paper and some dish rags and stuff, you're not gonna get over. I didn't say those words. I was like, "No," like this here. It's just unbelievable. There's so many people out there that's not genuine.

DISCUSSION

Like the poor single mothers in Edin and Lein's *Making Ends Meet,* the mothers in this study found ways to package income from a variety of sources or find others in their social networks to pay their bills. However, their income packaging strategies were fraught with a number of challenges. In households not receiving disability benefits, the only stable source of public benefits was nutrition assistance—SNAP or WIC. While crucial to women's budgets, SNAP and WIC can only legally be used to purchase food. TANF, on the other hand, provides the flexibility of being a cash benefit. Unless they were willing to commit fraud (like Gina), they lacked the stable source of income that welfare was for Edin and Lein's respondents. Living in public housing or receiving a housing subsidy eliminated an otherwise potentially large expense for disconnected women, but it also sometimes tied them to a place that was not safe. Doubling up with others could help them save on housing costs or provide a refuge when they could not afford rent, but this strategy usually meant living in very cramped and sometimes unhealthy quarters.

Family members and the men in women's lives—cohabiting partners, boyfriends, the fathers of their children—provided crucial support for quite a few women. However, relying on others to pay the bills and provide for their families negatively affected some women's sense of self-worth and autonomy. Several women had been able to count on a network member for financial help, but deportation, job loss, or death had changed their circumstances quickly. Most of the women in Los Angeles were living with a male partner, although this did not always equate to economic stability, nor did it signal that a woman was in a healthy relationship; several women described living with a partner for the sake of residential and financial stability rather than for love. Some of these findings are expected given what we know from previous studies about poor women's economic coping strategies, although the extent of support from nonresident former partners that we found was perhaps surprising, since previous studies have indicated that child support payments (let alone more substantial contributions) are sporadic.

Our findings also highlight the role that immigration status plays in becoming disconnected. While the citizen mothers in the Michigan sample had difficulty finding jobs during the economic downturn and slow recovery, the Los Angeles mothers always faced challenges securing employment, given their undocumented status. Many of the jobs they could find were off the books and paid very little. Once child care was factored in, the cost of taking a job outweighed any benefits. Immigration status also limited these mothers' options for receiving public benefits, at least for themselves. A number of mothers in Michigan lost TANF owing to time limits and other regulations, but undocumented mothers in Los Angeles did not qualify for benefits for themselves, and their status kept them from seeking out TANF for their citizen children. Finally, although not necessarily tied to immigration status, differences in cultural norms about a mother's role affected the route to disconnection. The belief among most of the Latina mothers (and their partners) in Los Angeles that a mother should stay home with her children when they are young had resulted in some voluntary exits from work. Mothers in Michigan did not discuss this as a reason for leaving jobs.

The study is not without its limitations. First, we rely on respondents' self-reports about the types of financial support they received, and those reports may over- or underestimate how much they truly received. People may underreport how much help they receive from others because of shame or stigma, or they may overreport if they are afraid of possible negative repercussions—for example, they may overreport the financial help they receive because they fear involvement from child protective services (see Desmond 2012). However, the in-depth interviews were framed as another part of the larger, ongoing survey study in which the respondents were already participating, not as a study of the economic survival strategies of a particular population that might be at risk, for example, for involvement from child protective services. Moreover, all respondents had already completed two to three in-person surveys before the in-depth interview. In these surveys, they were also asked to report on their sources of economic support, albeit in a close-ended fashion. Our comparisons of the survey data to the data gathered in the in-depth interviews show generally consistent reports of income from public assistance, although more financial support was uncovered in the in-depth interviews, possibly because of the different mode of data collection and the way questions were posed. For example, the survey would not have been able to document the practice of other family members directly paying the bills of the women we interviewed. In addition to receipt of public benefits, the longitudinal survey from which the Los Angeles sample was drawn assessed multiple indicators of child and family well-being, including maternal depression, food insecurity, and material hardship. The survey data generally align with the interview data. For example, in both data sources, about one-third of the women expressed some depressive symptoms, and another one-third reported food insecurity.

Second, our recruitment strategy may have resulted in an overrepresentation of women who had access to other forms of support. In Los Angeles, all participants had connections to the WIC program, which may have helped them form connections to other sources of support, such as SNAP. The Michigan participants were part of a random sample survey, but the sampling frame was census block units, so the survey respondents were somewhat clustered geographically. One of the census blocks contained a public housing project, where four of the qualitative study participants lived and where several others had previously lived before transitioning to Housing Choice (formerly Section 8 vouchers). Another census block included in the sampling frame contained a block of low-income housing units. These sampling artifacts contribute to a higher rate of receipt of housing assistance than one might expect—50 percent of the Michigan respondents compared to 23 percent of low-income renters nationwide (Sard and Fisher 2013).

Despite these limitations, our results have implications both for future research and for policy. First, our study again points to the challenges that researchers face when trying to understand the complex financial lives of low-income, single-mother families. Some of these families do have access to financial help beyond their own earnings and public assistance benefits. Income received from a family member or former partner may be difficult to capture in surveys or administrative data, particularly when that person takes over payment of bills. Not being able to account for this income may lead to overestimating the number of families that are truly without any economic resources. On the other hand, assuming that this income is stable and available for long periods of time may overstate the resources available to families during periods of disconnection from employment and cash assistance.

While the availability of private safety nets was crucial to these women's economic survival, at least some of the participants would have preferred to have been working and earning their own money. Public policy should not lose sight of the importance of creating employment opportunities for low-wage workers, nor should it overlook the need for a more comprehensive safety net. Many of these women had been attached to the labor market before the recession and wanted to work again yet were "long-term unemployed," or at risk of becoming so, and thus their future employment was less likely. During the Great Recession, more than half of states used TANF "emergency" funds that became available through the American Recovery and Reinvestment Act (ARRA) of 2009 to create subsidized employment programs for some portion of their TANF clients who were unable to find work (Pavetti, Schott, and Lower-Basch 2011). Perhaps some version of a subsidized employment program could be created for people who have otherwise exhausted benefits (both TANF and unemployment) to maintain or learn new skills and earn an adequate income. Guaranteed child care assistance for low-income workers would also allow more mothers of young children to enter the workforce. Mothers in the Los Angeles sample commonly reported the challenge of finding affordable and reliable child care in a local system that had a waiting list for child care subsidies. The high cost of care outweighed the little income they would earn, causing some mothers to prefer staying home with their children rather than work and pay a child care provider.

The findings also point to some systematic problems with TANF. For the Los Angeles immigrant participants, misinformation and misunderstandings about the program seemed to keep women from using it, even for their citizen children. Assuming that use of TANF among those who are eligible is a policy goal, reducing barriers to access through community outreach campaigns might increase use of the program. That mothers who were probably eligible for TANF and nutrition assistance only received SNAP or WIC suggests the possibility of using the SNAP or WIC application process as another opportunity for outreach—at least for a targeted subgroup of mothers. Second, the rhetoric around time-limited welfare receipt cast this policy tool as motivation for women to find work. But do time limits make sense in an environment where there are few jobs and no affordable child care? For women who receive no support from current or former partners, greater efforts toward securing child support payments could help lift them out of dire situations. Finally, immigrant mothers living with undocumented partners can quickly become disconnected if their partners are deported or cannot secure employment. Issues of immigration reform, although beyond the scope of this article, are clearly intertwined with economic disconnection.

REFERENCES

Avellar, Sarah, and Pamela J. Smock. 2005. "The Economic Consequences of the Dissolution of Cohabiting Unions." *Journal of Marriage and Family* 67: 315–27.

Blank, Rebecca, and Brian Kovak. 2009. "The Growing Problem of Disconnected Single Mothers." In *Making the Work-Based Safety Net Work Better*, edited by Carolyn J. Heinrich and John Karl Scholz. New York: Russell Sage Foundation.

Cancian, Maria, and Daniel R. Meyer. 2011. "Who Owes What to Whom? Child Support Policy Given Multiple-Partner Fertility." *Social Service Review* 85(4): 587–617.

Carlson, Marcia J., and Frank F. Furstenberg. 2006. "The Prevalence and Correlates of Multipartnered Fertility Among Urban U.S. Parents." *Journal of Marriage and Family* 68: 718–32.

Castro Martin, Teresa. 2002. "Consensual Unions in Latin America: Persistence of a Dual Nuptiality System." *Journal of Comparative Family Studies* 33: 35–55.

Danziger, Sandra K. 2010. "The Decline of Cash Welfare and Implications for Social Policy and Poverty." *Annual Review of Sociology* 36: 523–45.

Danziger, Sheldon, and David Ratner. 2010. "Labor Market Outcomes and the Transition to Adulthood." *The Future of Children* 20: 133–58.

Desmond, Matthew. 2012. "Disposable Ties and the Urban Poor." *American Journal of Sociology* 117: 1295–1335.

Domínguez, Silvia, and Celeste Watkins 2003. "Creating Networks for Survival and Mobility: Social Capital Among African-American and Latin-American Low-Income Mothers." *Social Problems* 50: 111–35.

Edin, Kathryn, and Laura Lein. 1996. "Work, Welfare, and Single Mothers' Economic Survival Strategies." *American Sociological Review* 61: 253–66.

———. 1997. *Making Ends Meet*. New York: Russell Sage Foundation.

Edin, Kathryn, and H. Luke Shaefer. 2015. *Two Dollars a Day: Living on Almost Nothing in America*. New York: Houghton Mifflin Harcourt.

Floyd, Ife, and Liz Schott. 2013. "TANF Cash Benefits Continued to Lose Value in 2013." Washington, D.C.: Center on Budget and Policy Priorities (October 21). Available at: http://www.cbpp.org/cms/?fa=view&id=4034 (accessed January 1, 2015).

French, Ron. 2012. "Welfare Reform: Back to the Drawing Board." *Bridge Magazine*, March 29, available at: http://www.bridgemi.com/2012/03/welfare-reform-back-to-the-drawing-board (accessed May 1, 2014).

Ha, Yoonsook, Maria Cancian, and Daniel R. Meyer. 2011. "The Regularity of Child Support and Its Contribution to the Regularity of Income." *Social Service Review* 85: 401–19.

Hogan, Dennis P., David J. Eggebeen, and Clifford C. Clogg. 1993. "The Structure of Intergenerational Exchanges in American Families." *American Journal of Sociology* 98: 1428–58.

Kroft, Kory, Fabian Lange, Matthew Notowidigdo, and Lawrence Katz. 2014. "Long-Term Unemployment and the Great Recession: The Role of Composition, Duration Dependence, and Non-Participation." Available at: http://www.korykroft.com/wordpress/KLNK_LTU_and_Great_Recession_june23_2014.pdf (accessed October 1, 2015).

Lichter, Daniel T., Zhenchao Qian, and Leanna Mellott. 2006. "Marriage or Dissolution? Union Transitions Among Poor Cohabiting Women." *Demography* 43: 223–40.

Loprest, Pamela. 2003. "Disconnected Welfare Leavers Face Serious Risks." *Snapshots of America's Families* 3(7). Washington, D.C.: Urban Institute.

———. 2011. "Disconnected Families and TANF." Temporary Assistance to Needy Families Research Brief 2. Washington, D.C.: Urban Institute (November). Available at: http://www.urban.org/sites/default/files/alfresco/publication-pdfs/412568-Disconnected-Families-and-TANF.PDF (accessed May 1, 2015).

Loprest, Pamela, and Austin Nichols. 2011. "Dynamics of Being Disconnected from Work and TANF." Report to the U.S. Department of Health and Human Services (USDHHS), Assistant Secretary for Planning and Evaluation (ASPE). Washington, D.C.: Urban Institute.

Loprest, Pamela, and Sheila R. Zedlewski. 2006. "The Changing Role of Welfare in the Lives of Low-Income Families with Children." Washington, D.C.: Urban Institute.

Mauldon, Jane, Richard Speiglman, Christina Sogar, and Matt Stagner. 2012. "TANF Child-Only Cases: Who Are They? What Policies Affect Them? What Is Being Done?" Washington: U.S. Department of Health & Human Services Administration for Children and Families (December 11). Available at: http://www.cfpic.org/pdfs/TANF-Child-Only-Cases--The-Report-12-19-2012.pdf (accessed January 1, 2015).

Miranda, Nannette. 2011. "Lawsuit Seeks to Stop Welfare Debt Collection from Children." ABC7 News, November 30, available at: http://www.abc7news.com/archive/8450446/ (accessed May 1, 2014).

Ojeda, Norma. 2011. "'Living Together Without Being Married': Perceptions of Female Adolescents in the Mexican–United States Border Region." *Journal of Comparative Family Studies* 42(4): 439–53.

Ovwigho, Pamela, Nicholas Kolupanowich, and Catherine Born. 2009. "Disconnected Leavers: The Circumstances of Those Without Welfare and Without Work." Report by the Family Welfare Research and Training Group. Baltimore: University of Maryland, School of Social Work.

Pavetti, LaDonna, Liz Schott, and Elizabeth Lower-Basch. 2011. "Creating Subsidized Employment Opportunities for Low-Income Parents: The Legacy of the TANF Emergency Fund." Washington, D.C.: Center on Budget and Policy Priorities (February 16). Available at: http://www.cbpp.org/sites/default/files/atoms/files/2-16-11tanf.pdf (accessed May 1, 2015).

Rosenbaum, Dottie. 2013. "SNAP Is Efficient and Effective." Washington, D.C.: Center on Budget and Policy Priorities (updated March 11). Available at: http://www.cbpp.org/cms/?fa=view&id=3239 (accessed January 1, 2015).

Sard, Barbara, and Will Fisher. 2013. "Chart Book: Federal Housing Spending Is Poorly Matched to Need." Washington, D.C.: Center on Budget and Policy Priorities (December 18). Available at: http://www.cbpp.org/research/chart-book-federal-housing-spending-is-poorly-matched-to-need (accessed May 1, 2015).

Sarkisian, Natalia, and Naomi Gerstel. 2004. "Kin Support Among Blacks and Whites: Race and Family Organization." *American Sociological Review* 69: 812–37.

Sinkewicz, Marilyn, and Irwin Garfinkel. 2009. "Unwed Fathers' Ability to Pay Child Support: New Estimates Accounting for Multiple Partner Fertility." *Demography* 46: 247–63.

Stack, Carol. 1974. *All Our Kin*. New York: Harper & Row.

Turner, Lesley, Sheldon Danziger, and Kristin Seefeldt. 2006. "Failing the Transition from Welfare to Work: Women Chronically Disconnected from Employment and Welfare." *Social Science Quarterly* 87(2): 227–49.

U.S. Department of Homeland Security. 2009. "Public Charge." Available at http://www.uscis.gov/green-card/green-card-processes-and-procedures/public-charge (accessed January 1, 2015).

Zedlewski, Sheila, Sandi Nelson, Kathryn Edin, Heather Koball, Kate Pomper, and Tracy Roberts. 2002. "Families Coping Without Earnings or Government Cash Assistance." Assessing the New Federalism Occasional Paper 64. Washington, D.C.: Urban Institute.